The Clydach Murders

The Clydach Murders

A Miscarriage of Justice

John Morris

SEREN

Seren is the book imprint of
Poetry Wales Press Ltd
Nolton Street, Bridgend, Wales

www.serenbooks.com
facebook.com/SerenBooks
Twitter: @SerenBooks

ISBN – 978-1-78172-392-0
Ebook – 978-1-78172-393-7
Kindle – 978-1-85411-394-4

A CIP record for this title is available from the British Library

The publisher works with the financial assistance
of the Welsh Books Council

Maps © OpenStreetMap contributors
openstreetmap.org

Printed in Plantin Light by Short Run Press Ltd, Exeter

Contents

'The house [at 9 Kelvin Road] was cleansed by one who was forensically aware.'

– Mr Justice Butterfield,
Swansea Crown Court, 24-27 June 2002
during the course of his summing up

Prologue

It was a crime that shocked the nation. During the early hours of Sunday 27 June 1999, three generations of one family, all female, living together in the village of Clydach in the lower Swansea Valley, were killed in a series of vicious attacks. Two years later, Mr Justice Butterfield, presiding over the trial of David George ('Dai') Morris, a builder's labourer and known petty criminal, described the atrocity as 'a murder of exceptional savagery'. Patrick Harrington QC, prosecuting counsel, described it as a 'massacre', and an 'orgy of savagery'.

Divorced mother of two Mandy Power (aged 34), her disabled and bed-ridden mother, Doris Dawson (80), and Mandy's daughters, Katie (10) and Emily (8), were brutally bludgeoned to death by a calculating assailant wielding a heavy four-foot fibreglass pole.

It was a killing on a scale previously unknown in Wales. It was the most horrific in regard to the violence inflicted on the victims; it resulted in the biggest murder investigation ever carried out by South Wales Police, involving over fifty detectives working full-time for almost three years; and it was by far the most expensive investigation in Wales up to that time, at a final cost of well over £6 million.

But despite the extensive publicity, the immense effort, the huge cost and time involved in bringing the case to trial, many consider that the truth of what really happened on that terrible Sunday morning has yet to be revealed. Moreover, justice may have miscarried and the man who was convicted of the murders might indeed be innocent. Neither his DNA nor his fingerprints could be found at the murder scene; the story told by the police was that he had wiped them all away. Furthermore, in order to destroy all potential remaining evidence, four fires were started in the house with the intention of razing it to the ground, thus obliterating all traces of the dreadful act.

However, owing to the presence of mind of a neighbour, that obliteration did not take place. Within minutes of smoke being seen rising from the back of 9 Kelvin Road, the emergency services were called. Morriston and Pontardawe Fire Services responded to what they assumed was an ordinary domestic fire, arriving at the now blazing house within just eight minutes of being alerted. Wearing breathing apparatus, firemen forced their way inside, even before the fire was brought fully under control, to search for anyone who might be trapped in the house.

One of the firemen, Neil MacPherson, brought out the first of the four occupants, ten-year-old Katie. She was laid on the ground where he tried to resuscitate her, but it was too late. Two more bodies were then brought out: another daughter, eight-year-old Emily, followed by the girls' mother, Mandy Power. They too were dead. The body of an elderly woman, Doris Dawson, Mandy Power's mother, was found in her bed.

What horrified the firemen was that none of the victims had been killed by smoke, by the fire or by accident. All had died as a result of extreme violence. Number 9 Kelvin Road was a crime scene, the address of one of the most shocking murders ever committed in Wales.

Then began the biggest murder hunt in Welsh history, and what also may be the greatest miscarriage of justice in Wales. The events that followed this terrible tragedy culminated in what can only be described as a travesty of justice.

As the police investigation progressed, integrity and the rule of law gave way to a fierce determination on the part of South Wales Police to protect their own. It appears that they were anxious to find a suitable suspect, frame him, and obtain a conviction at any cost. In 2001, 21 months after the crime, the police charged builder's labourer David George (Dai) Morris with the murders. Morris was convicted essentially on the basis of a single piece of evidence – his broken gold neck-chain, partially covered in blood, which was found at the crime scene. His litany of lies, lack of an alibi for the night in question and his previous criminal record formed a case for the prosecution based more on speculation than on hard fact. In 2002 at the Swansea Crown Court he was found guilty of the murders, and at his second trial in 2006 at the Newport Crown Court, Morris was again found guilty of the murders, and sentenced to four terms of life imprisonment.

This is the story of an appalling crime and the flawed police investigation that followed. It is based mainly on first-hand reports from the *South Wales Evening Post*, which kindly opened its archives to me, and recollections of witnesses who gave evidence at the Swansea and Newport Crown Courts. It also includes the memories of people who were not called to give evidence at either of the trials, but nevertheless had something important to say. It is the account of a major injustice and what happens when one of the greatest legal systems in the world is manipulated by the unscrupulous, in order to achieve a court finding that is entirely inconsistent with the justice it seeks to deliver and endeavours to uphold.

Part I

The murders at 9 Kelvin Road
and the flawed police investigation that followed

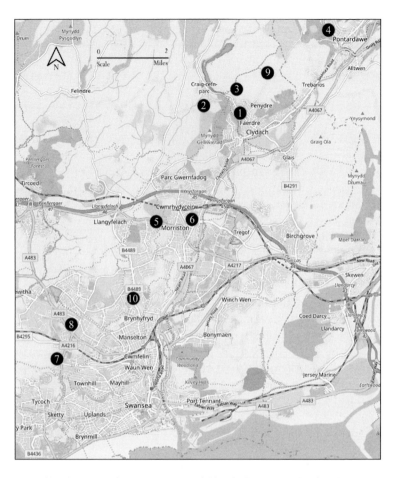

1. 9 Kelvin Road, Clydach – *home of Mandy Power and her family*
2. Rhyddwen Road, Craig Cefn Parc – *home of Dai Morris and Mandy Jewell*
3. New Inn Pub
4. West Crossways, Pontardawe – *home of Alison and Stephen Lewis*
5. Morriston Police Station
6. Morriston Fire Station
7. Cockett Police Station
8. Coedwig Place, Gendros, Swansea – *home of Dai Morris' parents*
9. The White Chapel
10. Treboeth

Chapter 1

It was 12.30 a.m. on a warm but rainy summer night. A minibus taxi stopped on a neon-lit road in a quiet Welsh village. An attractive female passenger and two small girls got out and climbed the short flight of steps leading to the front door of an ordinary suburban semi. The driver watched as the woman turned the key in the lock before she and the girls slipped inside, closing the door behind them. Almost three years afterwards, recalling aloud his thoughts at that moment for the benefit of a jury, the taxi driver said: 'They're safe now.'

Four hours later, at 4.27 a.m. on Sunday 27 June 1999 the Emergency Control Centre in Newport received a 999 call. It was the first of several urgent calls the Centre was to receive that night from an area north of Swansea. The message was immediately relayed to the South Wales Fire Service headquarters in Carmarthen which, in turn, notified the two fire stations nearest to the location of the alarm. 'Red Watch' fire crews at Morriston and Pontardawe, two small industrial towns to the north of Swansea, were instantly alerted to the emergency by a loud bell, a flashing red light and a fax message which spewed out simultaneously in the two fire stations.

The 999 call came from the Sunnybank district of Clydach, a sprawling village situated on the western slopes of the lower Swansea Valley. Minutes before, at 4.20 a.m. Robert Wachowski, a BP chemical worker, had looked out of his bedroom window after hearing banging and smashing noises coming from 9 Kelvin Road, the house almost directly opposite his home. His first thoughts were that someone was tampering with cars in the street but then, in the half-light, he saw clouds of white smoke billowing from the rear of the house. He wondered if someone had set fire to a bag of rubbish and rang the occupant of number 9, Mandy Power, on her landline. When she failed to answer, he tried her mobile number, but again got no reply. Wachowski dressed quickly, ran across the road, banged on the front door of the threatened house and shouted for Mandy to wake up. He then ran around to the back of the house, where he found that the kitchen was blazing fiercely.

Donald Jones, another neighbour, was woken by his mother, who ran screaming into his bedroom. He rushed out to help Wachowski. Together the two men hammered on the front door and windows and shouted warnings as they desperately tried to rescue the family they believed were trapped inside. As they attempted to force open the front door, they were beaten back by thick smoke. Running to the back of the house, they found the french doors swinging open, the double-glazed windows shattered and the window frames buckled by the intense heat. Again they were beaten back, this time by a wall of flames. Wachowski recalled later: 'I looked up at Katie and Emily's room and thought, "I hope they're not in there."' Desperate to help, he shouted to Rosemary Jones, who lived opposite number 9, asking her to ring for the fire service. Moments later a powerful Dennis fire engine, one of two on permanent standby at Morriston Fire Station, was on its way, and a fire support Land Rover followed closely behind.

Number 9 Kelvin Road, a semi-detached three-bedroom house, was built around the mid-1950s. It is one of about sixty houses, all of a similar style, rising on either side of Kelvin Road, between Gellionnen Road to the east and Tan Yr Allt Road to the west, at one point intersected by Carlton Road. The house occupies a slightly elevated site on the north side of the road. Six stone steps rising from the pavement meet a short path dividing a small patchy lawn fenced by low wrought-iron railings. From there it takes just three paces to reach the front door. A path on the right leads round the side of the house to the back garden.

During their journey, the fire crew maintained radio contact with South Wales Fire Service in Carmarthen. The crew assumed that they would be dealing with a straightforward house fire, but John Campbell, the commanding officer, was prepared for anything, or so he thought. Headquarters had received conflicting reports as to whether the occupants of the burning house were still inside, and no one knew for certain whether or not they would be looking for survivors. Shortly before the fire engine arrived, controllers confirmed that there was at least one person in the house.

Off-duty firefighter Adrian Humphries was the first emergency services worker to arrive at the scene. He lived in Kelvin Road, just a few doors away, and was dozing in his armchair when his wife shook him awake to tell him about the fire. He rushed to the burning house and asked if anyone was inside. Someone said, 'No, she's out.'

As the Morriston fire engine turned into Kelvin Road, crew member Neil MacPherson and his team strapped on self-contained breathing apparatus. He readied himself to lead the search for the people trapped inside the house. He and John Campbell were both 30-year veterans, with extensive experience of house fires, road traffic accidents and numerous other fire-related incidents. Up to that night, they thought they had seen it all.

Even before the fire engine came to a complete halt, Campbell had issued his orders. Onlookers moved aside and the crew saw for themselves that the house was well and truly ablaze. Campbell instructed MacPherson to lead a search for casualties or trapped individuals. Floodlights were turned on and directed towards the house while oxygen cylinders were prepared in anticipation of resuscitating survivors affected by smoke inhalation. Within seconds of the Morriston crew's arrival, a second fire engine, from Pontardawe, pulled up at the house. Now, ten firefighters were involved, plus those who had travelled separately in the Morriston support Land Rover.

Robert Wachowski told the firemen that the stairs were on the right, just inside the front door, then retreated to a safe distance where he and his other neighbours watched as the dreadful events unfolded. MacPherson, wearing a fire protection suit, was the first of a two-man team to force his way into the blazing house, kicking in the front door as he went. Fire officers Spencer Lewis, Huw Thomas and Peter Bringloe followed closely behind. Battling through the flames and thick blinding smoke, they felt their way upstairs on their hands and knees, their noses just inches from the stair carpet.

As they reached the landing, one of the firemen swept the floor with a gloved hand and discovered the first body.

MacPherson gathered up a limp little girl whom he described as 'light and small'. She was blackened by smoke. He carried her downstairs and out through the front door. As John Campbell went to help him, vomit spewed from the child's mouth over the front of Campbell's jacket, giving him the impression that she was still alive. They passed the child to Adrian Humphries, and together helped him lay her on the grass where MacPherson tried to resuscitate her.

Huw Thomas, a fireman from Pontardawe, found another small child upstairs as he felt his way on his hands and knees through the dense smoke. She too was carried downstairs and passed to Humphries. He later described the child as 'very grey-looking'. Then the firemen brought out a third body: a dark-haired young woman. Smoke had blackened her entire naked body and, oddly, a pink vibrator was lodged in her vagina.

All three bodies were laid on the ground and covered with blankets, leaving only their heads exposed. For several long minutes the firemen tried to revive them. While MacPherson continued working on the first little girl, Humphries worked on the second. MacPherson applied mouth-to-mouth resuscitation. Certain that he detected a heartbeat, he tried hard to coax a response from her.

At 4.41 a.m. a team of paramedics arrived and took over the medical care of the victims. Paramedic Eric Thomas ran to the three victims the firefighters were trying to revive. He helped those working on the young woman who, he saw, had an injury to the side of her face. He would say later that 'there was always a chance that she was alive, but, given the extent of her injuries, we decided then it was a lost cause and we stopped.' Clearly Mandy Power was dead.

Thomas' colleague, ambulance technician Barry Pierpoint, who had also tried to resuscitate one of the children at the scene, would later say that 'it was quite obvious that very serious injuries had been sustained'. He observed that the fire officers appeared to be 'quite shocked and distressed' by the condition of the three bodies.

The paramedics were unable to properly fit oxygen masks on the faces of the little girls. One of the paramedics noted that neither of them appeared to be breathing, and both had sustained extensive head injuries. Another paramedic said to Neil MacPherson, who was still trying to revive one of the girls, later identified as Katie Power: 'You're going to have to stop. I'm afraid they've all gone.' As MacPherson pulled his gloved hand away from the back of the child's head, he saw that it was covered in blood.

The firemen quickly realised that the injuries could not have been caused by the fire. Given their extent and nature, it was obvious that they had been deliberately inflicted. All efforts to revive the victims using first aid and oxygen ceased, and the medical team packed away their equipment and left.

MacPherson re-entered the burning house to search for more casualties. By now the fire was under control and the smoke was less dense. In an upstairs back bedroom, he found the dead body of an elderly woman still in bed. She too had sustained terrible facial and head injuries and was covered in blood. Leaving her where she lay, he retreated from the bedroom. On the landing he saw flesh, pieces of bone and pools of blood. Looking into the bathroom, he saw a bath, partially filled with water which contained more blood. Descending the stairs, he saw that the walls, doors and ceilings were also spattered with blood. He said later: 'I had never seen anything like this in one incident.'

It was clear that 9 Kelvin Road was a crime scene. It was a startling development, but fire crews often find themselves in unusual situations and have either been trained, or have learned, to deal with most of them. A short coded message was sent to the South Wales Fire Service: a dead body had been found. Code is used to prevent amateur radio enthusiasts from intruding into emergency services' wavebands to pick up and disperse sensitive information before the authorities might wish it to be released. The same code is used regardless of the number of deaths. The message does not state the cause of death, so the emergency services operatives who receive it have no way of knowing the number of bodies found, or whether death was the result of an accident or foul play. Despite having alerted their colleagues to the loss of life, only the personnel on the scene were aware of the extent or cause of the shocking discoveries.

The fire crew was simply not trained or properly equipped to deal with a crime of this magnitude. When Police Constable

Alison Crewe, an Acting Sergeant, arrived at Kelvin Road, she immediately realised the seriousness of the situation, and radioed her senior officer, Detective Inspector Stuart Lewis, who was also on duty that night, telling him he was urgently required. Lewis was an experienced police officer and had been a member of the South Wales Police Force for more than twenty years. He had investigated numerous serious crimes, including two murders that had resulted in convictions.

When Detective Inspector Lewis arrived at Kelvin Road, his seniority effectively placed him in charge of the crime scene. John Campbell, Eric Thomas and shortly afterwards Alison Crewe all told him that the victims had not died as a result of the fire but from injuries inflicted on them. Three of the bodies were still laid out on the lawn in front of the house, and Lewis could see this for himself. This was a multiple murder and demanded the highest level of priority and immediate action. But the house was still on fire and the crime scene was overrun by firemen whose primary concern was to make it safe and minimise risk, rather than to preserve evidence for use in any future criminal proceedings.

However, Detective Inspector Lewis knew full well the steps needed to be taken in a situation such as this: taking command, restricting access to the crime scene and preserving evidence so that the criminal investigation could begin promptly. He also knew that everything had to be done strictly by the book, otherwise valuable time might be wasted, important clues missed and even vital evidence contaminated and rendered useless for legal purposes, or even lost for ever. But to this day, for reasons known only to himself, Lewis took none of these steps and, instead, quickly removed himself from the scene.

Chapter 2

Between 1980 and 2000 South Wales Police gave an entirely new meaning to the expression 'trial and error'. Of all the police forces in Britain, South Wales Police has been responsible for some of the worst miscarriages of justice in the United Kingdom. By the time of the Clydach murders, no fewer than nine earlier murders investigated by the force had proved to be miscarriages of justice, and nineteen people had been freed after being wrongly convicted of crimes they did not commit. Had their trials been conducted before 1967, when the death penalty was abolished, those individuals would have been hanged.

In order to prove that a miscarriage of justice has taken place and to ensure that a conviction is quashed, new exculpatory evidence, which was not available at the trial, is required to show that the original conviction was unsafe. Alternatively, there must be proof of error by the trial judge, by the prosecution lawyers, or by the convicted person's defence team, or proof of corruption on the part of the police who had investigated the case. The waiting list for review is at least two years long, during which time the convicted person will remain in prison.

Many miscarriages of justice were caused by wrongdoing on the part of South Wales Police detectives. Evidence was routinely altered and fabricated. In some cases, detectives wrote statements themselves and then forced suspects or witnesses to sign them. In other cases, suspects were tortured, bullied or simply worn down by lengthy interviews into making untrue confessions. Vulnerable witnesses were 'leaned on' to make false statements implicating an innocent person in a crime; others were bribed, some intimidated. Prisoners serving time in jail were offered deals in return for signing false statements, and some detectives planted incriminating evidence where it was certain to be found, to frame innocent suspects for crimes they had not committed.

The practice of writing up notebooks at a later date than claimed – producing non-contemporaneous accounts of events – was exposed following the application of a modern forensic technique called Electro Static Detection Analysis (ESDA). Officers habitually wrote up their notebooks at a later time than they claimed. This is illegal and is also a disciplinary matter, but this unlawful practice nevertheless persisted as a simple means of obtaining evidence in order to achieve convictions.

In many cases later set aside by the Court of Appeal, ESDA testing proved that some officers lied about the times and dates when statements had been written. Often the statements were prepared only after officers had compared notes and colluded with their colleagues. This could be ascertained because forensic analysis revealed what had been written on pages below the page the statements were written on in the officers' notebooks, which included information that gave away what the officers had been doing.

In June 1999, two weeks before the Clydach murders, South Wales Police hit the national headlines when human rights lawyers and civil rights campaigners accused the force of 'corruption and incompetence on a massive scale'. They revealed that many of the murder cases the force had investigated over two decades were fundamentally flawed and were among the worst miscarriages of justice ever seen in Britain. The headline in the *Daily Express* on 13 June 1999 read: 'SHAME OF FORCE THAT DECIDED IT WAS ABOVE THE LAW'. The editorial outlined a number of cases in which South Wales Police detectives ignored both the legal and human rights of suspects in order to obtain convictions that were later revealed to be unsafe. A year later, the situation had not improved, and South Wales Police continued to tolerate illegal practices within its ranks in order to keep conviction rates high. A headline in *The Observer* on 15 October 2000 stated: 'CORRUPT FORCE IN FIRING LINE *sic*: PRESSURE GROWS FOR SOUTH WALES POLICE TO FACE INQUIRY OVER MISCONDUCT AND WRONGFUL IMPRISONMENTS'. But even though deep general concern and dissatisfaction persisted over the manner in which South Wales Police conducted many of its investigations, the Home Secretary, Jack Straw, was reluctant to agree to demands for a review.

Despite the pressure generated by the media, no inquiry was ever launched, although one was badly needed. There was little political will by the sitting Labour government to undermine the work carried out by South Wales Police, no matter how unlawful and insidious its practices were revealed to be. Bernard de Maid, a highly regarded criminal lawyer who represented two of the three defendants wrongfully convicted of the 1988 murder of Cardiff prostitute Lynette White, said: 'There has been, over the years, a corrupt clique of South Wales Police officers who have been responsible for various miscarriages of justice.' Satish Sekar, investigative author and civil rights campaigner, said: 'They [South Wales Police detectives] seem to decide who is guilty and then seek evidence to fit that scenario instead of allowing the evidence to lead them to the guilty.' Commenting on the Lynette White murder case in 2011, Sekar said: 'Innocent men were put behind bars following the murder.... The system is a disgrace.'

Between 1980 and 2000, thirty South Wales Police officers were temporarily suspended from duty as a result of using illegal and unacceptable investigative practices, but even where criminal charges were brought against them, no convictions resulted. Some officers were allowed to take early retirement on full pension, despite a catalogue of complaints recorded against them.

In one of these cases, it was shown that a senior detective had verbally and physically bullied suspects and vulnerable witnesses into making and signing untrue statements. In another case the same officer had handcuffed a male suspect to a hot radiator in order to force a confession from him. Other confessions were shown to have been fabricated, evidence vital to the defence team was not disclosed and notebooks and records were altered and lost.

All this is not to say that the entire corpus of the South Wales Police Force was corrupt. Of course it was not. But it is a recorded fact that the South Wales Police Force was responsible for more miscarriages of justice during this twenty-year period than any other police force in the UK. Those miscarriages of justice and the resulting wrongful imprisonments were the responsibility of a relatively small number of police detectives, but it was those few corrupt officers who were the root cause of the problem, and their wrongdoings tainted the force. Notable miscarriages of justice involving South Wales Police included the Darvell Brothers, the Cardiff Three, and the case of Jonathan Jones. A full list is included in the Appendix to this book.

All the miscarriages of justice for which the South Wales Police force was solely responsible were characterised by the same elements: dishonesty on the part of the responsible detectives, their rejection of a suspect's basic human and legal rights, and a determination to obtain a conviction at the cost of truth and justice. If framing an innocent person by police officers sworn to uphold the law was not bad enough, another custom that flourished within the ranks of South Wales Police was equally corrupt. This was the sinister practice of watching one another's backs. It ensured that a fellow police officer would escape the consequences of wrongdoing, no matter how serious the misconduct or criminal their actions might be.

Of all the miscarriages of justice set aside by the Court of Appeal, few were more shocking than the case of Stephen Miller, Yusef Abdullahi and Anthony Paris, known collectively as the 'Cardiff Three'. In 1988 they were framed for the brutal stabbing to death of Cardiff prostitute Lynette White, and sentenced to life imprisonment. It took eleven years for the case to be brought before the Court of Appeal when, in 1999, eight police officers were shown to have acted wrongfully during the murder investigation, and the Cardiff Three were set free. The responsible police officers were arrested and charged with conspiracy to pervert the course of justice. Some were charged with perjury. Despite the damning evidence against them, they all pleaded not guilty to the charges.

The reason why the police officers were so confident in their pleas soon became abundantly clear. Chief Superintendent Chris Coutts, an experienced police officer, was placed in charge of the investigation, and yet before their trial had even started, two sets of paperwork, vital to the prosecution case, went missing. The trial ended there and then, with formal verdicts of not guilty and all eight police officers walking free from court.

The following year, the missing documents miraculously reappeared. They had not been destroyed after all, but by that time it was too late. The case had been thrown out and the suspects could not be retried. On 16 July 2013 reports released by the Independent Police Commission and HM Crown Prosecution Inspectorate revealed a failure by the police and prosecution to control their files. It was justice denied to the Cardiff Three.

Meanwhile, during the same year, there was a growing clamour from all parties in the Welsh Assembly to formally ask the Home Secretary, Jack Straw, to launch a public inquiry into the activities of the South Wales Police. If granted, the potential consequences would be enormous. A public inquiry into so many miscarriages of justice would inevitably lead to questioning ministers in Parliament and loss of confidence in the Chief Constable of the South Wales Police and his force. Reputations would be shattered and careers ruined. It would be a crisis of monumental proportions from which it might take decades for the police force to recover. For all these reasons, the South Wales Police, under the leadership of Chief Constable Sir Anthony Burden, and on the brink of a new murder investigation in the aftermath of the Clydach house fire, was determined to avoid yet another miscarriage of justice. Their stated intention was to conduct this murder hunt properly, effectively and strictly by the book.

Speaking early on in the Clydach murder investigation, Detective Chief Superintendent Wynne Phillips, head of South Wales CID, put his reputation on the line when he vowed: 'I am determined that in the event of a trial there must be no appeal against a guilty verdict as a result of what we have, or have not done…. If there is, it must only be on legal grounds.'

But the investigation was doomed before it started. Corruption and systematic wrongdoing by officers in the South Wales Police, determined to get a conviction at any cost, were endemic and too deeply rooted. Furthermore, the consequences for any officer found guilty of misconduct were not onerous. Internal enquiries by officers investigating their own colleagues usually ended with no sanctions imposed. Court hearings were sabotaged, leaving guilty officers to walk free. Punishments or written warnings were of little or no deterrence. At the time of the Clydach murders, officers in the South Wales Police force had little to fear if they were caught out.

Detectives in the South Wales Police were not above the law, but they knew how the criminal justice system could be manipulated. Furthermore, they knew they could rely on their colleagues to support them. They were poachers turned gamekeepers, able to both commit crimes and to get away with them.

The Murders at 9 Kelvin Road

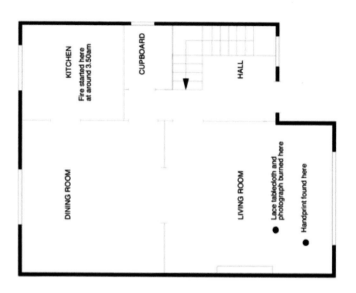

GROUND FLOOR PLAN

KITCHEN

Fire started here at around 3.50am

CUPBOARD

HALL

DINING ROOM

LIVING ROOM

- Lace tablecloth and photograph burned here
- Handprint found here

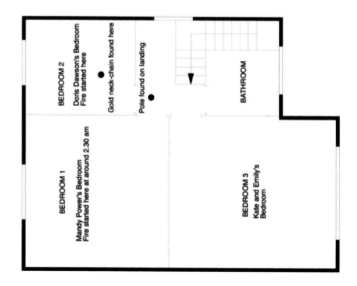

FIRST FLOOR PLAN

BEDROOM 2

Doris Dawson's Bedroom
Fire started here

Gold neck-chain found here

Pole found on landing

BATHROOM

BEDROOM 1

Mandy Power's Bedroom
Fire started here at around 2.30 am

BEDROOM 3

Kate and Emily's Bedroom

25

Chapter 3

When night-duty police officers at the Kelvin Road crime scene ended their shift at 6 a.m. on that fateful June Sunday morning, they made their way to police headquarters in Cockett, Swansea. On their arrival some 30 minutes or so later, they promptly handed in their reports to the duty officer. Only then, about two hours after the crime had first come to light, did South Wales Police realise that they were dealing with a serious crime. Valuable time had been lost, and there followed a frantic scramble to action as word of the murders quickly spread and the detectives on duty prepared themselves to deal with the situation.

In the event of a serious incident, such as rape or murder, weekend emergency cover was provided by senior detectives on a rota basis. On the weekend of 26/27 June, cover was provided by Detective Superintendent Martyn Lloyd-Evans, so the Clydach murders file landed on his desk. Second in command was veteran officer Deputy Detective Chief Inspector Chris Coutts, who, more than a decade earlier, had headed the disastrous Lynette White murder investigation.

Martyn Lloyd-Evans had been a police officer for almost thirty years. He had spent most of his career in the South Wales Police working as a detective inspector in Caerphilly and Cardiff. In the mid-1980s he worked with the Regional Crime Squad. For the eight years leading up to the Kelvin Road murders he had worked with the Major Crime Support Unit (MCSU), the police unit responsible for investigating serious crime. In his long career, Lloyd-Evans had been involved in more than 50 murder investigations. Even so, when he witnessed the extent of crimes inside 9 Kelvin Road, he was reduced to tears.

As soon as reinforcements arrived, the crime scene at 9 Kelvin Road was secured and a murder investigation began. By 7 a.m.

Police Surgeon Carl Harry had arrived to examine the victims for signs of life. Three smoke-stained bodies remained under blankets at the front of the house, while a fourth was in bed in a back bedroom of the house. The fire had been brought under control and the flames extinguished. The interior of the house and the outside walls above the windows of the rooms where the fire had burned were blackened by smoke. Throughout the house a thick layer of dark-grey ash had settled on every horizontal surface.

After examination, Mr Harry pronounced the victims dead. He then estimated the times of their deaths based on a formula by which the rate of body cooling is calculated, and the extent of rigor mortis. Later the bodies were removed to Morriston Hospital mortuary where full pathological examinations would be carried out over the next few days. Carl Harry's report would record in brief terms the injuries the victims had sustained, which, in his opinion, had caused their deaths. For all four victims his note recorded the same comment: 'The indications were of traumatic injuries being sustained prior to or around the time of death.'

As the Morriston and Pontardawe fire services rolled up their hoses, packed away their equipment and checked off their marker-pen tally to ensure that all the firefighters were accounted for, Dr Deryk James, a Home Office forensic pathologist, and two forensic scientists arrived at Kelvin Road to begin their investigations. Dr James confirmed Mr Harry's findings, recording the 'obvious blunt head injuries' sustained by all the deceased. He also noted the end of a pink vibrator protruding from Mandy Power's vagina.

Local journalists who had thought they were turning up to a house fire in Clydach found themselves reporting a multiple murder. The families of the victims were quickly traced and informed of the deaths. Michael Power, Mandy Power's former husband and Katie and Emily's father, was visited by police at Eynon's bakery in Pontardawe. He had been at home with his new partner, Sara Williams, at the time of the killings. Distraught, he could provide no explanation for the attack, nor, he told detectives, was he aware of any threats made against his former wife. His pain was so immense that he was unable to speak publicly for a month. When at last he did, he said: 'I have lost Katie and Emily, the two most important people in my life.' He then made an emotional appeal, on behalf of the police, to find the killer: 'These children could have been your children and I ask people to think about this and come forward to the inquiry team with any information you may have.'

Mandy's three older married sisters, Margaret Jewell, Julie Evans and Sandra Jones, and her brother, Robert Dawson, were also overcome with grief when they learned of the tragic deaths. Speaking on behalf of the family, Mandy Power's brother-in-law Peter Jewell said that they were struggling with their loss, but were confident that the police would catch the killer. 'We want the person behind bars. We will never get over our loss, but it will mean someone is off the streets.'

On the day after the murders, a press conference was called at Cockett Police Station headquarters at which news of the crime was announced to a packed assembly of journalists. A broadcast was made on national television, and an appeal called for witnesses to come forward. Speaking on behalf of South Wales Police, Detective Superintendent Lloyd-Evans said: 'Amanda, a devoted mother, came home with her two children at 12.30 a.m., I need to know what happened after that. Three generations of a family have died and a family has been devastated by this appalling crime. They have been brutally attacked and it is important that we get to the bottom of this as soon as possible.'

It was the worst multiple murder in the history of Wales and there was no obvious motive, but Lloyd-Evans managed to convey the impression that all was well in his investigation. From the clues he believed must have been left in the house, he was confident the police would have the killer in custody by nightfall. In reality, Lloyd-Evans and his team were feeling anything but confident.

Detective Inspector Stuart Lewis, the first senior police officer to turn up at 9 Kelvin Road and who had de facto control of the crime scene, had seen the horrifically injured bodies of the victims and knew they had been murdered. His rank placed a responsibility on him to take control of the situation and follow a strict protocol of preserving the crime scene against loss, contamination or damage, and reporting the situation to senior officers and the control, thus setting a murder inquiry in motion. Furthermore, he was expected to remain at the scene of the crime until reinforcements arrived. It was vital to follow proper procedures if the police were to stand the best chance of catching the murderer quickly. And for reasons that soon became clear, Stuart Lewis should have contacted his superiors in order to have himself removed from the case.

But instead, within minutes of being informed by John Campbell, Eric Thomas and police officer Alison Crewe that the victims had died as a result of the injuries inflicted on them and not from the fire, Stuart Lewis hurriedly abandoned the scene of these horrific murders. Estimates by witnesses of the time Lewis remained in Kelvin Road range from five to fifteen minutes. He gave no plausible explanation as to why he was leaving, nor did he organise a senior police officer to replace him. It was a gross dereliction of duty and a serious disciplinary offence.

The crime scene and all operational procedures were consequently left to Police Constable Alison Crewe, then an Acting Sergeant, who had summoned Lewis to the scene in the first place. Also on duty at this time was Constable David Williams, who had accompanied Crewe to Kelvin Road. In an understatement of monumental proportions, Crewe said later: 'I was surprised he [Detective Inspector Lewis] left the scene so suddenly.'

Fifty officers were quickly assigned to the case and began their hunt for a killer. While the trail had not yet gone cold, it had certainly cooled, and some of the detectives were annoyed about the unnecessary delay. At this point they cast around for someone else to take the blame, and their eyes quickly settled on a likely candidate. The police accused fire officers of trampling all over the crime scene, removing three of the bodies and failing to preserve evidence which, they said, amounted to gross negligence on the part of the fire service. This was both untrue and unfair. The first duty of the firemen was to preserve life, followed closely by their second duty, which was to bring the fire under control. Preserving evidence was not their immediate responsibility: that was a job for the police. In any event, the firemen had informed Detective Inspector Stuart Lewis of the crime, so if valuable evidence was lost or damaged as a result of delay, the police had no one to blame but their own.

In the internal disciplinary inquiry that followed, Stuart Lewis gave no explanation for his abrupt departure from the crime scene, nor did he clarify why he had failed to report the murders to his superior officers. The account he eventually gave at a disciplinary hearing which followed the inquiry was considered to be untrue. ESDA testing proved that Stuart Lewis' account of the incident, which he recorded in his notebook, was written two days *after* the event and, even then, some of it had been altered. These questions remain unanswered to this day. It was, and still is, a highly unsatisfactory state of affairs.

What *is* known for certain is that when Stuart Lewis returned to Morriston Police Station, he reported the fire to a superior officer but, incredibly, not the murders. In the police station, he made a lengthy private telephone call and was seen feeding numerous coins into a payphone that was located in the public waiting area. Police Constable Geraint Usher, who had accompanied Lewis from Clydach to the police station, observed Lewis on the telephone talking about events in Kelvin Road to a person who was never identified.

Why did Stuart Lewis use a payphone in a public area of the station to make his call when he had a private phone in his office? The telephone in his office would have logged his call; the payphone did not. It was the only phone in the building that he could have used if he did not want his call to be traced. Even though all this activity took place during his work shift, Lewis never divulged the identity of the person to whom he had spoken. Neither would he say what they had discussed.

It later emerged that these were not the only occasions that Stuart Lewis had behaved oddly that day. When his shift ended later that morning, he returned to his home in Pontardawe, showered and went to bed. He mentioned nothing about the murders to his partner, even though he was aware that the victims were well known to his brother and sister-in-law. She found out about the murders only when two police officers called at their home during the afternoon to speak with him about the crime. But even more crucially, Lewis was found to have been absent from his police station office between midnight and 3 a.m. – the very time when the murders were believed to have been committed. His unmarked red Peugeot police car was also missing from the police station's car park. He was on duty at the time and should have been catching up with paperwork in his office. Several police officers later gave evidence that they had looked in on Lewis during these hours, but he was nowhere to be seen.

Yet, despite all Stuart Lewis' wrongdoing, his flagrant disregard for police regulations and protocols, the unconscionable delay in commencing the biggest murder hunt in the history of Wales, which could be laid squarely at his feet, Lewis was never brought to book or faced disciplinary sanctions. He was not demoted as a result of his conduct and continued to work until his retirement from the force.

And if all this might be considered bad enough news for a police force struggling to repair its tattered reputation in the wake of so many miscarriages of justice, worse would follow. As the boiling anger of Detective Superintendent Martyn Lloyd-Evans and his team increased with each new revelation of wrongdoing within the force, it now turned to acute embarrassment as another shock development came to light.

Stuart Lewis has two brothers: Chris, who is younger, and Stephen, his identical twin brother. Stephen was a serving police officer, a sergeant in South Wales Police based in Neath, at the time of the murders. At 9 a.m. on Sunday morning after the fire, Stephen Lewis and his wife Alison – a former police officer – turned up at 9 Kelvin Road, which now was a cordoned-off crime scene. Barriers had been erected at either end of the road, preventing all traffic except official vehicles from entering the hitherto quiet residential street.

The couple confirmed the identity of the victims with officers at the scene, and then Alison Lewis seemed to become extremely distressed. The reason why soon became clear. As the police investigation progressed, it was revealed that she had been having an affair with one of the victims, Mandy Power.

Quickly departing the murder scene, Alison and Stephen Lewis returned to their home at 8 West Crossways in Pontardawe, where she collapsed in paroxysms of grief. Also present in her home at this time were Neath solicitor Joanne

Anthony, Anthony's daughter Victoria, and Kimberley Wilson, a friend of Alison Lewis. Joanne Anthony later described how, inconsolable in her apparent grief, Lewis held out her hands while tears streamed down her face as she called out to her erstwhile lover. Victoria would later describe Lewis as being 'in a very distressed state'.

Saying that she could not go on living without Mandy, Alison went upstairs to a bedroom. Her husband Stephen and Joanne Anthony followed her and then restrained her from jumping out of a first-floor window.

On 7 July, ten days after the murders, Alison Lewis booked herself into Cefn Coed psychiatric hospital in Swansea, where she stayed for 14 days. While she was there, she was kept on a 24-hour suicide watch. Two police officers stood guard outside her room. During this time detectives investigating the murders could not question her unless her doctors agreed that she was sufficiently mentally competent to understand the nature of the questioning. Alison Lewis failed to cooperate with medical staff and refused to leave her room while the officers were on guard, even when she was expected to attend a fire drill. No statement could legally be obtained from her at this time, although she voluntarily provided samples of her saliva for DNA testing.

Alison Lewis' husband also knew Mandy Power. Sergeant Stephen Lewis had met her at their home in Pontardawe when she visited on two or three occasions. In fact, on Friday 25 June, little more than 24 hours before the murders, Mandy Power had joined the Lewis family and their twin four-year-old daughters, Catrin and Rhiannon, for a barbeque. Mandy's own children, Katie and Emily, had stayed with their father that night on an access visit at his home in Pontardawe.

On the day that Alison Lewis was admitted to Cefn Coed Hospital, a South Wales Police spokesperson confirmed that Stephen Lewis had temporarily flown to Germany with his daughters, 'to avoid the adverse publicity' that was gathering in the lower Swansea Valley.

By this point it had become known that a senior South Wales Police officer and his ex-police officer wife had been intimately involved with one of the murder victims, and another related police officer had inexplicably abandoned the crime scene. So it might have been prudent for Sir Anthony Burden, Chief Constable of South Wales Police, to have handed the investigation over to another police force. Such a transfer of responsibility would have removed any suspicion that South Wales Police might, yet again, be seeking to look after their own. It would also eliminate any temptation by fellow officers to leak to their colleagues' sensitive information that might hinder the investigation and prejudice its outcome.

And, although its significance would not become known until later, there was another reason why the investigation should have been handed over to another police force. Alison Lewis, her husband Stephen and brother-in-law Stuart knew a number of police officers in the South Wales Police both as work colleagues and friends. Many of these officers were working on the murder investigation. Thus, as the Lewis' involvement with one of the victims became known, their connection to colleagues involved in the case would throw further suspicion on the force as one unable in this instance to act with disinterest and integrity.

There was yet another issue which should have increased pressure on the Chief Constable to consider whether his force should continue investigating the murders, and this would have come to light at the time if the investigating police officer had not been silent on the matter. Alison Lewis knew Martyn Lloyd-Evans well: they had worked together at Llanishen police station in Cardiff several years previously. But this extraordinary disclosure would not become public knowledge until Alison Lewis revealed the association in an HTV Wales interview many months later.

Remarkably, South Wales Police and Sir Anthony Burden retained responsibility for the conduct of the case, even though officers in the force would inevitably find themselves investigating their colleagues. The lessons of recent history unlearned, this decision meant that, in a time-honoured tradition, police officers were able to watch out for one another. Confidential information crucial to the investigation could be passed on by detectives involved in the case to their fellow officers Stephen and Stuart Lewis, who were not entitled to receive it. In the event, this is *exactly* what the Lewises later claimed did happen.

Stuart Lewis' early-morning disappearance from Swansea Police Station, and his incomprehensible act of abandoning the crime scene, Alison Lewis' sexual relationship with one of the victims, and other incriminating evidence that soon came to light, which *prima facie* implicated the Lewises in the crime, was more than sufficient for them to be arrested and brought in for questioning. Yet, astonishingly, Detective Superintendent Lloyd-Evans did not take this seemingly obvious step. That moment was unaccountably delayed for more than a year. On 4 July 2000, in a series of three dawn raids, Alison Lewis and her husband Stephen were arrested on suspicion of murder, while Stuart Lewis, Stephen's identical twin brother, was arrested on suspicion of conspiracy to pervert the course of justice.

But despite the substantial weight of evidence against them, it was not the Lewises who would stand in the dock for the Clydach murders. That unfortunate position would be occupied by someone else altogether, a man who would be convicted of the killings on the strength of a single piece of evidence, lies and his lack of a solid alibi. It was David George (Dai) Morris, a builder's labourer with a police record for robbery and violence, who swore on his children's lives that he had had nothing to do with the crimes.

Chapter 4

As the media circus and restless crowds waiting outside 9 Kelvin Road on the morning of the murders grew larger, the fire-gutted house was taped off before being filmed, photographed, catalogued and forensically examined in minute detail. The investigation and the search for evidence in and around the house took almost three weeks to complete. It would turn out to be the longest crime scene investigation ever carried out in Wales.

A routine police video was taken of the crime scene. Apart from a brief introduction, it was a silent movie. Every harrowing detail left in the aftermath of the crime was preserved in a 40-minute film. Nothing was omitted for fear of missing some vital clue, and out of respect for the victims, all of whom displayed the most appalling injuries. The video would play a key part in the two trials that would follow.

Claire Galbraith, a forensic scientist, was one of the first experts to enter the burned-out house on Sunday morning as the hunt for evidence and the murder weapon began. Also on the investigative team were forensic scientists Robert Bell and Dr Michael Barber, who was a footmark and fingerprint specialist; Michael Appleby, an expert in DNA analysis, and scene of crimes investigators Gerald Williams, David White and John Rees. Two Home Office pathologists were present: Dr Deryk James, who would later conduct the postmortem examinations, and Dr Peter Vanezis, who had practiced forensic pathology for more than twenty years. Other forensic scientists would be drafted in later, each a specialist in their own field. One of these was Dr Jonathan Whitaker, a leading expert in DNA profiling.

Detective Superintendent Martyn Lloyd-Evans made an announcement to reporters at Cockett Police Station, telling them 'the inquiry is still in its infancy'. Speaking of the manner in which the victims were killed, he said: 'We believe all members of the family were struck with a heavy object – some sort of implement perhaps.'

Interest among the waiting crowds intensified as detectives continued the investigation and questioned neighbours. They watched as drain covers in the street were lifted off, manholes were searched and probed with torches as police hunted for the murder weapon and any evidence connected with the crime.

All this activity took place under the gaze of UK national television cameras, a battery of radio microphones and a gaggle of newspaper reporters, some local, others from farther afield. News of the murders quickly spread and an anxious public wanted to know all the details. Journalists mingled with neighbours in Kelvin Road, gathering whatever newsworthy items they could.

One reporter discovered that it was not the first time 9 Kelvin Road had provided the stage for human tragedy. Forty-five years earlier, in 1953, a previous owner of the house had accidentally shot himself dead while trying to kill a rat in the garden. Shocked neighbour Shirley Macmillan described Mandy to milling reporters as 'a pretty girl with very friendly children'. She said: 'She was a devoted mum – always with her kids. We are all devastated.'

Local councillor Sylvia Lewis, who knew both Michael Power, Mandy's ex-husband, and her bedridden mother, Doris Dawson, spoke aloud the words everyone else was thinking: 'This is terrible, terrible, terrible. There seems to be no motive.' She explained that widowed Doris Dawson had 'suffered a brain haemorrhage several years earlier and was in poor health. Even so, she always put a brave face on things, and was well liked.'

At about noon on the day of the murders, a young witness, Nicola Williams, from Sunnybank in Clydach, appeared at the crime scene. She told detectives that on the previous evening she and a female friend had driven up to Cardiff for a night out. They returned early in the morning, arriving back in Clydach at around 2.20 a.m. At this time there was just a slight drizzle. Ms Williams dropped off her friend in Vardre Road and continued driving home alone. When she turned right off the main Lone Road into Gellionnen Road, she saw a man ahead of her walking quickly up the hill towards the junction with Kelvin Road. As she drew closer to him, she decreased her speed to a crawl and lowered her window. When they were level with one another, she looked directly at the man to see if he was someone from the village whom she knew. At the time, he was passing under a streetlight and he turned to face her, so she saw him clearly. But she did not recognise him and so drove on home without thinking any more about it.

Later that morning, when Nicola Williams heard about the murders, she remembered the man, realised her sighting might be important, and left for Kelvin Road immediately to pass on her information. She described him as being in his thirties, six feet tall or a little more. He was wearing dark jeans or trousers and a shiny bomber jacket which she said 'looked like something police wear', and he was carrying a bag under his arm.

On Wednesday 7 July, Nicola Williams attended Cockett Police Station by appointment to meet a police e-fit operator. There she provided an image of the man she saw which she believed was a good likeness and around 90 per cent accurate. Attempting to identify the type of jacket this man was wearing, police accompanied Nicola Williams to several clothing shops, some of them as far afield as Cardiff, but, despite their efforts, she was unable to find anything that resembled the police-type jacket she said the man had been wearing.

Less than a week later, on 13 July, Detective Superintendent Martyn Lloyd-Evans appeared on BBC *Crimewatch* when he appealed directly to the public for their help in catching the murderer. It was the first of three appearances he was to make on this popular programme, and he also appeared on HTV's *Crimestoppers*. But even though he now possessed an e-fit image of a man who had been seen walking towards Kelvin Road at 2.20 a.m. on the morning of the murders, he made no reference to him nor, inexplicably, did he show his image in any of the programmes. This was an astonishing omission, since the man was a person of interest to the South Wales Police whom they would surely have wished to question in relation to the crime if only to eliminate him from the inquiry, and here was an opportunity lost to show his likeness to the programme's four million viewers.

Chapter 5

The manner in which the four victims were attacked and killed was established by pathological examinations conducted at Morriston Hospital, and by a thorough forensic examination of evidence obtained from inside the house. Human tissue found on the floor and blood spatter patterns left on the floor, walls, ceilings, doors and doorframes, furniture – and in one room, a radiator – told their own story, while forensic pathology reports of the injuries sustained by the victims confirmed the experts' findings.

Even though the front door had been damaged by neighbours who had reported the fire, and kicked in afterwards by the fire crew, there were no obvious signs of forced entry by anyone else. This meant that if the murderer had gained access to the house by the front door, he or she must have been let in, or have been in possession of a key.

Lying in the charred debris on the landing, close to where the bodies of Katie and her mother were found, investigators came across a thick plastic-covered pole about four-feet long. It was pointed at one end and blood could be seen on its tip. It was a heavy, blunt instrument, consistent with the type of weapon police believed had been used in the attack; a thorough forensic examination would tell for certain. It had already been recorded on video; it was now photographed *in situ*, bagged and tagged and sent off to the Home Office crime laboratory in Chepstow.

A mobile phone belonging to Mandy Power was discovered in one of the smoke-blackened rooms. It was checked for messages and was expected to reveal useful information, but nothing helpful to the investigation was apparently found. A photograph of the two little girls, charred in a deliberate attempt to burn it, was found in the lounge. Two of the family's kittens were found to have died in the fire, while two adult cats survived in the house and a third kitten was later found alive.

Dr Michael Barber began the search for fingerprints. Those found would be checked against persons who had a legitimate reason for being in the house, isolating those who did not. Any fingerprints that could not be identified would be referred to the Police National Computer data base where they would be cross-referenced against the fingerprints of known criminals.

Forensic scientist Robert Bell's investigation discovered that the first of four separate fires had been started in Mandy Power's bedroom at around 2.30 a.m., while the last, and the major cause of the blaze, had begun in the kitchen at around 3.50 a.m., just 37 minutes before smoke was spotted. Burned matches were discovered near the source of one of the fires, indicating the way in which the fires were started. The black, calcified remains were photographed, then carefully bagged and tagged. Forensic examination would detect any DNA or partial fingerprint left on the matches, and establish which make of matches was used.

Claire Galbraith's investigation established the likely chronology of events. Her findings were based on the murder victims' injuries, on bloodstain evidence found inside the house and on the murder weapon. Her opinions were later confirmed by reports following postmortem examinations of the victims. It took three weeks to complete the postmortems, and the bodies were examined over several days. So extensive were the injuries that, unusually, the victims were X-rayed inside their body bags.

A chemical reagent, Luminol, was used to find traces of blood left at the crime scene. Luminol exposes blood molecules so small that they are invisible to the naked eye. This chemical is an invaluable tool for forensic investigators and is widely used to help establish the order of events at a crime scene.

Blood spatter patterns and expired blood, breathed out as a fine mist by a person who has sustained wounds to the face, throat or lungs, can reveal the actual and relative positions of the attacker, the victim and anyone else present. They also help investigators to build up an accurate picture of what happened during the attack.

A chemical test called the 'Christmas Tree Stain' was used extensively throughout the house in Kelvin Road to detect semen. If traces of semen were found, it would indicate that sexual activity involving a male had occurred. When viewed under a microscope, the stain colours the heads of the sperm red and the tails green, which is where the test derives its name, since a positive stained slide looks a little like a decorated fir tree. But no traces of semen were found either on Mandy Power's naked corpse, her underwear, her outer garments, her bed, on anything else, or anywhere in the house.

Claire Galbraith was of the opinion that all the killings had taken place upstairs and might have involved more than one attacker. She said: 'Doris Dawson was attacked sitting or lying in her bed, Katie was attacked and beaten on the landing, Emily in the girls' bedroom. Mandy Power was injured in her own bedroom before going into her mother's room.'

Mandy Power, her mother and daughters were all struck repeatedly with the same heavy pole. The heads of each of the victims were hit with such force that their skulls were smashed and extensive bone damage was caused to all four individuals.

Claire Galbraith said the forensic evidence showed that Doris Dawson was the first to be killed, while Katie was probably the last. The defenceless pensioner was struck a blow directly to her face with the pole. Such great force was used that her skull was crushed and her upper jaw was split away from it. Several further blows were directed to her upper body, and she died from a combination of shock and colossal head and chest injuries. Hanging from her bedroom ceiling was a smashed light bulb. Blood spatter evidence showed that it had been broken when it was struck during one of the blows inflicted on the old lady. The breakage had caused a fuse to blow downstairs. A television set resting on a chair in the children's bedroom had been lifted onto the bed. The chair was taken to the downstairs lavatory where the murderer stood on it to reach the fuse box and repair the blown fuse. The television set was covered in blood; the chair was not. This meant that whoever killed Doris had ample time to mend the fuse before carrying out any further killings. It confirmed the findings of Claire Galbraith that the 80-year-old was killed first. It also meant that the murderer was almost certainly in the house *before* Power and her children returned home. Emily's body was found in her bedroom 'still in a cowering position', and it was her blood that was found on the television set.

The order in which Mandy and her daughter Emily died was less certain. It appeared that Emily was killed in her bedroom by a single blow, or perhaps by multiple blows from the pole. Dr Deryk James said: 'Eight-year-old Emily was probably unconscious from one of the first of fifteen blows rained down on her.'

Forensic tests showed that Mandy Power was attacked in her own bedroom. She too had been smashed in the face with the pole. A bloodied tooth knocked from her jaw was found on the floor. An expired mist of blood breathed onto the carpet, the doorframe, and oval blood droplets on the floor, pointed at one end, indicated the path she had taken as she fled from the bedroom. Analysis of the white blood cells and DNA fingerprinting revealed it to be Mandy Power's blood.

Her flight from danger took her onto the landing where she continued to expirate a fine mist of blood which forensic investigators later found on the carpet and walls. The direction and impact angle of the blood drops showed that Mandy Power's head was about five feet above the floor and moving towards her mother's bedroom. She had entered the bedroom where her murdered mother lay dead in her bed. Badly injured, Mandy Power was bleeding but still conscious. The drops of her blood on the floor were now circular, indicating the point at which she stopped moving or running away.

Examination of Mandy Power's head found the shape of a Maltese cross indented in her skull. It corresponded with the same distinctive shape on a chest of drawers in her mother's bedroom. This injury confirmed that she had either been deliberately thrown, or had fallen against the heavy piece of furniture. An analysis of blood spatter patterns at this point showed that her head was less than two feet above the floor.

More blood spatter patterns over a wide area and more expirated blood found on the walls and floor showed that Mandy Power was attacked again in her mother's bedroom and struck repeatedly with the pole. Tiny drops of blood from the pole made dotted red lines on the ceiling, walls, carpet and bedroom furniture, each line of small red dots representing a blow. The victim might have tried to defend herself and her daughters at this point by fighting back. It was suggested that she may even have managed to scratch her attacker's face. She had certainly sustained defensive injuries to her forearms, but routine fingernail clippings and scrapings under the nails found no evidence of foreign DNA to confirm that Mandy Power had inflicted any injury upon her attacker.

As she died, so her expirated blood and the pattern it made on the carpet indicated the point where she had fallen to the floor, though the texture of the carpet made the pattern indistinct. The position and shape of the blood spatters also showed in which direction her head was turned when she finally succumbed to her injuries.

Even after Mandy Power's death, the remorseless attack continued. The murderer continued to rain down blows on her lifeless body. Pathological examination revealed later that she had sustained 38 separate injuries, and 15 blows were directed to her face and head alone. Her skull was broken into ten separate pieces. Marks on her neck suggested that an attempt had also been made to strangle her. Mysteriously, after the attack, a silver wrist watch had been placed on her wrist.

At some point between the time when the violence began and when Mandy Power's body was left to be consumed by the fire, all her clothing was removed. Her T-shirt was found on the floor close to the partition wall between her and her mother's bedrooms. Mandy's denim wraparound skirt and her tights were found in the downstairs hallway, suggesting that this was where the attack on her had begun. A pink, battery-operated vibrator was found pushed deep into her vagina, with only the circular plastic end exposed. A statement by pathologist Dr Peter Vanezis, read out in court later, said he 'believed the pink vibrator found in Mandy's body was pushed into her either when she was immobile or unconscious or after she had died'.

Eight-year-old Emily was found partially undressed, as though she had been getting ready for bed. Blood spatter patterns showed that the little girl was attacked in the bedroom she shared with her older sister Katie, almost certainly as she cowered in terror. She sustained severe facial and skull fractures from powerful blows, and even after she was dead her merciless assailant repeatedly hit her.

Ten-year-old Katie, still wearing her outdoor clothes and thought to be the last to be killed, was attacked on the landing with a determination and viciousness that beggars belief. A violent blow to the back of her head probably killed her instantly. A forensic examination of the pole found Katie's blood on the tip, and it was this evidence which determined that she was probably the last to die.

More blood on the floor, this time drops from the pole itself, led to the place where it had been discarded on the landing at some time after the attack, close to where the bodies of Mandy Power and Katie were found.

The extensive injuries inflicted on the victims had a devastating effect on police officers who attended the crime scene, and the fire crew, to whom the brigade counsellor provided several weeks of therapy. Several police officers also required professional trauma counselling to help them cope with what they had witnessed at 9 Kelvin Road. The reaction of fireman Neil MacPherson had been immediate. Distraught by what he saw inside the house and frustrated that he could do nothing about it, he had lashed out with his boot at the banister spindles, smashing them on his way downstairs.

For some, not even professional treatment was enough. Terry Williams, a mortuary attendant in Morriston Hospital, recognised the victims as his neighbours when their bodies were brought in. Helping pathologists with the grim task of examining them for clues gave him nightmares. Psychiatric treatment failed to cure him and he eventually left his job. Chris Bevan, a South Wales Police employee who had been instructed to clean up the crime scene, was so traumatised by what he saw that, three years later, he broke down and attempted to take his own life. Few people who witnessed the bodies or the crime scene in the aftermath of the murders were unaffected.

The murder weapon was examined microscopically by forensic scientists in the Home Office crime laboratory in Chepstow. They established that it was made of solid fibreglass and coated with plastic. It weighed one kilo, was 130cm long (about four feet) and 2cm (roughly one inch) in diameter. The scientists cut it in half so that it could be further examined. Traces of blood were found on the pole which exactly matched the profiles of Mandy Power and her daughters, but not that of Doris Dawson. Nevertheless, Claire Galbraith felt there was extremely strong evidence to show that the pole had been used to attack all four victims. The shape of the pole matched precisely some of the injuries that were inflicted on the old lady. She thought it was possible that blood from her injuries had either been flung off the pole as it was used to batter the other victims, or it had been wiped off before being used to batter the remaining victims. If this was the case, it confirmed that there was a delay between the time of Doris Dawson's murder, and the time when the rest of the family were attacked. Further microscopic examination of the murder weapon allegedly failed to detect any other DNA or fingerprints, and the only blood found on the pole was that of the other three victims.

But trace evidence was discovered. Known as the Locard Exchange Principle, this cornerstone of forensic science establishes that every contact made with another person, place or object results in an exchange of physical materials. Whether a human hair, a flake of skin, fibres or another material, something tangible is always left behind.

A blood-soaked white sports sock was found in Mandy Power's bedroom. Claire Galbraith tested the sock and identified traces of fibreglass and plastic from the murder weapon. She said: [it] 'might have been used by the killer as a glove.' And on the pole she discovered a single tiny strand of white cotton which was identical to the cotton used to make the sports sock. More strands of the same white cotton were also found on a blood-stained envelope found in the house. This discovery established that the killer had worn a sock over at least one hand to avoid leaving fingerprints when wielding the pole during the attack.

Other evidence was also found. Dr Michael Barber said that two bloody handprints from a left hand were found on the downstairs living room carpet near the television set, close to where video cassettes were kept. He examined a number of marks on the carpet, using chemicals, ultraviolet light and lasers, to confirm that two of the handprints were made in blood. Looking at one of the handprints, in particular, Dr Barber said that it could have been made either by a hand covered in blood, or by a hand inside a blood-stained sports sock.

In order to test his theory, Dr Barber carried out an experiment. Using sterilised horse blood to soak a sports sock, he placed his hand inside it and pressed down on a piece of the carpet that had been sent to him from the crime scene. He said the mark he made was effectively indistinguishable from the mark found on the carpet inside 9 Kelvin Road, although he also said that that mark could have been made by a bare hand. The locations of the handprints were recorded and photographically preserved for later analysis. The blood-stained sock was bagged and tagged and joined the rest of the evidence waiting to be transported to the Home Office crime laboratory in Chepstow.

On the carpet in Doris Dawson's bedroom, lying in some blood next to a dinner plate, where Mandy Power had been attacked, investigators found a piece of jewellery. It was a heavy, 9 carat gold unisex St Christopher neck-chain, 20 inches long, with circular links; it was bevelled at the edges and hallmarked 1989. Its jump ring and fastener were missing and a piece of wire had been used to make a temporary repair. The discovery of this broken chain suggested that Mandy Power had tried to defend herself and her daughters, and had ripped it from her assailant's neck in the struggle. This was by no means certain and the temporary repair suggested that there could easily have been another, innocent, explanation for the chain being found on the bedroom carpet. The broken gold chain was bagged and tagged, and taken away for forensic examination.

Tests carried out on the neck-chain proved that the blood on the chain was Mandy Power's, although, it was claimed, no DNA or fingerprints could be found on it. Relatives were questioned about its ownership, but no one knew at that time to whom the chain belonged and its significance was not immediately realised. When enquiries among the family were exhausted, the police suspected that it might belong to the killer.

Scene of crimes investigator David White made a curious find when examining Doris Dawson's body. She lay on her back in bed in the same position in which fireman Neil MacPherson had discovered her. MacPherson had not touched her body then, nor had it been moved since. Her head was resting on a blood-saturated pillow, her face battered and her nightdress blood-soaked. She was recognisable only by her gold wedding ring. Doris Dawson died of catastrophic injuries. Afterwards, the killer had packed paper around her body and set it alight. This was presumed to have been an attempt to destroy all evidence of the crime, but the fire quickly went out.

However, in the middle of the old lady's abdomen and placed on top of her nightdress, White found an engagement ring. No one knew to whom it belonged or from where it had come. Whether this was a symbolic gesture of some sort, or the killer's cryptic message, White was unable to say. An empty ring box was discovered on the floor of the living room, but whether the mystery ring had come from this box could not be established. The engagement ring was photographed where it was found, then it joined the silver watch placed on Mandy Power's wrist, with all the other evidence sent for forensic analysis.

As a team of police officers searched for evidence in the back garden and tool shed, the first of hundreds of tributes began arriving at 9 Kelvin Road. Bunches of flowers and soft toys, one a large pink and white teddy bear, were placed on the front lawn. They soon stretched from one side of the garden to the other. When there was no more room, the display overflowed onto the pavement. As the investigation inside the house progressed, forensic investigators had to step over the bouquets to get into the house. Children had picked wild flowers and put them into milk bottles; others were bought from florists and donated in bouquets by sympathisers, neighbours and friends.

Several gifts had messages attached. One note signed 'Rob' read: 'Farewell to two beautiful girls and two lovely mothers.' Detectives carefully examined even these tokens of affection, searching for clues that might lead them to the killer. People who had never known Mandy Power and her family brought flowers and gifts in a show of support and sympathy. The colourful floral display, which grew larger by the day, was in stark contrast to the fire-damaged, smoke-blackened house, which had once been the home of the family whose lives had been so brutally taken.

Chapter 6

What happened that night in 9 Kelvin Road was a crime that continued to dominate the news in Wales and the rest of Britain for months. South Wales Police were hounded daily by the media and were under intense pressure to make an arrest. Four innocent people had been murdered in their own home, and their killer was still at large.

The motive for the murders was unknown and Detective Inspector Martyn Lloyd-Evans told reporters that few useful clues had been found at the crime scene. Since discovery of a motive frequently leads to the perpetrator of a crime, the need to discover the reason behind the attacks became crucial.

Enquiries by detectives established that the heavy fibreglass pole used as the murder weapon had come from the nearby New Inn. This pub, standing a little back from a bend in the road, is located on the outskirts of Craig Cefn Parc village on the road leading to Clydach. Kelvin Road is less than a 15-minute walk away. Alan Cook, a previous landlord, had used the pole to reach a switch high up on the wall to turn the outside lights on and off. Glynn Hopkin, a pub regular and the previous occupier of 9 Kelvin Road, had asked Cook if he could have the pole for his wife Jayne, because she was nervous about intruders when she was alone in the house and he wanted to give her the pole to defend herself in case anyone tried to enter the house.

In April 1998, Hopkin took over the lease of the New Inn and moved in as its landlord. This left 9 Kelvin Road empty, though a few pieces of furniture and the pole were left behind. Hopkin then let the house to Mandy Power and her family. When they moved into the partly furnished house, the pole was effectively part of the fittings. In a grim irony, Mandy Power kept it to protect herself and her family.

On 1 July 1999, the same day that rumours of Mandy Power's affair with former policewoman Alison Lewis became public knowledge, detectives escorted twenty members of the victims' family to the house to see the crime scene. To enter, they had to walk through the sea of colourful flowers, and step over cuddly toys at the front door. On their way in, Mandy's sisters Sandra Jones and Julie Evans stopped for a moment and placed their own flowers and a large white teddy bear near the door with a note attached that read: 'Love you forever. God bless you. Lots of hugs and kisses.' After viewing the terrible aftermath of the murders and what remained of the fire-gutted home, the family members left, several in tears. All were shocked into silence.

By the simple process of eliminating 80-year-old Doris Dawson and the two little girls as the reason for the killings, Mandy Power was considered to be the person most likely to be at the centre of this dreadful catastrophe. The investigation, therefore, focused on her. The empty ring box on the lounge carpet, the engagement ring on her mother's corpse, the silver watch placed on Mandy Power's wrist and the attempt made to destroy a photograph of the two little girls brought an element of mystery to the crime. The brutal manner of Mandy Power's death – beaten, then stripped and a vibrator pushed into her vagina – gave her murder a sexual twist.

The police investigation quickly began examining Mandy Power's life, especially her love life, to see what in her past might provide clues. Family, friends and neighbours were all inter-viewed to help detectives build as full a picture as possible of the attractive young mother and her tragically short life. Police appeals on British television asked witnesses to come forward to reveal what they knew.

Police enquiries were far-reaching and stretched back to Mandy's schooldays. They established that in 1982, when she was just sixteen, Amanda 'Mandy' Dawson met Michael Power, a baker, her first serious boyfriend. Four years later they married with the blessing of Mandy's family. In May 1989, Mandy gave birth to their first child, Katie, and two years later, in May 1991, their second child, Emily, was born.

In the mid-1990s problems developed within their relationship when Michael took up golf, leaving Mandy feeling ignored and unloved. She found work as a part-time care assistant in a Clydach nursing home which gave her independence, while the income she earned increased her self-confidence and improved her social life. By 1996 the love and sex that Mandy wanted from the marriage had deteriorated to the point where, in desperation, she looked elsewhere for both. She began an affair with Richard Franks, a local taxi driver who used to drive her to work. The relationship did not last long and she attempted reconciliation with Michael, but it failed. In March 1998, Michael left the marital home and the marriage was over.

Even before the decree absolute finally dissolved the marriage, Mandy began to revel in her new-found freedom. She was in her early thirties, she was attractive and relished the attention male admirers gave her. She enjoyed affairs with several men, some of whom were married. All were traced by the police and investigated. One of these men was Robert Wachowski, the neighbour who had tried to rescue her and her family on the night of the fire. They had first met some months earlier when he had found a bottle of wine she had left on his doorstep with a note attached to it inviting him out for a drink. He accepted her offer, they got on well together and the relationship flourished, quickly becoming sexual. But Wachowski was just getting over a divorce and, even though his small son, David, enjoyed playing with Katie and Emily, he did not want the relationship to become serious and it fizzled out after only a few weeks. Their friendship continued, however, and Wachowski retained Mandy's number on his mobile phone. Wachowski told detectives that he knew about her relationship with Alison Lewis because she had discussed it with him. He recalled her telling him that they sometimes argued fiercely.

Another lover, Howard Florence, 36, was a former golf professional who worked at Nevada Bob's golf shop in Swansea.

When detectives questioned him about his relationship with Mandy Power, Florence lied repeatedly about the extent of his involvement with her. This, he explained later, was because he was married and did not want Yvonne, his wife of 17 years, to find out. Finally, he was forced to admit the truth about the affair. He told detectives that he and Mandy met about once a week and they always had sex on these occasions. He said 'Mandy was very shy of exposing her body and would cover up under the bed clothes.' Sometimes, he said, they used a vibrator during sex. Their physical relationship lasted for 18 months and ended in December 1998, although they kept in regular phone contact. Their last phone conversation had taken place on Saturday, 26 June 1999, the day before the murders. It was later established that Power carried around with her a photograph of Howard Florence, even after their relationship ended. On St Valentine's Day 1999 Florence sent Mandy flowers. By his own admission, he still had 'strong feelings for her' and said he 'would have continued the affair had she not, by then, met somebody else' – her new partner Alison Lewis.

Howard Florence said that sometimes when he telephoned Mandy the phone was answered by a woman, whom he assumed was Alison Lewis. He maintained that Mandy told him several times that Stephen Lewis, Alison's husband, knew of her affair with his wife. This was despite Stephen Lewis insisting later, under oath in court, that he had not known of his wife's relationship with Mandy until the morning of her death.

Mandy Power was clearly a warm, sensitive and vibrant young woman, devoted to her widowed mother, doting on her daughters, close to her brother Robert, her older sisters Margaret, Julie and Sandra, and loyal to her relatives and her many friends. Elizabeth Evans, who enjoyed evenings out with Mandy on a regular basis, said that : 'Mandy was fun to go out with. We had a brilliant laugh.' Lisa Sullivan, who sometimes acted as Mandy's babysitter said: 'Mandy was a really happy person who lived for her two girls. The children were getting to a really nice age and you could tell they were going to grow up to be lovely people. They were my little angels – my little rays of sunshine.'

But family and friends who were close to the recently divorced Mandy also worried about her. They felt that she was vulnerable and too trusting; that she did not recognise danger, but saw good in everyone. Mandy's sister Julie Evans said that Mandy had described Alison Lewis as 'possessive and jealous', and Mandy's close friend of twenty years, Manon Cherry, said: 'Alison Lewis dominated Mandy's life.'

Elizabeth Evans, who knew Mandy well, hinted that jealousy could have been the motive for the murders. Regrettably, she never explained her reasons for suggesting this. Another female friend, who did not wish to be named, said: 'Mandy was very attractive. Her personality made her shine; a lot of people were instantly attracted to her. She drew people to her like a magnet.' But, she continued, Mandy 'attracted people who tried to take over. She became stifled, but she was too nice to say so. I know that she worried over certain relationships.' Which relationships the friend unfortunately failed to specify.

Three weeks before her death, Mandy was seen in the company of a woman in the Farmers Arms pub in Clydach. A female witness who saw them together and overheard some of their conversation said she was discussing a 'problem relation-ship'. She gave the police a description of the woman Mandy was talking to, but despite their efforts they were never able to trace her.

The person with whom Mandy had become so deeply involved in the six months before her death was former South Wales Police officer Alison Lewis. This relationship naturally brought Lewis into the police spotlight, and while officers continued to make their enquiries elsewhere, others began the task of investigating Alison Lewis, her husband, South Wales Police Sergeant Stephen Lewis, and his twin brother, Detective Inspector Stuart Lewis.

It was quickly discovered that Alison Lewis was active in women's rugby. She was a club member and an outstanding player with an international reputation, having won seven caps for Wales. The police contacted rugby clubs in the Swansea Valley and a list was drawn up of registered members. All of them were traced and questioned. Officers also contacted local gay and lesbian groups in the area in their efforts to find out more about Alison Lewis.

While these enquiries were taking place, the police made another media appeal on 2 July which resulted in some 500 calls being received via the murder incident line. Incredibly, the police still made no mention in the programme about the unidentified man carrying a bag in the Kelvin Road area whom Nicola Williams had seen on the night of the murders.

It was established that on the Saturday evening, just hours before the murders, Mandy Power and her daughters had gone to the home of her nephew, Stephen Jones (a Dyfed Powys police constable, the son of her sister Sandra) to babysit for him and his wife Christine. As midnight approached, taxi driver Kevin Duffy picked up Stephen Jones and his wife from the Sunnybank Club in Clydach where they had been celebrating Stephen's parents' wedding anniversary. Duffy drove them to their home in Craig Cefn Parc, dropped them off, collected Mandy Power and her children and headed for Kelvin Road. Duffy was the last known person to have seen Mandy Power and her daughters alive.

Following the 2 July media appeal, Rosemary Jones, an elderly pensioner and widow who lived opposite 9 Kelvin Road, called the police to say that a car, which she had recognised as a diesel by its distinctive sound, had pulled up outside the house at about 12.45 a.m. on the morning of the murders. She then heard a car door open. Someone got out, she heard the car door close, and this was followed by the sound of footsteps going towards 9 Kelvin Road. Since this was about 15 minutes after Mandy Power and her children had arrived home, the information was naturally of great interest to the detectives.

In a subsequent witness statement, Rosemary Jones said she had looked out of her window and saw that the car's passenger was now inside the house, although whether the figure was male or female she was unable to say. Nor did she know if the person had let themselves into the house, or had been admitted by someone already inside.

By now, the ground floor light had come on. This seemed to indicate to Rosemary Jones that whoever had entered the house had turned on the light. She saw the silhouette of a person's head inside the house through the pane of frosted glass in the front door. Then the upstairs landing light went on. The front lounge curtains were open at this time, though they were normally closed at night. Upstairs, in the front bedroom where the children slept, the curtains were also open. This, Rosemary Jones believed, suggested that everyone in the house was still awake, though perhaps not 80-year-old invalid Doris Dawson.

These events were also witnessed by Rosemary Jones' adult son, Wayne. He too saw the shape of a head behind the frosted glass in the door, but was also unable to say whether the person was male or female. Their sightings would, however, enable the police to estimate the approximate height of the unknown person.

Less than a week after the murders, more than 100 witness statements had been taken and the murder hunt was already the biggest in Wales. A forensic science spokesperson confirmed that the house was still being searched for trace evidence: DNA, fingerprints, skin, hairs, blood particles and any human tissue that did not belong to the victims.

In a further announcement on national television, Detective Superintendent Martyn Lloyd-Evans said: 'Whilst we are delighted with the hundreds of telephone calls received, we are disappointed with the lack of response to our call for help following the clues we have had.' Inexplicably, yet again no mention was made of Nicola Williams' sighting of the man walking near Kelvin Road on the night of the murders.

Some callers put forward names of individuals whom they said police should interview. Several of them mentioned builder's labourer Dai Morris and he quickly became a 'person of interest' to the murder team.

Within two days of the murders, David George (Dai) Morris had been traced to the council flat he shared in Craig Cefn Parc village with his girlfriend, divorcee Mandy Jewell and her eight-year-old daughter Emma. At the time of the murders, Morris, a banned driver, did not own a car, though Jewell's flat in Rhyddwen Road was within easy walking distance of 9 Kelvin Road, perhaps 25 minutes at most.

Burly, heavily tattooed Morris, aged thirty-eight, was the father of three girls on whom he doted, Laura, Adele and Janine. His ex-wife Wendy had divorced him several years earlier after he physically abused her. Morris, originally from Gendros, a quiet suburban district of Swansea, was well known to the police and had a history of petty crime and violence, some of it directed towards women. Morris revelled in his reputation as a hard man, although he was not a practitioner in the martial arts. This fact would assume crucial significance at his trial. He was known as the Enforcer in the village where he now lived, and as the Nonce Basher in Swansea prison where he had spent several months for robbery and conspiracy to rob, before being moved to Dartmoor prison to complete a five-year sentence.

Morris' relationship with Mandy Jewell began in 1995. Both he and Jewell enjoyed a drink and the couple had had their share of ups and downs. He was very fond of Jewell's daughter, Emma, whom he treated as one of his own daughters. Sometimes after arguing with Jewell, Morris retreated to his own rented accommodation in Llangyfelach Road, Treboeth in Swansea. He said that 'this gave her the time she needed to cool down'. He described their relationship as 'very volatile. We could get on for a week or two and then have a big argument and then I'd leave.' Morris also rented a council flat in Arennig Road, Penlan which he used from time to time, having taken on the tenancy some time after the murders.

Mandy Jewell, an attractive Yorkshire girl, worked in Eynon's bakery in Clydach. She had lived in the Swansea area for the previous ten years and for five of those years she occupied her ground floor council flat in Craig Cefn Parc with her husband Andrew Jewell, a local man, from whom she later separated. Before moving to Rhyddwen Road, Jewell lived in Pendre in Clydach where she met Mandy Power, a neighbour. They were both pregnant at the time: Mandy Power with Emily, she with Emma. They struck up a friendship which lasted several years, but they began to drift apart in 1998. The following year their relationship took a major blow. In April 1999 Power told Jewell and several other people close to her that she was suffering from cervical cancer. The following month they discovered that this claim was a lie. Christine Pugh, a friend and neighbour of Mandy Power, rang the hospital that Mandy said she was attending, and discovered that she did not have cancer. What made matters worse was that Mandy Power had simulated symptoms exhibited by Mandy Jewell's mother who really did have cervical cancer. Hurt by this discovery, Jewell and Power stopped speaking to one another for several weeks. Jewell later said: 'I believed what I had been told. I was really scared for her…. I thought she was dying.'

In statements given to the police two days after the murders, Dai Morris and Mandy Jewell claimed that on Saturday 26 June they had gone to the New Inn in Craig Cefn Parc for a few drinks. They sat in the lounge bar where they stayed for the next few hours, drinking and chatting with friends and watching rugby on the pub's large-screen TV. Wales were playing South Africa at the inaugural rugby match that day in the recently opened Millennium Stadium in Cardiff. Kick-off was at 5.00 p.m. and the Welsh team went on to win 29-19, so there was a celebratory atmosphere among the customers. When closing time came at 11.00 p.m., Morris and Jewell spent a few minutes finishing their drinks, left the pub and walked home, taking a short cut through the woods. They arrived back at their flat about 11.30 p.m. They then went to bed together. The first they knew about the deaths, they agreed, was at about 7 a.m. on the Sunday morning when Mandy Jewell received a telephone call from Alison Lewis. Jewell knew Alison Lewis well because of her relationship with Mandy Power. Their statements were filed and the investigation moved on.

On 6 July, Richard Morgan, coroner for Swansea and Gower, received the results of the Home Office pathologist's report. The four bodies were then released to the relatives so that they could make the funeral arrangements. The inquest was formally opened, but was adjourned immediately, pending completion of the police investigation.

On 13 July, another broadcast was made on BBC's *Crimewatch*, when Detective Superintendent Lloyd-Evans made a further public appeal for help to the programme's huge audience. Afterwards, 40 calls were received by the studio and a further 40 calls by the incident room at Cockett Police Station, but none of them provided any helpful information.

Nearly three weeks after the murders, on 17 July, the forensic investigation at 9 Kelvin Road ended and the house was sealed. Lloyd-Evans confirmed that it was the longest time ever spent at a murder scene by South Wales Police. By now, more than 1,000 people had been interviewed, 280 witness statements had been taken and 300 messages received in connection with the investigation.

Even more puzzling than Lloyd-Evans' unwillingness to publicise Nicola Williams' e-fit image of the mysterious man was his response when he received the report, that week, which contained the results of the forensic investigation undertaken at 9 Kelvin Road. At first the police were certain that there would be numerous clues left in the fire-damaged house to help them identify the killer, and Martyn Lloyd-Evans was confident of an early arrest. The house was stripped of its contents; the bathroom suite was removed in its entirety, the water drainage pipes taken right down to the sewerage system, all the furnishings were packaged and hundreds of items were sent away to the Home Office crime laboratory in Chepstow for forensic examination.

The team of investigators had spent almost three weeks minutely examining the house and practically everything it contained. But, according to Lloyd-Evans, the results had been negative. No useful evidence leading to the identification of the killer had been found, either in the house, or on any of the hundreds of items taken away for analysis, including the murder weapon. He claimed there was no DNA or fingerprints on anything or on any object that the murderer might have handled, touched or seized: they had all been wiped away. Indeed, at some stage, after the murders had taken place and with four bodies lying only feet away, the murderer had coolly gone into the bathroom and used the shower over the bath to wash blood-soaked clothing and afterwards had used the bath to wash away any remaining blood.

Lloyd-Evans said he did not want the contents of the report to be made public. The few reporters who knew about it agreed to postpone publishing the findings that, they were assured, the report contained. The detective superintendent did, however, tell reporters that the killer may have been male or female, and that more than one person could have been involved. In other words, he did not tell them anything at all.

This left reporters with the image of a brutal killer who possessed the scientific know-how to destroy DNA and finger-print evidence which might otherwise have led to his or her identification. Thus was born the myth that the murderer was someone who was 'forensically aware' – a person who was conscious of the type of clue that might be left behind to lead to their identification – which eventually became one of the hallmarks of the Clydach murder case.

Certainly no DNA or fingerprints belonging to the man who would stand trial for the murders were discovered anywhere in 9 Kelvin Road. But evidence which came to light much later showed that DNA and fingerprints from an unknown male *were* found in the female-only household. Why then was Detective Superintendent Martyn Lloyd-Evans so reluctant to make public the forensic report?

An unnamed scene of crimes officer, a university lecturer in forensics consulted by the author, said that in a crime of this brutality, 'Tracking down and eliminating every bit of biological debris left behind would have been impossible, even for the cleverest criminal. DNA fingerprinting allows the forensic investigator to use even the smallest piece of genetic material to identify an individual who was present at the crime scene. The forensic investigation should have at least found hair follicles or dead skin cells in the bathwater. While conditions might have made it difficult to extract DNA, a genetic profile could have been extracted from a single cell immersed in water, even for a long time, sufficient to identify the Kelvin Road killer.' Yet, unbelievably, no DNA was reported as having been found in the bath or bathwater.

One explanation suggested for the lack of useable DNA was that the murderer might have poured bleach into the bath which would have the effect of destroying DNA. But the scene of crimes investigator also said that if it *was* bleach which had been used, it could not have been ordinary bleach. It would have to be a special type of *oxygen-producing bleach* – such as Vanish – which has the effect of destroying DNA completely. Ordinary bleach does not have this effect, and traces of DNA may still be detected, sometimes even years afterwards.

An enquiry by the author directed to South Wales Police to establish whether or not bleach had been used, and if so, the *type*, was met with silence, though if this special type of bleach had been used, such knowledge as to its effect on DNA went far beyond that usually possessed by anyone not trained in forensics. Likewise, an enquiry made to South Wales Police to establish whether or not DNA *had* been found in the bath, and if so, why the discovery had never been made public, also received no reply. Commenting on the forensic investigation, the scene of crimes investigator said, "It is simply not credible that no DNA or trace evidence leading to the murderer could be found [at 9 Kelvin Road]."

The final obstacle to the forensic investigation was the series of fires lit in four locations throughout the house, each started with the obvious intention of eliminating whatever evidence remained. Of all the methods employed by criminals to destroy evidence of their crime, including DNA and fingerprints, fire is by far the most effective. When the first fire failed to spread, three further fires were started, but only the fourth fire in the kitchen took hold. This led to the blaze which might have destroyed the house and any remaining evidence the killer had failed to get rid of. But the house had not burned down. The fire had been quickly brought under control, preserving such evidence as there was. Realisation of this might have caused the murderer to panic, acting in a manner inconsistent with his or her normal behaviour, which later might be difficult to explain.

Perhaps there was another reason why no DNA, fingerprints or trace evidence which belonged to the man who was eventually convicted of the murders could be found in 9 Kelvin Road. Not, as South Wales Police and later the prosecution insisted, owing to his being 'forensically aware' and wiping them all away, but quite simply, because he was never there?

As the end of July drew near and no appreciable progress had been made, a public campaign appealing for help was launched. Nicola Williams' e-fit image, however, had still not been made public. On 26 July, posters were put up in shops, post offices, pubs and libraries and on the internet, asking anyone who knew anything about the murders to get in touch with the police. It was a fruitless exercise which drew no worthwhile results.

On Friday 30 July, the streets of Clydach were packed with thousands of mourners who fell silent as the cortège of four hearses and several funeral cars slowly made its way to the small church of St Mary's. The coffins of Mandy Power and her mother Doris were covered with wreaths of white roses. Wreaths in the shape of teddy bears and a cross lay on the two small white coffins of Katie and Emily. One by one the coffins were carried into the church to the strains of the family's favourite song, 'My Heart Will Go On', from the film *Titanic*. The congregation sang three hymns: 'The Lord is My Shepherd', 'The Old Rugged

Cross', and 'All Things Bright and Beautiful'. A poem entitled 'Peace', written by ten-year-old Katie seven weeks before her death, was read out. It told of her love of nature and the safe, starry sky. Stephen Jones, Mandy's nephew, recited 'Mandy', a poem he had written as a moving tribute to his aunt. It told of her love for her children, and of life, and of her warm generous personality. He said he 'wanted everyone to know the real Mandy'.

The poignant service was too much for some to bear. For others, the grim reality of the terrible tragedy struck home and they were overcome with grief. The Reverend Nigel Griffin urged anyone with knowledge that might lead to the killer to come forward. He said the four coffins should be enough to prompt whoever was shielding the killer to act. The clergyman's words fell on stony ground.

After the church service, all four victims were laid to rest. They had lived together, and now they were buried together in a single grave on the grassy slopes of Coedgwilym Cemetery in Clydach, on the Brecon Road.

Chapter 7

When the Home Office pathologist's report came back, it showed the extent of the terrible injuries inflicted on the victims. Mandy Power had been extensively battered, but there was no bruising, tearing or other injury to her private parts consistent with rape, or attempted rape. A small speck of DNA resulting from sexual activity was found on the inside of one of Mandy Power's thighs. More identical DNA was also found on the pink vibrator pushed into her vagina.

Forensic analysis proved that the DNA discovered on Mandy Power's thigh and on the vibrator was not hers. A comparison analysis quickly found a match. The DNA came from the epithelial cells in the vaginal fluid of Alison Lewis, her lover. This suggested that Mandy Power and Alison Lewis had engaged in sexual activity *shortly* before the murders. But this was contrary to the evidence that Alison Lewis had given to the police. She said that the last time she had had sex with Mandy Power had been early on the morning of Saturday 26 June – some 20 hours before the murders.

When questioned about the nature of her relationship with Mandy Power and events leading up to the last time she had seen her alive, Alison Lewis told detectives that on the evening of Friday 25 June, she had invited Mandy Power to her home in West Crossways for a barbeque. There, Power joined Alison, her husband Stephen and their twin four-year-old daughters. By 10.00 p.m. the twins were already in bed and Stephen had also retired for the night, leaving the two women alone. According to Alison Lewis, they had made love in the living room, using a strap-on dildo that Mandy Power had bought for them to use a few weeks earlier. Afterwards, Lewis left Power on the sofa and joined her husband in bed. Stephen woke at 5 a.m. the following morning and left for work in Neath shortly afterwards. Alison Lewis left the bed and joined Power in the living room where they again had sex and dozed for the next hour. They both then went upstairs to the marital bed where they made love for a third time. Later that morning, Lewis drove Power home. Doris Dawson was in the house. Mandy's daughters had been dropped off earlier by their father. Kimberley Wilson, a gay friend of both Mandy Power and Alison Lewis, was also in the house. Wilson had returned from a short stay in Ibiza the previous day and had stayed overnight in 9 Kelvin Road, sleeping in Mandy Power's bed.

In her statement to the police, Alison Lewis claimed that she took a bath at 9 Kelvin Road before driving to Pontardawe Leisure Centre where she did a workout, dropping off Mandy Power in Clydach village on the way. That morning, she said, was the last time she seen Power alive.

Power's nephew Stephen Jones cast doubt on one of the details in Alison Lewis' testimony. Crucially, he said that when Mandy Power arrived at his home to babysit on the evening before the murders, he noticed that she was 'freshly showered'.

The significance of his comment was this: Mandy Power suffered from psoriasis, a common but lifelong disease which manifests itself as dry, red, scaly patches on the skin. Sufferers are often uncomfortable and may bathe frequently to soothe the itch and rid themselves of dead skin which can be produced in large quantities. Mandy was so troubled by her psoriasis that she was known to shower four or more times a day. Personal hygiene was vitally important to her and it is certain that she would have showered perhaps several times between the time Alison Lewis said she had had sex with her on the morning of 26 June, and the time of her death, less than twenty hours later.

The key issue from a forensic evidence viewpoint is that it was extremely unlikely that DNA from Alison Lewis would have remained on Mandy Power's thigh since early on the Saturday morning if she had showered in the meantime. And Power 'almost certainly' had taken 'several showers' during the course of the day. In other words, the evidence indicated that the pair's sexual contact took place much later than Alison Lewis claimed, and some time *after* Mandy Power had taken her last shower.

On the basis of the discovery of this DNA evidence alone, South Wales Police would have been justified in arresting Alison

Lewis on suspicion of the murders. But while she became a 'person of serious interest', she was not arrested at this time.

Further police enquiries into Alison Lewis – much information being provided by women's rugby club members and the local gay and lesbian community – revealed a truly extraordinary woman. From the age of twelve, Lewis' ambition was to become a police officer. During her school years, she had developed a crush on an older female teacher, although she said she did not then consider that she might be a lesbian.

Alison Lewis excelled at sport and studied karate, for which she trained up to eleven times a week. She qualified as a second dan black belt and won the Welsh Ladies' Championship four times. She also won the British Ladies' Championship on four occasions. At the age of sixteen she became the youngest person ever to represent Britain at senior level karate. These were remarkable achievements for a teenager.

As part of her karate training, Alison Lewis also became proficient in the use of weapons. One of these was the *bō*. This deadly pole-like weapon, usually made of hard wood, is about six feet long and often thicker in the centre than at the ends. This allows the user to grip the pole tightly with both hands to block and counter an attack with a variety of strokes, all designed to defeat, maim or even kill an opponent. Just one end of the weapon is used when striking an opponent. A shorter four-foot long version is known as a *jō* and differs from a *bō* in that both ends of the weapon are used against an opponent. It is similar, though not identical, to the pole used as the murder weapon.

At eighteen, Alison Lewis applied to join the South Wales Police. She was ideal police material: intelligent, physically fit and very tough. In 1986 she was accepted into the force and began her police training. As part of her ten-week induction course in Bridgend, she was taught how to use the police baton and learned how to strike, jab, block or bludgeon an aggressor. By the time her course was complete, she had become an efficient combatant, deadly with weapons and without – a formidable opponent. Her police training programme also included current forensic detection techniques, such as how to find and preserve evidence of a crime. This included blood detection and analysis, taking and distinguishing fingerprints, footprints and handprints, as well as finding, collecting and analysing DNA.

Alison Lewis was also taught Police and Criminal Evidence interrogation and interview techniques. She knew the carefully laid traps detectives arranged and she watched as unwary suspects walked into them time and again. Lewis knew what evidence was needed to charge a suspect with a crime, and the importance of obtaining sufficient evidence so that the Crown Prosecution Service would take a case to trial.

Her first posting in the police force was to Llanishen in Cardiff. In 1990 she met her future husband, Stephen Lewis, in Bridgend on a police driver training course. A year later they married and the wedding ceremony took place in Alison's home town of Pontypridd. She was then posted to Neath where her husband was based. A semi-detached police house was provided for them in Pontardawe where, in 1995, their twin daughters were born. It was here that they were living at the time of the murders.

In 1992 Alison Lewis developed a stress-related illness after attending a suicide in the village of Bryncoch, near Neath. An old man had gassed himself and Lewis gave evidence at the inquest. She subsequently became depressed, left the police force and was pensioned off on the grounds of ill health. Soon afterwards, her illness notwithstanding, she began playing women's rugby and excelled at this sport. She played on the wing for Ystradgynlais, was picked to play for Wales and went on to win seven caps. Kimberley Wilson said that Alison Lewis was known as a 'bitch' by her fellow players because of the rough nature of her play.

It was at this time that Lewis became aware of her physical attraction to women and she had her first sexual encounter with a fellow rugby player in 1996, the relationship lasting for several weeks. She began visiting gay pubs and clubs in and around Swansea, Neath and Pontardawe, seeking out lesbians with whom she enjoyed numerous sexual relationships. She said that her sex life with her husband at this time was almost non-existent and she had sex with him only when she had to. This, she said, was to maintain the impression that she was happily married when in fact she was not.

In the summer of the same year, Michael Harris and a friend, Welsh welter-weight boxing champion Geoff Pegler, were enjoying a drink in the Tredegar Arms pub in Swansea. Alison Lewis and a girlfriend were also in the pub, caressing one another in the lounge bar. When Pegler objected to this public display of affection and suggested that they remove themselves to somewhere private, Lewis flew into a rage, followed him outside and, without warning, knocked him to the ground with a single punch.

In November 1998 Alison Lewis and Mandy Power met for the first time. Alison Jones, a mutual friend and a member of the Swansea Uplands women's rugby team, took Alison Lewis along to 9 Kelvin Road where Mandy Power was hosting a tarot card reading. During the course of the evening Alison Lewis found that she was sexually attracted to Mandy, but believed her to be heterosexual. They struck up a friendship and, over the course of the next two weeks, the two women met several times. Once or twice Mandy cooked dinner for her new friend. The attraction was mutual and their relationship became sexual. This was Mandy Power's first lesbian relationship.

According to Alison Lewis, on almost every occasion when the two women met, they had sex. Mandy owned at least three vibrators. One she kept in a bedside locker, the second was the strap-on dildo, stored in a box, the third was the pink vibrator, kept on top of her wardrobe, which was found lodged in her vagina after she was murdered.

Alison Lewis said the relationship was difficult because, like her other sexual encounters, it was conducted behind her husband Stephen's back. She claimed he had no knowledge of her affair until the morning of the murders when she was unable to conceal her secret from him any longer. The women had split up on two occasions; the first time for two weeks in January 1999 when Mandy became jealous of Alison's relationships with other women; the second in May when Mandy lied about having cervical cancer. On that occasion they separated for a week. After the break-ups came making up and, according to Alison Lewis, their relationship became stronger and more intense. When Stephen Lewis had a day off work, Alison would leave their twins with him so that she could meet Mandy in 9 Kelvin Road.

Alison Lewis provided detectives with an alibi for her where-abouts at the time of the murders. She said she was at home in bed with her husband for the entire night, though she had got up twice to attend to one of her daughters.

Stephen Lewis told detectives that they had arranged a barbeque at their home on the evening of Saturday, 26 June. He went to bed at around 10.00 p.m., before his wife, and slept soundly until 5.00 a.m. when the alarm woke him for work. His shift in Neath started at 6.00 a.m. To the best of his knowledge, his wife had been in bed with him all night. Within twenty minutes of waking, Stephen Lewis and Constable Gareth Thomas, a work colleague who came to the house to collect him, were on their way to Neath Police Station. Thomas later described Stephen Lewis as being in a 'relaxed, normal mood' when they left West Crossways at 5.18 a.m.

Alison Lewis said in a statement given to detectives that she first knew of the deaths was when she was awoken by a phone call at 6.06 a.m. from Mandy's friend and neighbour, Christine Pugh. Lewis said she rang her husband and told him the news, then waited for him to return home from work. They went to Kelvin Road together to learn the facts at first hand, arriving at the cordoned off crime scene at around 9.00 a.m. They then returned to their home where Alison Lewis appeared to have been overcome by a grief so great that it led her to attempt suicide. This was followed on 7 July by a 14-day stay at Cefn Coed psychiatric hospital.

This account did not sit well with eyewitness recollections. Two of them placed Lewis at the crime scene very close to the time of the murders. Neighbours of Mandy Power, Timothy and Manon Cherry, who lived almost opposite number 9 at 16 Kelvin Road, were woken by the commotion caused by the fire at around 4.30 a.m. They said at 6.00 a.m. they saw Alison Lewis, whom they both knew, outside in the street. Timothy Cherry watched as Lewis approached his wife and then buried her head in his wife's shoulder. The evidence given by Manon Cherry was that Alison Lewis appeared freshly showered and smelled strongly of soap. Cherry also described her as being 'startled and jumpy'.

Two more eyewitnesses placed Alison Lewis at the scene much earlier than she had stated in her statement to the police.

Taxi drivers and lovers Carol Ann Isaac and Beverley Lewis of Clydach Cabs also swore under oath that they saw Alison Lewis, and spoke to her in Christine Williams' Kelvin Road home early that morning. Their statements, though given separately to detectives, tallied in nearly all important aspects. They said that a few minutes past 6.00 a.m. on the morning of the murders they were awoken by loud banging on the bedroom window of their ground-floor council flat in Morriston. It was Beverley's mother, Lorna Lewis, and her business partner Beryl Hawkins, owners of Clydach Cabs. When the night shift at the taxi company office changed at 6.00 a.m., Lorna and Beryl had turned up for work and were told about the fire by the telephone operator whose shift had just ended. Mandy Power and her family were all believed to be dead, they said. Not only was Mandy Power a good friend of Carol Ann and Beverley, she was also a frequent customer of the taxi company which often ferried Mandy's daughters to and from school. Because the two women had turned off their mobile phones to get a good night's sleep, they could not be contacted, so Lorna Lewis and Beryl Hawkins drove to Morriston to give them the news and bring them to Kelvin Road.

Several weeks earlier, radio controllers in the taxi company had passed on the news that Mandy Power and Alison Lewis were 'seeing' each other. Since that time, Carol Ann Isaac and Beverley Lewis had got to know Alison Lewis well. Alison Lewis used the taxi company frequently to get to and from her home in Pontardawe, and Alison and Mandy had recently attended Carol Ann's fiftieth birthday party in the Carpenters Arms in Clydach.

Having told Carol Ann and Beverley the news, the four women climbed into the taxi and travelled immediately to Kelvin Road, arriving between 6.30 a.m. and 6.45 a.m. The house was not yet a cordoned-off crime scene, no detectives had arrived, and there was just Alison Crewe on duty. The fire services were still busy clearing up and it was obvious that there had been a major catastrophe.

Carol Ann and Beverley called to neighbour Christine Williams' house, next door to number 9 Kelvin Road. Williams confirmed that Mandy Power, her mother and two daughters had all perished in the fire and she invited them inside. In the living room, seated in an armchair and in floods of tears, was Alison Lewis. Beverley went to her and put an arm around her shoulders to console her. She expressed their sadness for her loss, and told her how sorry they were.

Both Carol Ann and Beverley gave the police identical descriptions of Alison Lewis' appearance. They said that she was wearing a spotless white T-shirt, white shorts, white sports socks and white trainers. Her hair was soaking wet, and she smelled fresh and clean. They did not think she could have been caught in the rain because there had been no showers during the previous hour.

Gary Beynon, a staff nurse in Morriston Hospital, a gay man and a close friend of Mandy Power, also knew Alison Lewis. On the Saturday before the murders, Beynon had spent two hours talking with Mandy in her home. In his statement to the police, he described her as 'flirtatious with men and a man-eater', adding that he 'never felt she was a committed lesbian'. He recalled that Alison Lewis appeared to be in some sort of relationship with a woman called Meryl James because he had overheard Lewis talking to her on the phone. This was at a time when Mandy Power and Alison Lewis were supposed to be seeing each other exclusively.

At 7.15 a.m. on the morning of the murders, Gary Beynon received a telephone call from Alison Lewis, who said: 'Mandy Power's dead. They're all dead; they died in a fire.' Beynon left his home immediately and drove straight to Kelvin Road where he saw firemen clearing up. Without stopping, he drove on to Alison Lewis' home in Pontardawe, arriving at about 7.35 a.m. When he arrived, Lewis was alone, though more friends and her husband Stephen turned up at the house shortly afterwards. In his statement describing Alison Lewis, Beynon said: 'She appeared fresh as if she had recently showered or washed.'

When Alison Lewis was questioned by detectives about these witnesses' statements, she denied that meetings with Manon Cherry, Carol Ann Isaac, Beverley Lewis and Gary Beynon ever took place. She also denied that she had bathed or showered that day. She said she had not, in fact, bathed since the morning of the previous day (Saturday 26 June), when she took a bath at 9 Kelvin Road.

Alison Lewis further denied that she had been in Kelvin Road at the time claimed by the three women and Timothy Cherry. Thereafter the detectives (and later counsel in *both* trials who prosecuted Dai Morris) suggested that the four witnesses were either 'mistaken' about the time they said they had seen her, that Carol Ann Isaac must have been under the influence of sleeping tablets or, quite simply, they had made it up.

But Carol Ann Isaac and Beverley Lewis insisted they were not mistaken. They persisted in their claims until on a day when they were planning to attend a charity fund-raising concert for the victims' families in Manor Park near Clydach, the police arrested them on what both Isaac and Lewis describe as 'trumped-up charges'. Isaac told the author that she felt that she and Beverley Lewis were being given a warning not to interfere in the police investigation. After 24 hours in police custody, they were released without charge. To this day, Carol Ann Isaac adamantly maintains that they had both told the truth about the morning of the murders.

But Carol Ann Isaac said something else too. In the weeks leading up to the murders, she and Beverley Lewis occasionally socialised with Mandy Power and Alison Lewis. Once while they were in a pub drinking and talking together, Alison pulled a key from her pocket, twirled it playfully and said: 'Look what I've got.' It was the key to the front door of Mandy Power's home. When she was questioned about this in court, Alison Lewis denied ever having a key to 9 Kelvin Road. Carol Ann Isaac also expressed her opinion in court that Alison Lewis did not like Mandy Power's elder daughter Katie. Coincidentally, it was Katie who sustained the greatest injuries in the attack. Gary Beynon confirmed Alison Lewis' dislike of Mandy's children, but he disagreed about which one she favoured the least. He thought it was eight-year-old Emily. He told police: 'Alison Lewis could just about take to Katie but did not like Emily.'

The statements made by these witnesses contrast sharply with Alison Lewis' own protestations of love for the family, including Mandy's elderly mother. After Dai Morris' first trial ended, she said: 'I have felt the loss of Mandy, Katie, Emily and Doris more than anyone will ever know.' But whilst struggling with her extreme grief in Cefn Coed Hospital, she astounded medical staff by exchanging sexually explicit texts with a partner, Meryl James, one of which read: 'Shall we screw now or shall we screw later?'

Furthermore, on 1 October 1999, Gary Beynon called into H2O, a gay club in Swansea. Clutching one another in a loving embrace were Alison Lewis and Meryl James. The two women were clearly enjoying each other's company as they danced slowly and closely together. But as soon as Lewis spotted Beynon watching them, her demeanour changed instantly to one of intense grief.

After Alison Lewis' admission to Cefn Coed Hospital, she was constantly monitored by at least one staff member, but more usually two. During her hospitalisation, Lewis frequently became hostile towards nursing and medical staff and often had to be physically restrained. So powerful and skilled in fighting was she that it took up to eight specially trained staff members to overpower her.

Her friend Joanne Anthony confirmed that one day Alison Lewis had 'gone berserk' in the hospital, losing control, striking out at medical staff and putting her fist through a window. Dr Peter Donnelly, who was in charge of her case in Cefn Coed, initially labelled Lewis' condition as 'acute grief reaction'. He warned Lewis that unless her behaviour improved, her treatment would be withdrawn and she would have to leave the hospital. Just a few days later Lewis checked herself out of Cefn Coed of her own accord.

Another male Cefn Coed Hospital staff member, who lived in Clydach, said he saw a red Peugeot car outside 9 Kelvin Road at midnight on the night of the murders and told detectives about it. This was important information because when Stuart Lewis was investigated by Superintendent Alec Davies for the Police Complaints Authority, it emerged that he was driving alone that night in an unmarked police car. Lewis claimed that he 'could not remember' where he was between midnight and 1.17 a.m. The car log, which would have revealed Lewis' whereabouts, could not be found. Several other witnesses also said they saw a red Peugeot in Clydach at around this time. But, he said, the detectives expressed no interest in this sighting and, as far as he was aware, did not pursue this line of inquiry.

Chapter 8

On 9 July 1999, Detective Superintendent Martyn Lloyd-Evans announced to a packed national media press conference that he was confident of catching the killer, but this time he warned that murder investigations sometimes take weeks, months, and even years to solve. It seemed to be a strange prediction to make so soon in the murder investigation when just days before he had announced that he expected to make an early arrest. But, notably, Lloyd-Evans had now learned that former South Wales Police Officer Alison Lewis had been intimately involved with Mandy Power, and that Lewis' husband Stephen Lewis, a serving Sergeant in South Wales Police, also knew the victims.

By now the investigation was well under way and detectives continued their trawl for information, placing posters in shop windows and appealing for help directly to the general public. Still, neither the e-fit image composed with the help of Nicola Williams was made public nor, it seems, was the sighting of a red Peugeot car in Kelvin Road at midnight on 26/27 June followed up.

On the one hand, Lloyd-Evans had his superiors, the victims' families, the media and the general public on his back, all clamouring for an arrest. On the other hand, he had only the Lewises to offer as potential suspects. He must have found himself in a dilemma. He was under immense pressure to find the murderer, but the political and public ramifications of any suggestion that South Wales Police officers were involved, whether serving or retired, were unprecedented and enormous. The government of the day had no political will to undermine its own police force by ordering a public inquiry, or, for that matter, taking any steps that might bring the force into disrepute. This had already been shown by the refusal of the Home Secretary to launch a public inquiry into police corruption which the Welsh Assembly had urged on him.

The problem Lloyd-Evans had was that the evidence against the Lewises was beginning to stack up. Stephen Lewis' story was that he had retired to bed before his wife on the evening before the murders and had slept soundly through the night until 5.00 a.m. Alison Lewis said she had followed him to bed after 10.00 p.m. and had stayed there all night, with the exception of two occasions when she got up to attend to one of her daughters. This, however, was impossible to corroborate. Because her husband insisted he had slept through the night of 26/27 June, Alison Lewis did not have a valid alibi at the time of the murders.

Stephen Lewis maintained from the outset that he knew nothing about his wife's affair with Mandy Power until the morning of the latter's death. But evidence given by two witnesses, Mandy's nephew, police officer Stephen Jones, and her ex-lover Howard Florence was that he *did know*. Why might he have been lying about this? Was it because if he admitted that he knew of the affair before Mandy Power's death, this disclosure might have influenced the jury when reaching its verdict?

A witness, Mandy Power's friend and neighbour, 19-year-old teenager Louise Pugh, the daughter of Christine Pugh, claimed that she overheard Stephen Lewis threatening to kill Power. A few days before the murders, she was in her home when she heard raised voices outside. Looking out, she saw Stephen Lewis on the doorstep of 9 Kelvin Road pointing his finger at Mandy Power shouting: 'If you do not keep away from my wife, I will kill you.' Under police questioning Lewis, at first, denied making such a statement, only to admit it in another statement the following day.

Stuart Lewis, together with his police car, went missing between midnight and 3.00 a.m. on the morning of the murders, so he had no alibi either. He would say later that he could not remember where he was between midnight and 1.17 a.m. Not only did Stuart Lewis *not* have an alibi, he was not in his office, where he claimed to have been in the three-hour period during which the murders were carried out. This included the time at about 2.20 a.m. when Nicola Williams saw a man with a bag near Kelvin Road; her description almost exactly fitted the appearance of either of the Lewis twins. Furthermore, within minutes of arriving at the crime scene and discovering that the house had not burned down as the murderer had planned,

Stuart Lewis abruptly left the crime scene and acted in a manner inconsistent with that of a serving police officer, which conduct has never been satisfactorily explained.

Lloyd-Evans wanted to make an arrest for the Clydach murders and much of the evidence in his possession pointed towards the Lewises as likely suspects but, inexplicably, he delayed taking any steps against them for over a year. The evidence of Alison Lewis' DNA on Mandy Power's thigh and on the vibrator seemingly was pushed aside. The statements of Timothy Cherry, Manon Cherry, Carol Ann Isaac and Beverley Lewis, in which they all swore that they had seen Alison Lewis in Kelvin Road early on the morning of the murders, were disregarded. The police disbelieved Isaac and Lewis' claim that Alison Lewis had a key to 9 Kelvin Road; the two women's claims and those of Gary Beynon and Manon Cherry that Alison Lewis had smelled of soap and appeared to have showered shortly after the fire were all ignored. And Alison Lewis' behaviour in Cefn Coed Hospital, demonstrating an unstable personality, seems to have been regarded as irrelevant. Stuart Lewis had never explained his reasons for leaving the crime scene so abruptly, and just days before the murders, Stephen Lewis had threatened Mandy Power's life. Just how much evidence did South Wales Police need to have before arresting three of their own?

By the end of the summer of 1999, Lloyd-Evans and his team were in possession of enough evidence to arrest and charge the Lewises on suspicion of involvement in the murders. Yet, for reasons that have never been explained, they did not arrest them until more than a year later. By then, Alison Lewis had moved to her parents' home in Pontypridd, Stephen Lewis had gone abroad temporarily with his daughters, and Stuart Lewis had moved house. Whatever the outcome of the investigation, South Wales Police would have satisfied critics that they were doing their job properly if they had arrested the Lewises earlier. Delaying their arrests for a year merely led to suspicions that they were not.

And could jealousy have been the motive for the crime? According to Gary Beynon, while Mandy Power had eyes only for Alison Lewis, she was 'never a committed lesbian'. This statement, while appearing to be contradictory, explains much of Mandy Power's complicated love life. While she was certainly involved in a sexual relationship with Alison Lewis, it was by no means monogamous. The evidence points to Mandy Power simultaneously enjoying other sexual relationships with men.

Unfortunately, what Mandy Power said to witnesses from time to time cannot always be relied upon as the truth. Her claim to have had cervical cancer earlier that year was exposed as a lie, while her statement to Gary Beynon that she was 'frightened of Dai Morris' may have been said to conceal the fact that she was involved in a sexual relationship with him.

Other examples of Mandy Power being economical with the truth included her deceiving Alison Lewis into believing that she was no longer in contact with her married lover Howard Florence. In fact, the pair often talked on the telephone, their last phone conversation taking place on the day before the murders. When Alison Lewis found out about this call, she had 'flipped' and flown into a rage. On Valentine's Day 1999, while Mandy Power's affair with Alison Lewis was in full swing, she received flowers from Howard Florence. On the same day, and (almost certainly) unbeknownst to Lewis and Howard Florence, her mobile phone records showed that she made numerous calls to Dai Morris in his apartment. This was at a time when he was separated from Mandy Jewell. Morris would later describe Mandy Power as 'just a sex-mad woman'.

The evidence was that Alison Lewis' husband Stephen *did* know of her affair before the morning of the murders, even though he swore on oath in court that he did not. Moreover, he had delivered a threat against Mandy's life, which Louise Pugh had overheard.

On 7 September 1999, the BBC recorded a full reconstruction of the crime for their weekly programme *Crimewatch*. Detective Superintendent Martyn Lloyd-Evans appealed once again for witnesses to come forward, and pleaded with the killer's family to provide the police with information leading to an arrest. Astonishingly, he yet again withheld the e-fit image which had been in his possession for over two months. About thirty phone calls were made to the studio after the transmission, and a further twelve calls were received by the Cockett Police

Station incident room that night, but no names of potential suspects were received.

By late September detectives had interviewed more than 2,000 people, but little useful information was forthcoming. A £30,000 reward for information leading to the capture of the killer yielded no response. In mid-November South Wales Police turned to leading police investigators from other jurisdictions for ideas on how best to find the killer. These included the team who had hunted for the killer of Jill Dando (Barry George was wrongfully convicted of the murder in a miscarriage of justice, and later was acquitted on appeal) and detectives who had tracked IRA and Loyalist killers. Lloyd-Evans gave the impression that they were doing everything possible to find the murderer, but this was far from the case. After almost five months, he had still not made public the e-fit image composed from Nicola Williams' description of the man with the bag she had seen walking towards Kelvin Road – the man she would subsequently pick out unhesitatingly in a video identity parade twenty-one months after the murders: South Wales Police Officer Sergeant Stephen Lewis, Alison Lewis' husband.

The New Year came and went and still no arrests had been made. By now, South Wales Police had visited more than 1,000 homes. They had interviewed almost 5,000 witnesses, of whom 1,700 had given statements, and the cost involved had exceeded £1 million, none of which had taken the investigation any further.

As the fifty detectives continued their hunt, Chief Constable Sir Anthony Burden announced that the police would 'do what it takes' to bring the killer to justice, while Detective Superintendent Martyn Lloyd-Evans, speaking with his characteristic confidence, stated: 'We're just a phone call away from nailing the killer.' A satellite office set up in Cardiff had brought new encouragement to the detectives. Lloyd-Evans said: 'No doubt we'll soon be knocking on the killer's door. New information is coming in every day.' He might easily have added 'and all of it useless'.

By mid-February 2000 the police were running out of ideas

and were stung by criticism of the amount of time the investigation was taking. Grasping at straws to appease the public, Assistant Chief Constable Tony Rogers decided to invite people behind the scenes to show them what went on in a murder investigation. At an event in the Dylan Thomas Theatre in Swansea on 11 March 2000, journalist Vincent Kane, *Crimewatch* presenter Nick Ross, and criminal psychologist Adrian West explained the processes involved in a criminal investigation.

An additional reason for organising this event was that the rumour mill had been working hard ever since revelations of ex-policewoman Alison Lewis' relationship with Mandy Power had become public knowledge. Fingers of suspicion pointed directly at the Lewises, and at Alison Lewis in particular; murmurs about their suspected involvement were becoming louder and more difficult to ignore.

The police had warned Alison Lewis about the dangers of returning to her home in Pontardawe following her discharge from Cefn Coed Hospital. It was believed she could become the victim of a revenge attack. But following an apparent marital rift, which both she and Stephen Lewis claimed was the result of his discovery of her infidelity, she went to stay with her mother in Pontypridd. Even there, she could not escape the gossip and suspicion and on 20 February 2000 her 70-year-old mother, Anne Powell, pleaded for her daughter to be left alone. This had no effect and the mutterings continued.

As the police investigation limped slowly forwards, DNA testing commenced on 25 March when mouth swabs were taken from everyone who had had access to 9 Kelvin Road around the time of the murders. The publicly stated intention was to subject the samples to analysis at the Home Office lab to isolate DNA which the police believed could identify the killer. Lloyd-Evans announced there were 'no plans for a DNA resident sweep. We have such a mass of evidence coming in that we need to eliminate people. Information is coming in and is just as strong.'

This was hyperbole. Lloyd-Evans was telling the public what he thought they wanted to hear, not the truth. As South Wales Police knew very well, DNA belonging to Alison Lewis had been found on Mandy Power's thigh and on her vibrator, and Stephen Lewis' fingerprints had also been discovered in 9 Kelvin Road, even though in the first statement he had given to the police he had denied ever going into the house. But, according to South Wales Police, no other DNA evidence was found. So why were samples taken from persons having access to 9 Kelvin Road when there was, according to the police, nothing to test it against?

In late May 2000, two weeks after a headstone for the murder victims was erected at Coedgwilym Cemetery, Lloyd-Evans addressed a meeting of villagers at Clydach Community Hall. 'The jigsaw in the hunt for the killer of a Clydach mother Mandy Power and her family is almost complete,' he told them. This was untrue. The police were nowhere near to making an arrest and the investigation had effectively stalled.

A third BBC *Crimewatch* appeal was planned to coincide with the anniversary of the murders a month later, the villagers learned, and there were now 58 officers working on the scaled-up investigation. Lloyd-Evans assured the residents: 'I am adamant and convinced we will get a result. It is not a question of if, but when. It is a very difficult thing to arrest someone with enough evidence to make sure they remain in prison for the rest of their lives.'

In mid-June, the police held a news conference and released an e-fit picture of a woman they wanted to interview. It was later posted on the internet and was shown on *Crimewatch*. The image showed a dark-haired woman in her mid-thirties, five feet five inches tall, wearing a black dress and a lot of jewellery. She was identified by two witnesses who claimed they saw her in Kelvin Road entering Mandy Power's house on the night of the murders. She never came forward and was never traced.

Another person whom the police wished to interview was the woman seen talking to Mandy Power three weeks before the murders in the Farmers Arms pub in Clydach. She was described as aged 23 or 24, had cropped hair, was of medium build and had a diamond stud on one side of her nose. She was never traced either. How, it might be asked, could South Wales Police hope to find the murderer if they were incapable of finding a close confidante of one of the victims, with such a distinctive appearance?

As the first anniversary of the murders approached, murmurs from the public turned into a deafening roar, as people publicly expressed their unease and dissatisfaction at the lack of progress and the length of time it was all taking. Speaking at a news conference at Cockett Police Station on 21 June, Mandy's brother, Robert Dawson, said the family was devastated by the thought that someone was sheltering the killer. Privately, he stated his concern that there had been no arrests. Mandy's sister Julie said they too would have liked an arrest, though she understood it was a difficult inquiry. She expressed her confidence in Lloyd-Evans and his team and said she was convinced someone was withholding information. Lloyd-Evans reassured both of them that he and his team were doing everything possible, statements were being constantly reviewed, and he was planning to place a mobile incident room in Kelvin Road.

On 23 June, 9 Kelvin Road was sold. An advertisement for the sale read 'Quick sale required due to relocation of vendor'. The house had been boarded up for the best part of a year, thus generating no rental income for its owner, publican Glyn Hopkin. The house, which had originally been bought for £39,000, fetched just £7,000.

On the anniversary of the murders, floral tributes began appearing outside the house. Reporters revisited Kelvin Road to evaluate progress. Reflecting on this, Clydach resident Eileen Jones commented: 'We all want to see for ourselves who was capable of this hideous killing. No one can rest easy at night till they're caught.'

On 27 June the promised mobile incident room was set up in Kelvin Road where it remained for just two weeks. Officers talked to dozens of people, hoping to jog their memories. They visited pubs and clubs in search of witnesses, and from midnight until 4 a.m. every morning officers were stationed at the Mond, a bronze statue commemorating Ludwig Mond, founder of Europe's largest nickel refinery in Clydach. Lloyd-Evans assured anyone who still listened: 'We will get a result with this inquiry.'

As posters in shop windows curled and faded, so the police pleas for information all but disappeared. It was a graphic illustration of the time the investigation was taking. Lloyd-Evans' announcements were sounding more and more empty. Many spoke privately about their doubts; others said in public that they were dubious about the ability of South Wales Police to conduct an effective investigation.

The pressure on Martyn Lloyd-Evans and his team to produce results was enormous. Something had to be done before the situation reached breaking point. And something *was* done – though it later became obvious that it was more spin than substance. Early on the morning of 4 July 2000, and perhaps with no more evidence against them then than they had possessed a year before, Lloyd-Evans finally arranged for the arrest of all three Lewises.

Alison Lewis was arrested on suspicion of murder at her mother's home in Morien Crescent, Pontypridd. She was roused from her bed, handcuffed, and plastic bags were put over her hands. She was taken from the house while neighbours looked on. Stephen Lewis was arrested at the family home, 8 West Crossways, Pontardawe, also on suspicion of murder. It was only now that a full forensic search was made of his home and his car. Stephen's identical twin, Stuart, was arrested at his home in Ashwood Drive, Gellinudd in Pontardawe on suspicion of conspiracy to pervert the course of justice.

While the Lewises were taken to separate police stations in Swansea, Morriston and Neath, Alison and Stephen's West Crossways home was cordoned off so that it could be forensically searched. A team of investigators moved in and removed from the house clothing and other items in a dozen or so black plastic bags. The contents would be examined for traces of blood and any evidence linking them to the crime scene, although what the police hoped to find more than a year after the event was anybody's guess. The arrests seemed very much like an act carried out to appease critics of the South Wales Police.

Searches continued at the Lewis' homes in Pontardawe and Pontypridd, and a similar number of black evidence bags were removed from each of them. Alison Lewis appointed Gareth Jones, a Neath solicitor, to act for her, while her husband and brother-in-law were both represented by Swansea solicitor David Hutchinson. A former Detective Inspector in the Metropolitan police, Hutchinson was an experienced criminal advocate and a familiar figure in Swansea Magistrates Court and the city's Crown Court. For more than two decades he had worked at Goldstones Solicitors. This small practice, located at the lower end of Walter Road, predominantly dealt with legal aid cases. Hutchinson's office was only a few hundred yards from Swansea Magistrates Court which he attended frequently. He was also a duty solicitor, which meant that he could be called out at any time, day or night, to advise criminal suspects of their legal rights while they were being held in custody.

Hutchinson began preparing for the Lewis brothers' defence in the event that criminal charges were brought against them. At one point it was suggested that he had consulted privately with Swansea barrister Peter Rouch QC, to help him decide whether or not Stephen Lewis should agree to take part in an identity parade. Rouch later denied having given Lewis any advice through Hutchinson.

The day the Lewises were arrested, an angry crowd of some 150 people descended on Morriston Police Station in Sway Road where it was believed Alison Lewis was being held. Her solicitor Gareth Jones walked up the front steps of the building to shouts of 'String her up!'

It was only then – some 13 months after she had seen him – that Nicola Williams was at last given the opportunity to identify the man she had seen in the vicinity of Kelvin Road on the night of the murders. She was shown a police video identity parade and *immediately* picked out the man she believed she saw; she had no doubt it was the same man. The person she identified was South Wales Police Sergeant Stephen Lewis.

However, the e-fit image resembled more closely Stephen's biologically identical twin brother Stuart Lewis. Even so, it was only Stephen whom South Wales Police chose to produce for the purposes of the identity parade. Stuart was never required to take part. This anomaly has never been explained, even though Stuart never accounted for his movements at the time of Nicola Williams' sighting. But no matter how damning the evidence against the Lewises might have seemed, South Wales Police were certain to look after their own.

The Police and Criminal Evidence Act sets out the conditions in which an arrested person may be kept in police detention, and the provisions of the act must be complied with. If they are not, the detention becomes unlawful. Usually a period of detention where a person has not been charged will be limited to 24 hours but this period can be extended to 96 hours. The clock starts ticking as soon as a suspect arrives at the police station.

While held in custody at the various police stations, the Lewises were subjected to intensive questioning by the investigating detectives in a series of taped interviews. In her statements Alison Lewis repeatedly denied responsibility for the murders. She told detectives that she and her husband Stephen were both at home on the night in question and that she heard him get up twice and return to bed. She claimed that he had not known of her sexual relationship with Mandy Power until after the murders. On 6 July a witness overheard Alison Lewis talking with her solicitor during a break between interviews at Morriston Police Station. He heard a male voice saying: 'You've got to come up with something' and a female voice reply: 'I didn't do it, I couldn't do it. He did it. I've got babies of my own.'

In the first of 34 taped interviews Stephen Lewis gave to detectives, he denied that he had ever been inside 9 Kelvin Road. However, his fingerprints had been found in several parts of the premises, including two of the upstairs bedrooms, on a number of items in the house, and in the tool shed in the garden, under which, according to Alison Lewis' later testimony, the murder weapon was kept. When confronted with this incontrovertible evidence, Lewis changed his story and confessed that he had, after all, been in the house. Not only that, but he also admitted that he might have touched the video cassettes, the burned photograph of the two little girls, and even the murder weapon. He claimed by way of explanation that he had once delivered a box of nappies to the house and had moved a tumble dryer into the garden shed for Mandy Power.

Had the fires in the house not been extinguished, they might well have burned it to the ground, destroying all the evidence it contained, which was, no doubt, the murderer's intention. This would have included DNA belonging to Alison Lewis, and Stephen Lewis' fingerprints. In this event, no one would have known that Alison Lewis' DNA had been found on Mandy Power's thigh and on her vibrator, nor the truth about Stephen

Lewis, which he was eventually forced to confess: that he *had* been inside 9 Kelvin Road.

When asked if he had ever threatened Mandy Power, Stephen Lewis at first denied this. But when confronted with Louise Pugh's sworn statement that she had heard his threat, he admitted that he had, but then claimed it was said as a joke.

While he was held in custody, Stuart Lewis was subjected to 22 interviews. He also denied any involvement in the murders. He refused to say why he had left Kelvin Road so suddenly on the morning of the murders, or to whom he had spoken on the public telephone he used in Morriston Police Station.

As the 24-hour mark approached, the time limit for the Lewises' detention was extended by a further 12 hours on the authority of a police superintendent, and the questioning continued. As the 36th hour approached, an application to detain them for a further period of time was made to the Swansea Magistrates Court, sitting in private. The Lewises arrived at the Swansea Magistrates Court in separate security vans, so that they could be present when a police application was made to detain them further. The streets outside the court were cordoned off as an angry crowd turned up again. The case was given priority and heard first. The magistrates granted the application and gave the police a further 36 hours to continue questioning their suspects. Speaking to reporters from the steps of the court following the hearing, Gareth Jones told them that his client, Alison Lewis, denied committing the crimes.

The Lewises were returned to their respective police stations that evening. South Wales Police now had until 3.00 a.m. on 8 July to either charge or release their suspects. As the time limit approached, they were released without charge, but given police bail, which required them to report back to Swansea Central Police Station on 7 October.

Alison Lewis immediately went into hiding. The windows at her mother's home in Pontypridd were boarded up as a precaution against revenge attacks. Stephen and Stuart Lewis were both suspended from duty on full pay. The police made no announcement that they had even arrested anybody, though by that time, and as a result of Gareth Jones' later public denial, it was common knowledge that they had.

If the public were losing confidence in South Wales Police before the Lewises were arrested, their release on bail meant that now confidence was lost completely. Pressure was mounting on them to explain what was happening. South Wales Police authority member and City and County of Swansea leader, Councillor Mike Hedges, demanded a statement from Sir Anthony Burden, to make it clear 'where the inquiry is going', and he called for changes in the investigation team.

When contacted by the author in May 2013, the Professional Standards Department at Police Headquarters in Wootton Hall Park, in Northamptonshire confirmed that the decision on whether or not to transfer an investigation to another police force still lies entirely within the discretion of the Chief Constable of the particular police force involved. Despite all the criticism of the manner in which the case was being handled, Sir Anthony Burden steadfastly refused to transfer the case to another force.

Two days after the Lewises were released, tensions continued to rise as condemnation of the police became more vocal. Councillor Mike Hedges again echoed the unhappiness of the public when he said: 'Support for the police investigation appears to be on a knife edge.' Again requesting a statement from Sir Anthony Burden, he said, 'It is a matter of huge local concern.' Councillor Hedges was backed by Graham Davies, a trustee of the Dawson memorial fund. Davies told a reporter from the *South Wales Evening Post*: 'I have never felt so let down in my life as when I heard the news last Saturday morning.'

Clydach councillor Roger Smith told the reporter, 'People are asking why the arrests took so long to happen and there was great disappointment on Saturday morning.' Clydach villager Kenneth Thomas repeated the criticisms when he said, 'I don't understand why South Wales Police were allowed to continue the investigation, knowing the suspects wore some of their own.' Another Clydach villager, Susan Griffiths, called for a fresh investigation. She said: 'We seem to be no closer to knowing the truth now than we were a year ago.' Jean Phillips from Craig Cefn Parc told reporters: 'the investigation is a disgrace … it's horrifying,' And Jean Healey, head teacher at Katie and Emily's school, confessed, 'I too am disappointed.'

Clydach councillor Denise Preece called for the detective team investigating the murders to be replaced, insisting that murder squad detectives from South Wales should not have handled the investigation. A childhood friend of Mandy Power, Councillor Preece called for the entire police investigation team to stand down and a new team to be installed. Seventy-year-old Graham Davies, a trustee of the Dawson memorial fund, supported Preece and agreed that Lloyd-Evans should be replaced and a fresh team brought in. He said: 'There are no words to describe the whole episode [of arrests and releases] other than one big cock-up.'

Chapter 9

Responding to the weight of criticism that was building up against him personally, and also against South Wales Police, Detective Superintendent Martyn Lloyd-Evans told reporters on 21 July 2000 that he felt 'the arrests showed progress was being made'. This might have been true if the Lewises had been charged, but that had not happened, and to all intents and purposes the three had been freed.

Two days earlier, on 19 July, Welsh Office minister David Hanson had agreed to visit Clydach after the MP for Gower, Martin Caton, told the House of Commons that it was rapidly becoming known as 'a murder village'. A visit by the minister, Caton believed, would help to lift the stigma. Later that year, Hanson visited Clydach where he discussed regeneration issues with a range of agencies, but predominantly to boost the image of the village in the aftermath of the tragedy.

In order to restore confidence in the police and reassure the public that the investigation was proceeding properly, Councillor Mike Hedges, magistrate Peter Muxworthy, and members of the South Wales Police Authority Layla Hoque and Brian Mackerill were invited to visit the investigation room in Cockett Police Station where they were briefed on the investigation. The day after the visit, the group announced that it had every confidence in Lloyd-Evans and his team. They had, however, learned only what South Wales Police had wanted them to know. Whether or not they were told that ex-policewoman Alison Lewis' DNA had been found on Mandy Power's thigh and her vibrator, along with Sergeant Stephen Lewis' fingerprints, is unknown.

On 9 September, Lloyd-Evans flew to the United States for a week. He had meetings with offender profile experts at the FBI's behavioural science laboratory in Quantico, Virginia. He intended to learn from their experience of multiple murders and to examine psychological profiling methods. On his return, he announced that he had learned 'valuable lessons'. What those lessons were Lloyd-Evans never explained and there was nothing to show that they in any way advanced the investigation.

On 7 October, police bail for the Lewises was extended until December. According to Lloyd-Evans, 'This decision has been taken because a great deal of information has been coming into the incident room which the team are currently working through.' The Lewises were once more bailed on 12 December, this time until 22 January 2001. By now 3,150 statements had been obtained, the police had visited 987 homes, officers had spoken to 6,580 people and received 3,150 messages, but were still no closer to charging anyone. Meanwhile, Kelvin Road was struggling to get back to normality, and neighbours welcomed the builders who had been employed by the new owners of number 9 as they moved their tools and equipment into the derelict house to start a major refurbishment.

In the New Year, word began to circulate that the police investigation would soon be scaled down, though these rumours were quickly scotched. On 10 January 2001 the police made an announcement that they were 'close to discovering the origins of the gold neck-chain' that had been found at the crime scene.

Assiduous detective work had determined that the 9-carat gold neck-chain was made in Italy in 1989 and had been imported into Britain the same year. It had probably cost around £280 and was bought from Argos, Ratners, H. Samuel or H. Jones, all of which sold jewellery in Swansea. But the police did not know who might have purchased the chain, and, despite all their efforts and media pleas for help, they were unable to find out. The chain was clearly a dead end at this point, yet Lloyd-Evans insisted: 'It is a line of inquiry which is very much open.'

By the third week in January, building work had finished at 9 Kelvin Road and the house had taken on an entirely new look. No longer displaying evidence of the tragedy that had taken place there, it now had bright daffodil-yellow paintwork, new windows and garden walls. Inside the house a complete refurbishment had been undertaken.

If the house appeared to have moved on, the critics had not. Satisfaction with the manner in which the investigation was heading was now at an all-time low. Janet Llewellyn of Tanycoed Road, the westerly extension of Kelvin Road, said: 'We feel as though the police have been fooling people by arresting them [the Lewises] and letting them go.' Other local people were also vocal. John Richards of Craig Cefn Parc commented: 'The police should be stepping up the investigation, not winding it down.' John Davies, a newsagent in Vardre Road, said aloud what many people were thinking: 'The whole village is bewildered that it has taken so long and nothing has arrived.' And Terry Wallington, Clydach Labour Party chairman, called for a public meeting in the village to discuss the lack of progress. He claimed that the investigation had been poorly handled from the start. Detectives even failed to examine the contents of a skip just 50 yards from the murder scene. What Wallington thought they might have found in it he failed to say.

A further shock was in store for everyone who was hoping for progress in the case. In what might be seen as a major instance of 'passing the buck', someone in authority had decided that the Lewises were not going to be charged, but clearly thought that the decision might be better received by the public and the media if it were delivered by a police authority unconnected with the case. On 21 January, a spokesperson for South Wales Police announced: 'The Crown Prosecution Service at York was asked to advise, rather than the Crown Prosecution Service in Swansea, because of the South Wales Police connection with the suspects.' This was all very well but by this stage it was far too late to convince anyone that the investigation was being properly run.

On 22 January, the three Lewises were formally told in the presence of their solicitors that no charges would be brought against them, although the two brothers continued to be suspended from duty. The next day a spokesperson for South Wales Police announced publicly that, on the advice of the Crown Prosecution Service, the Lewises would not be charged with the murders. It was shattering news. The explanation given was that there was little likelihood of getting convictions against anyone with the evidence so far obtained. Furthermore, the spokesman said, the investigation team was likely to be disbanded, with most officers returning to ordinary duties. This was a hammer blow to the hopes for justice of the Power family and the village of Clydach.

Few people, if any, were fooled by the apparent wish of South Wales Police to have the evidence reviewed. They hoped that the announcement would be seen as the 'independent' decision of the York Crown Prosecution Service and nothing to do with South Wales Police, whereas it had everything to do with them.

Even the *South Wales Evening Post*, which had covered the investigation closely from the outset and rarely, if ever, criticised it, had this to say on 23 January: 'Nobody would presume to suggest that this has caused them [South Wales Police] to stint in their efforts in any way. Arguably, the opposite might apply, but it would be natural for people to feel an outside force should have been brought in in such unusual circumstances.'

While the first part of the newspaper statement was undoubtedly generous to South Wales Police, if not entirely accurate, people were indeed expressing their concerns at the objectivity of the South Wales Police and it reflected a widespread view that another police force should have been brought in to carry out the murder investigation. Nevertheless, Gareth Jones, acting for Alison Lewis, and David Hutchinson, acting on behalf of the Lewis brothers, closed their files and submitted their bills for payment.

Following the announcement that charges would not be pressed against them, Stephen Lewis told reporters he was 'a broken man' who 'would have told them where Lord Lucan was' [if he had known]. Stuart Lewis said he had no idea that his arrest and subsequent release was going to happen. 'I started going through a whole range of emotions. I felt relieved but, on the other hand, angry. I have been dragged through it all. I have also been protesting my innocence. I have lost everything – my job, my reputation and my girlfriend.'

Alison Lewis complained bitterly about her arrest and treatment, claiming that while she was held in custody, she was subjected to 23 interviews by detectives. 'I was interrogated. I was tortured with my grief for four long days,' she said. 'The police put me through hell for four days, but I didn't do it. I'd never hurt anyone. I loved Mandy and my only guilt is that I was not there to protect her on the one night she needed me. That night I was in bed with my husband in Pontardawe. That's my guilt.'

Alison Lewis later consulted London solicitor Nogah Ofer, who specialised in civil actions against the police, over the mental anguish she claimed she had suffered during her detention in police custody. The outcome of any negotiations or financial settlement is unknown.

The Lewis brothers delayed their response to their situation, although by mid-March they had challenged their suspensions from duty. Significantly, in the context of what transpired in subsequent court proceedings, David Hutchinson continued to act as the Lewis twins' solicitor and in March 2001 he wrote to both the South Wales Police and to the Independent Police Authority demanding that they investigate his clients' grievances.

In the meantime, as shock in the small village community metamorphosed rapidly into anger, Sir Anthony Burden boldly assured residents that the hunt for the killer would never end. Behind the scenes, however, plans were being quietly finalised to scale down the size of the team working on the investigation.

Chapter 10

When the case against the Lewises was dropped, the public began to ask what exactly had gone wrong. If there was enough evidence to arrest the Lewises in the first place, then surely there was enough evidence to charge them. However, in the complex sphere of criminal law, the legal concepts of 'arrest' and 'charge' are poles apart.

Working in tandem with the police, the Crown Prosecution Service (CPS) is the government department responsible for the public prosecutions of persons charged with criminal offences in England and Wales. The CPS is headed by the Director of Public Prosecutions, who is directly responsible to the Attorney General, the chief legal advisor to both the Crown and the government. The CPS's role in maintaining law and order requires it to advise the police on the appropriate charges to bring against a suspect, considering the strength and sufficiency of any gathered evidence, deciding which cases to take to court, and prosecuting the person or persons charged.

Today, the CPS works by a code of conduct which is set out in a public document. *The Code for Crown Prosecutors*, issued by the Director of Public Prosecutions in 2010, provides the general principles that Crown Prosecution lawyers should follow when making decisions on cases that come before them. There are two factors to consider when taking the decision to prosecute:

> 1. *Is there enough evidence against the defendant?* Crown Prosecutors must consider whether or not the police have provided them with sufficient evidence to be used in court, and possess evidence that is reliable, i.e. of good enough quality, to provide 'a realistic prospect of conviction'. If there is insufficient evidence, the prosecutor will advise the police of the additional evidence required to meet its minimum standard. If the police cannot produce the further

evidence required, the case may be discontinued, with no further action being taken against the suspect or suspects.

2. *Is it in the public interest for the CPS to bring the case to court?* Even if there is sufficient evidence, a prosecution will take place only when the Crown Prosecution Service considers it to be in the public interest; in other words, that it is worthwhile to prosecute.

The CPS will start or continue a prosecution only where a case passes both these tests.

Before the introduction of the code, the rule of thumb was the same. A prosecution would be commenced only if the evidence the police produced was considered sufficient, if it gave the CPS a better than a 50/50 chance of obtaining a conviction, and if it was 'worthwhile'.

This was how the CPS decision-making process had worked for two decades. The system was designed with the best of intentions – to protect the innocent and convict the guilty – but it has the added hidden benefits of saving police time and conserving public funds. If there is insufficient evidence to launch a prosecution, any charges brought against the accused are dropped and the case will never proceed to trial. This is not to say that a person suspected of committing a criminal offence is innocent; it merely means that the police have not provided the Crown Prosecution Service with *enough* evidence to meet their 50/50 minimum standard.

Should a criminal somehow possess the forensic knowledge necessary to destroy evidence left at a crime scene which might lead to his or her identity becoming known – evidence such as DNA or fingerprints – then crime scene investigators may find that any remaining evidence fails to meet the CPS minimum standard. At this stage, unless the police can find sufficient further evidence, no court proceedings will be commenced, and any charges will be dropped. If the suspect is in custody, he or she will be released. In many such cases, criminals known or believed to have committed a criminal offence will have 'got away with it' merely for want of sufficient evidence that could prove beyond a reasonable doubt that they were guilty.

However, in serious cases, such as assault, rape and murder, the investigation will not end merely because of an insufficiency of evidence leading to a suspect. Rather, it will try to find more evidence until the CPS is satisfied that it has enough evidence to be reasonably sure of achieving a conviction. Alternatively, it will move on until it finds another suspect against whom sufficient evidence can be found. Or, if such a person cannot be found, then the case will remain 'open', perhaps to be reinvestigated in years to come. By this time, new evidence might be forthcoming, or improved investigative techniques may help police to make a breakthrough, leading them to a new suspect. This occurred in the Lynette White murder case, following the development of Second Generation Multiplex Plus where DNA taken from a 14-year-old boy, not even born at the time of the killing, led police to the real murderer, the teenager's uncle, killer Jeffrey Gafoor.

But long before this point is reached, some police officers give in to pressure, lose their integrity, and become prepared to break the rules because they are determined to identify a suitable suspect, ensure that they 'find' sufficient evidence to charge them with the crime, and make certain that a prosecution is brought, followed by a conviction. One rule of justice – that a person is presumed innocent until proven guilty – simply ceases to apply; the demands for retribution outweigh a suspect's basic legal and human rights and provide the genesis of a miscarriage of justice.

If South Wales Police was losing the confidence and, more importantly, the support of the media and public, it was under-standable. Not only had they arrested, and then released, three suspects for the murders without charging them, but extensive efforts to trace key witnesses had met with failure. Some twenty months after the murders, a number of people whom the police had wanted to interview had still not been located – this notwith-standing the fact that more than 50 detectives had been involved in the inquiry and they had carried out literally thousands of enquiries.

The missing witnesses included the following five individuals:

The unnamed woman Mandy Power was seen speaking to in the Farmers Arms, Vardre Road, Clydach, on a weekday some three weeks before the murders. Presumed to be a friend in whom Mandy Power had confided, she was described as aged

23 or 24, with short cropped hair, of medium build and with a diamond stud on one side of her nose.

The second was a white male aged between 25 and 30, who went by the name of 'Mark'. He was seen in the Three Compasses pub in Clydach at 12.30 a.m. on the morning of the murders just before he took a taxi to the junction of Gellionnen Road and Kelvin Road. He was described as 5'10" tall, of stocky build, with short black hair, gelled back. He was clean-shaven and wore a gold earring in each ear.

A third was a dark-haired woman who took a taxi from the Mond in Clydach to Kelvin Road at around 1 a.m. on the morning of the murders. She was in her late twenties or early thirties, 5'5", thin or petite, with long black wavy or frizzy hair with a full fringe, seen wearing a black skirt or dress, high-heeled shoes and gold jewellery. She might have been carrying a small black bag.

A fourth was a young woman with long black hair, seen at around 12.45 a.m. near a public telephone kiosk beside the bronze statute at the Mond. She was wearing a Puffa-style jacket and was talking to a number of youths.

The fifth person the police wanted to trace was a man who got out of a Hackney (London-style) taxi at 5.35 a.m. in Port Tennant, Swansea – some 10 kilometres distant from Clydach – on the morning of the murders. The reason the police were so interested in him was that he was reported as being heavily blood-stained. Described as a white male, he was in his late twenties with short collar-length hair. He was wearing a short-sleeved T-shirt and had an elastic bandage on his left arm which was free from blood. An intensive campaign, accompanied by a thousand leaflets pushed through letterboxes in Port Tennant, failed to identify him.

Extensive enquiries succeeded in tracing none of these people. This despite the fact that two of them at least, both with distinctive appearances, seemed to have been friends of Mandy Power and therefore, one would think, be relatively easy to find.

The question as to whether or not it was ethically proper for the murder investigation to have been conducted by South Wales Police was finally answered by Alison Lewis herself. On 8 February 2001 she appeared in an HTV Wales interview in which she said she knew several people involved in the inquiry. Not only that, she admitted that Martyn Lloyd-Evans had been her Detective Inspector when they had both worked at Llanishen. Her admissions showed that widespread suspicions of a personal connection were proved to be correct. It was a highly unsatisfactory state of affairs and it should have made Lloyd-Evans' position untenable.

The day following the broadcast, calls flooded in, all demanding an independent probe into the police investigation. Swansea City Council leader, Mike Hedges, said: 'I'm shocked, and, in retrospect, it would have made a lot of sense for an outside force to have been brought in.' Comparing his own position on the council with that of the leading detective inspector in the police force, he explained: 'We have extremely stringent rules in council where we have to declare any interest or relationship with anyone involved in any business.' Hedges summed up the feelings of the general public by adding, 'Now there will be a complete lack of belief in what has happened and there will be a feeling of Clydach being let down.'

Councillor Hedges was supported by Clydach Councillor Roger Smith, who said: 'If Alison Lewis' claims are substantiated, then I would call on the Chief Constable to immediately investigate. And any officer involved should be immediately removed from the case and fresh people moved in…. The question needs to be asked – why did they not declare an interest at the beginning? I have every confidence in the integrity of senior officers and the investigation team, but if these claims are substantiated, the public perception of the investigation in Clydach will sink to an all-time low.'

A South Wales Police spokesman contemptuously declined to comment on the allegations when he ought to have done the exact opposite and come clean. The South Wales Police should have either admitted the allegations and somehow made amends, or rebutted them in their entirety. They did neither. Incredibly, the status quo continued and the long-held suspicions that hunter and hunted were in league continued to fester.

But eleven days after Alison Lewis' interview, public attention was diverted away from the South Wales Police and their responsibility for the Lewis debacle, as a new and more fitting suspect for the murders was found. It was David George Morris. He was exactly what the police wanted, and he was handed to them on a plate.

Chapter 11

On 19 February 2001, the police made a 'breakthrough' when a tip-off was received from an unexpected source. It was then less than a month since the case against the Lewises had been dropped for what was officially termed 'lack of sufficient evidence'.

An off-duty policewoman, Deborah Powell, was enjoying a night out with friends in Swansea. During the course of the evening, Powell spoke to Kim Crowley, an old acquaintance whose husband Michael was a fireman, and she mentioned something that caused Powell's ears to prick up. The previous year, fireman and part-time builder Eric Williams, who was carrying out some building work on Kim Crowley's house, had told her something odd which, she thought, might have a bearing on the Clydach murders. Williams had said that his cousin Dai Morris, who worked for him as a part-time labourer, had admitted to him that he had had sex with Mandy Power at her home just two days before the murders. This was information of potentially colossal proportions. It was news the police were hoping for, and Deborah Powell, realising immediately its tremendous importance, quickly passed on the information to the investigation team.

Eric Williams was traced and grilled extensively by the police. He was Dai Morris' second cousin and he told the police everything he knew, most of which Morris had himself told him. Morris, he said, had been involved in a long-standing sexual relationship with Mandy Power. On the Friday morning before the murders, Morris and Power accidentally met in Clydach then went back to her home for sex. Morris carelessly left his broken gold neck-chain behind when he left. Morris told Williams that he had meant to retrieve his chain the following day, Saturday, but he did not get an opportunity to do this because he was with his girlfriend all day. Shortly afterwards Williams bought him a replacement chain.

The detectives warned Williams to keep his mouth shut and say nothing to Morris about what they now knew. Williams duly obliged, but privately worried whether or not he had done the right thing in helping the police to build a case against a relative, and one whom he believed was innocent of the crime.

The investigation involving Dai Morris commenced with extreme prejudice. At 7.10 a.m. on Tuesday, 20 March, barely a month later, South Wales Police Detective Sergeant Wayne Thomas, accompanied by two other police officers, arrived at Mandy Jewell's Rhyddwen Road flat in Craig Cefn Parc. Jewell let them in. Dai Morris was in bed. Detective Sergeant Thomas arrested Morris on suspicion of the Clydach murders and led him outside in handcuffs. Morris made no protest. Then, in full view of his neighbours, he was placed in a police car and driven to Morriston Police Station where he was held pending the arrival of a solicitor.

Mandy Jewell was also arrested on suspicion of conspiracy to pervert the course of justice. She too was taken away in handcuffs and driven to Neath Police Station for questioning. The small flat was then subjected to an intensive forensic search for evidence linking Morris to the murders.

In Penlan, Swansea, police raided an empty council house registered in the name of Morris' ex-wife, Wendy. They hammered on the door, shouting for her to open up. But housing records had not yet been updated and Wendy and her family had moved to another council house several weeks previously. Other officers tracked her down at her workplace in Tesco, Fforestfach, and at 10.30 a.m. they turned up at the supermarket and took her away for questioning.

On the same morning, Dai Morris' mother, Shirley Morris, was taken from her home in Gendros to 'help the police with their enquiries'. Although it was evident that she was in poor health, Mrs Morris was questioned for eleven hours. During this time, she became distressed about her elderly mother who suffered from Alzheimer's disease and was at home alone. She needed to ask someone to feed her mother and look after her. Despite her pleas, she was refused permission to use the telephone to make arrangements for the old lady's care. As the day wore on, Shirley Morris became ill, but even so, no doctor was called to attend to her. It was early evening by the time her anxious daughter, Debra Thomas, tracked her down to Swansea Central Police Station and demanded to see her. Only then was Shirley Morris released and almost immediately collapsed from exhaustion.

Meanwhile, in Morriston Police Station, Dai Morris, who was unaware of his mother's detention, realised that he was in deep trouble because he was now the main suspect, in fact the *only* suspect, for the Clydach murders. In addition, he was frantic with worry that his girlfriend Mandy Jewell would find out about his sexual relationship with her best friend, the deceased Mandy Power. And Detective Sergeant Phillip Rees was anxious to begin questioning him. Morris needed his brief.

At the same time that Morris was being arrested, a small group of criminal lawyers from Swansea were attending a legal conference in Bristol. A late, unexpected cold spell had brought heavy snow to south Wales and the west of England, and some of the lawyers wondered if they should even try to make the long journey back to their homes in Swansea when the session ended, or book into a hotel for the night. For one of the lawyers, the decision was made for him when a telephone call came through from Morriston Police Station. A shaky voice on the other end of the line asked for David Hutchinson.

Following the call, and despite the risk of driving on icy roads, Hutchinson announced to the other lawyers that he was leaving early and returning to Swansea to represent Morris. Hutchinson's fellow lawyers were aware that he had already represented the Lewis brothers and knew the broad facts surrounding the case. They saw only too clearly the dangers presented by the potential conflict of interest. Two veteran Swansea solicitors, one of whom had previously acted for Morris, tried to talk Hutchinson out of acting for Dai Morris.

Critically, not only had David Hutchinson acted for the Lewis twins when they were suspected of involvement in the murders, he was in fact still acting for them. Only days earlier, he had written to the South Wales Police and the Independent Police Authority, demanding that they investigate the Lewis brothers' grievances. Now he was proposing to act for another suspect for the murders, who would, in all likelihood, try to blame the Lewises for the crime. In these circumstances Hutchinson could not do his best for two parties with opposing interests; besides, it was prohibited by the strict rules of his profession. His fellow lawyers told Hutchinson that, quite apart from the potential conflict of interest, if he won or lost the case, he would be a marked man. If he won, South Wales Police would be humiliated by their perceived 'defeat' and be out to get him. If he lost, Dai Morris would exhaust all his appeals procedures and then blame Hutchinson for his misfortune. But Hutchinson refused to change his mind or listen to reason. He left his colleagues to make their own arrangements for the evening and drove back to Wales and the police station where Morris was being held. It was a disastrous decision that eventually cost Hutchinson his career.

In Morriston Police Station solicitor David Hutchinson and Dai Morris were given the use of a police interview room, rather than the usual consultation room in which solicitor and client could talk privately. A twin-deck tape recorder was fixed to the wall and a green light above the door was supposed to come on as an indication that an interview was taking place. But unknown to Morris and Hutchinson, the interview room was bugged. A secondary device had been installed so that conversations could be monitored elsewhere in the police station. The bug did not have the effect of activating the green light.

Listening in on their private conversation, was Detective Inspector Shane Ahmed of the South Wales Police. Ahmed wrote down the conversation he claimed he had heard on a series of Post-it notes which, he said, was the only paper available to him. As a result of what he heard and wrote down, he believed that Morris had incriminated himself.

Afterwards, Ahmed telephoned Detective Superintendent Martyn Lloyd-Evans, who arrived hot foot from Swansea. The detective inspector told his superior officer what he had heard and showed him the Post-it notes' record of the conversation. It appeared to place Morris at the crime scene at the time of the murders.

This apparent cloak-and-dagger behaviour seemed to be a throwback to the 1987 case involving the Darvell brothers. South Wales Police had bugged conversations between the two brothers which strongly suggested their innocence, but wilfully kept this evidence hidden from the brothers' defence lawyers in order to wrongly convict them. (See Appendix.) This time, Ahmed claimed, the bugged conversation suggested guilt on the part of Dai Morris. The Post-it notes were shown to Hutchinson in the hope of forcing an admission from Morris. Hutchinson denied that his client had admitted guilt. Lloyd-Evans was forced to agree that what had been overheard did not represent the entire conversation, and no confession was obtained.

This incident on the day of Morris' arrest, which would later be described by his trial judge as an 'inadvertent error', set the tone for the rest of the investigation.

Prior to Morris' arrest the police swiftly established that he had a substantial criminal record. Crucially, as far as the police were concerned, some of it was for robbery and violence, and it also included the physical abuse of women. By the time of the Kelvin Road murders, however, Morris had been going straight for several years, receiving convictions only for minor driving offences. Nonetheless, he became deeply unpopular in the village of Craig Cefn Parc. Sylvia Lewis, the local village councillor, told journalists that one person had moved from the village in order to get away from him (Morris denied this allegation), while others were known to cross the road to avoid him. In many people's view, the police would be doing everyone a favour if they could get him off the streets and sent to prison for a long time. Whether Dai Morris was guilty of the murders or not, as far as the police were concerned they had found their man: they were not about to let another suspect slip through their fingers. From the moment the investigating team got Dai Morris in their sights, he was a dead man walking.

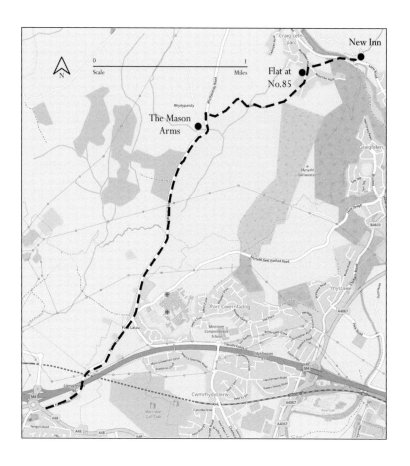

Chapter 12

When Dai Morris was arrested on 20 March 2001, the police had little enough evidence upon which to hold him, let alone charge him with a multiple murder, and hope to make it stick. All the police knew for certain was what his cousin Eric Williams had told them, and this was circumstantial evidence at best.

Morris' fingerprints were nowhere to be found in 9 Kelvin Road; neither was his DNA. An indistinct, bloody handprint discovered on the carpet in the living room was checked against his handprint, but two leading experts agreed later that it was not Morris'. The lack of clues left at the scene of what was considered to be a brutal spur-of-the-moment crime was unprecedented. The incredibly thorough clean-up operation to remove fingerprints and destroy DNA, including DNA in the waste traps removed from under the sink and bath, was attributed solely to Morris.

Detectives had deduced that the killer had removed blood-soaked clothes from the crime scene, but a Luminol test can detect traces of blood on clothes after many months – or even years – of repeated washing. Blood finds its way into stitching and into the soles of shoes, materials and fabrics which is virtually impossible to remove. Blood can even be detected in crevices and cracks in floorboards, and inside washing machines. An intensive forensic search of the flat that Morris shared with Jewell found no DNA or traces of blood belonging to any of the Kelvin Road victims.

For months after his arrest, almost up until four days before his trial began, the police were unable to prove that the broken neck-chain found in Mandy Power's house belonged to Dai Morris. He was asked many times if he owned the gold neck-chain and just as often he denied that he did.

But Morris' alibi to have spent the night of the murders in bed with Mandy Jewell quickly fell apart. Under intense police questioning, Jewell admitted that she had not, after all, gone home with Morris on the Saturday night before the murders. Neither, she said, did she open the door of her flat for him in the early hours of Sunday morning, countering another statement Morris had made. Finally, she admitted she had let him in that morning, but did not know at what time.

Following Jewell's admission, Morris gave detectives an account of his movements after leaving the New Inn, which he insisted were true. He said he could not go to the flat he shared with Jewell because of an argument they had had in the pub. She was angry with him and he knew she would not welcome him home. Instead, he had decided to walk to his parents' home in Gendros to spend the night there. He had a key to the house but had lost it, so that meant he would have to 'knock his parents up'. But by the time he reached Llangyfelach roundabout, he was 'getting soaked' and realised he was in the wrong over the argument with Jewell. He changed his mind about going to his parents' home, turned around and walked back to Jewell's flat, arriving some time before 3.00 a.m. This meant that he had no alibi for the time of the murders.

The route Morris had taken, according to the prosecution, involved a 3.2-mile walk from the New Inn to the roundabout at Llangyfelach. A police officer completed the trip on foot in 55 minutes, which was much less than the time Morris said it had taken him to complete his journey.

In fact, neither the distance nor the time involved, as suggested by the police, were accurate. The distance between the New Inn and Jewell's Rhyddwen Road flat measures 0.3 miles, while the further journey from the flat to the Llangyfelach roundabout adds another 3.2 miles. Adding the return journey back to the flat of 3.2 miles makes a total of 6.7 miles, more than double the distance suggested by the police; therefore, more than double the time. This meant that the police estimate of the time taken by Morris to walk from the New Inn to Llangyfelach roundabout and then back to the flat was grossly underestimated. And unlike the police officer walking the route, Morris was walking in near pitch-darkness and in no particular hurry. He had also consumed perhaps seven pints of lager, which probably would have slowed his progress, and taken shelter from periodic rain showers. As Morris' defence barrister, Peter Rouch QC, would point out later, Morris had, according to the prosecution case, taken substantial quantities of amphetamines, and these too would also have a slowing effect. What all this meant was that Morris' claim to have taken almost three hours to walk the distance was much closer to the time he said he had taken than the time the police proposed.

Twenty-four hours after Dai Morris' arrest, the police were granted another 12 hours to continue questioning him. While Morris was being interrogated, detectives descended on Morris' former home in Swansea. The house was searched thoroughly and stripped right back to the bricks and mortar. Carpets and furnishings were all removed for forensic examination. A neighbour, Maria Stephens, said: 'They've stripped most of the house and taken the floorboards up, taken bags of whatever out of the house; they've been through the attic and everything.' A number of black plastic bags containing a variety of items were removed from the house and taken away for forensic examination. Nothing even remotely connecting Dai Morris with the murders was found.

A kilometre away, a similar search was taking place in the home of Dai Morris' elderly parents, Brian and Shirley. No evidence connecting him with the murders could be found there either, and the hunt moved on to a nearby wood after someone reported that something had been burnt there. The wood was also thoroughly searched. Yet again, nothing whatsoever was found to link Dai Morris to the murders.

Before the 12-hour extension ended on 21 March, the police applied for further time to continue questioning Morris. The roads to Swansea Magistrates Court were sealed off as Morris was again brought before the justices. After an hour-long session, a further period of 24 hours' detention was granted. Even this extension proved insufficient for the police to gather enough – or any – evidence to charge Morris with the murders, and he was taken before the justices yet again when a further 24-hour detention period was obtained.

On 23 March, despite an almost total lack of evidence against him, David George Morris was formally charged with the murders of Mandy Power, her mother Doris Dawson, and

Mandy's daughters Katie and Emily. The following day, a special committal hearing was scheduled for Swansea Magistrates Court: the first step in sending Dai Morris for trial to Swansea Crown Court. Once again, roads leading to the court building were closed off. Morris arrived at 8.30 a.m. amidst tight security and was placed in a holding cell. Because he was a potential target for a revenge attack, all spectators attending the hearing were searched for weapons as they entered the courtroom.

At 10.00 a.m. sharp, the court proceedings commenced. The chairman of the bench was senior magistrate Howard Morgan JP. The Crown Prosecution Service was represented by solicitor Bryn Hurford, while David Hutchinson represented Morris. The accused was clean-shaven, his dark hair was short and neat; he wore a dark grey open-neck shirt and dark trousers. He spoke just once to confirm his name.

The proceedings lasted for just a few minutes. Morris was committed for trial at Swansea Crown Court and a preliminary hearing was set for 3 April. Reporting restrictions were not lifted. The media could report only basic facts: the accused's name, address, age, occupation, the charges he faced, the identity of the court, the names of the magistrates, his legal representatives, whether or not bail and legal aid had been granted, and the fact of his committal for trial. After the short hearing, Mandy Power's family issued a statement, which read: 'Our family has endured almost twenty-one long and agonising months since the murders of Mam, Mandy, Katie and Emily to hear the news we have received today.'

This was all well and good and partially satisfied the public's demand for justice, but the extent of the evidence against Morris at this time amounted to this: an uncorroborated statement made by Eric Williams that Morris said he had had sex with Mandy Power two days before the murders when he left in her house his neck-chain, and that he (Williams) had bought him a replacement neck-chain. There was no admission, DNA, finger-prints or any other evidence linking Morris to the crime. Yet all the publicity surrounding his arrest and committal for trial suggested that there was.

On 26 May 2001 it was announced that the trial would begin on

8 April 2002. Several Clydach villagers objected to the delay without realising that South Wales Police had yet to build a case about Morris to be sure of achieving a conviction. On 5 November 2001, the allegations of murder were formally put to Morris at a hearing in Swansea Crown Court to which he assertively replied: 'Not guilty'.

Even if Morris' denials about owning the broken neck-chain were proven to be untrue, detectives must have feared that if he genuinely had been intimately involved with Mandy Power, he might be able to come up with a reasonable explanation as to how the neck-chain was found at the crime scene – an explanation that a jury might accept. But South Wales Police detectives were not about to let the small matter of lack of evidence stand in their way. The pressure was on to find hard evidence linking Dai Morris to the crime and the search continued unabated.

In the absence of hard evidence, however, there was another, disarmingly simple option available to the detectives. When used to maximum effect, the technique is potentially shattering since it could make a totally innocent person appear to be guilty of a crime: it is called *character assassination*, and it was this practice that was used to devastating effect against Dai Morris. In his case the police did not have to *prove* that he had a bad character; he had already done that for himself by virtue of his long criminal record.

Aside from citing his criminal record, the police had a plethora of character witnesses to choose from. Dai Morris was not well liked in the village where he lived. Several witnesses who had given statements in the early days of the investigation were visited again. This time they were questioned even more closely about their recollections of the events leading up to the murders and, more specifically, about how these involved Dai Morris. By now, any memories about the night of the murders were almost two years old and therefore likely to be hazy. One of these witnesses was Mandy Jewell's next-door neighbour, Janice Williams.

Janice Williams was a friend of Mandy Jewell and had known Mandy Power since they were teenagers. One of several conflicting statements she gave to investigating detectives provided the police with much of what they needed to build their case against Dai Morris. Williams had spent the afternoon and most of the evening before the murders with Jewell and Morris. Though broadly similar to Jewell's and Morris' accounts of their evening at the New Inn, it differed somewhat, and it was those differences that became a root cause of Dai Morris' problems.

Janice Williams said that on the Saturday afternoon before the murders she and a man called Michael Randerson went to the Masons Arms pub in the small nearby village of Rhydypandy. At some point during the afternoon, Mandy Jewell and Dai Morris joined them there for a drink. Morris and Randerson did not usually get on, but they put up with one another on that day. After a while, Williams and Randerson said they were leaving to go and watch the televised Wales v. South Africa rugby match in the New Inn, Craig Cefn Parc – some mile and a half distant from the Masons Arms. Jewell and Morris spontaneously decided to join them, taking Jewell's eight-year-old daughter Emma with them. The New Inn was packed with customers when they got there but they managed to find a table at the far end of the busy lounge bar.

Janice Williams told detectives that during the afternoon and evening Morris drank eight pints of lager, though this was almost certainly an exaggerated figure. He was dressed in a white Adidas T-shirt and jeans, or possibly jogging pants, she said. Most damagingly for Morris, she said he was wearing a heavy gold neck-chain similar to the one displayed in the murder publicity posters.

According to Janice Williams, after they had been in the pub for a short time Randerson announced that he was going to fetch his girlfriend, Fay Scott, and bring her back to the New Inn. After he left, Williams told Jewell and Morris that Fay Scott was a bit stuck-up. Morris took this as a challenge and made a bet that he could 'pull her', or words to that effect. When Randerson arrived back with his girlfriend, Dai Morris immediately turned on his charm. Morris was deemed to have won his bet when Scott wrote down her telephone number and handed it to him. If Randerson had disliked Morris before, now he truly despised him, and Jewell was humiliated. This humiliation soon turned to anger and a full-scale argument developed between the two men.

Janice Williams claimed in one of her statements that, in the course of their row, Morris began 'slagging off' Jewell's friend Mandy Power, calling her 'evil', a 'cow' and 'a bitch'. She said Morris grew increasingly angry whenever anyone, including Mandy Jewell, tried to defend Mandy Power's character. 'The more I tried to calm him by saying her good points, the more irate he was getting – so I stopped talking about it.' She said that Morris' 'eyes were bulging and he was furious'. Then Jewell and her daughter Emma left the pub without Dai Morris. By now, it was around 9.00 p.m.

In yet another statement to the police, Janice Williams stated: 'His eyes were big and wild and manic, and he was very quiet. It was very frightening and I don't frighten easily.' Separately, she noted: 'He did not usually go there [the New Inn pub] and people did not like him there.'

Morris vehemently denied these damning claims about his aggressive manner that evening. Neither was Williams' account corroborated by anyone else sitting at their table, or by any of the many customers in the lounge bar. Michael Randerson said he did not see Morris behave in the way Williams described, nor did Fay Scott. Mandy Jewell agreed that his demeanour was nothing like that described by Williams. Pub landlord Glyn Hopkin said he did not notice unpleasantness of any sort, and nor did his wife, Jayne. Jeff Jewell, Mandy Jewell's father-in-law, who was also in the pub and gave Mandy and Emma a lift home, made a statement in which he said Morris most certainly did not behave in the manner Janice Williams had described. Nevertheless, her statements subsequently formed a key part of the prosecution case during the murder trial: that Morris had exhibited a strong – even manic – hatred of Mandy Power shortly before her death.

Janice Williams' unfavourable, often contradictory, statements about Morris continued and were used by the police to build their circumstantial case. She said that soon after 7.00 a.m. on the morning of the murders, she was woken by a distraught Mandy Jewell who told her about the deaths of Mandy Power and her family. Williams said she comforted Jewell in her garden and, while there, she noticed Morris drinking lager in the garden, which she thought was unusual for that time of the day. She said he usually wore a short-sleeved shirt or went bare-chested, but on this day, even though it was quite warm, he was wearing a lumber-jacket style long-sleeved shirt. She also claimed that she saw a scratch on his nose which had not been there the previous evening.

By way of explanation, Morris described Janice Williams to the author as an alcoholic, addicted to prescription drugs and sex, and someone who possessed a vivid imagination. There may be more than a grain of truth in this. Williams gave several statements to detectives in which she described Morris' character differently each time. Had all her statements been read out, the inconsistencies would have been obvious. In one statement given to detectives when she was sober, she described him as a 'regular guy' and said she could not remember whether or not he was wearing his heavy gold neck-chain in the New Inn. When in drink, Williams told detectives an entirely different story; that Morris 'definitely' was wearing a gold neck-chain on the night of the murders. Yet the prosecution relied upon only the incriminating statements in court.

While giving her evidence during the trial, Janice Williams swayed in the witness box and slurred her words, giving every appearance that she was drunk. In a television interview immediately after she had given her evidence, subtitles had to be added, because she was incoherent.

If it were not for the incriminating statements Janice Williams gave to the police – statements not corroborated by anyone else – the prosecution would have been unable to show that Morris was angry enough with Mandy Power to wish to harm her. The prosecution *needed* statements of the type Williams provided in order to make its case against Morris. But other conflicting statements Janice Williams gave to detectives, which were not used, confirm that she had perjured herself in the witness box and given false evidence against Morris.

Why Janice Williams should have given false testimony to the police incriminating Morris in the murders was explained by Dai Morris in a letter to the author. As an alcoholic, he wrote, Williams was susceptible to police pressure and would have told them anything she thought they wanted to hear. Statements she gave them while in drink differed significantly from those she gave when she was sober. Furthermore, Williams, he said, had developed a fondness for him that he did not reciprocate. Morris said that on several occasions after Jewell had left for work in the mornings, Williams called to the flat and would try to initiate sexual relations with him. When he refused to become physically involved with her, he believes she became embittered towards him and this was her way of taking revenge.

Shortly after Morris' arrest, 'Mr A', an old friend, came forward offering his support to the Morris family. He became their confidant, accompanying them everywhere, including the various jails where Morris was being held on remand. 'Mr A' stayed close to the family during the two Crown Court trials in 2002 and 2006, and listened closely while Morris talked to his nearest and dearest.

'Mr A' was a crook with a long criminal record, mainly for drug-dealing. He had recently been caught with a stash of drugs imported from Amsterdam in the boot of a car he had hired. Normally, owing to his extensive criminal record, he would have faced prosecution followed by a long stretch in prison but, strangely, this did not happen. Other things did however. Snippets of conversations that Morris and members of his family had made during prison visits where 'Mr A' had been present were later repeated to Morris by the police in an attempt to force him to confess his 'guilt'. 'A' was almost certainly a police spy. It was an unusual technique which had worked well in the past and had led to convictions in difficult cases. But these efforts to elicit incriminating evidence failed. Throughout the entire police investigation and two Crown Court trials, 'Mr A' was never able to report anything to his police handlers that the prosecution needed in order to strengthen its case. Nothing he heard, and inevitably passed on, ever amounted to a confession or implicated Morris in the crime. In one letter Morris wrote to me, he said quite simply, 'There was nothing to confess.'

Did South Wales Police do a deal with 'Mr A'? It is a question raised by several people. Did they promise to drop all criminal charges against him on the drugs arrest in return for information and for help he might give that would lead to Dai Morris' conviction for the murders? Whatever the truth of the matter, the fact is that 'Mr A' was never prosecuted for the serious drugs offence for which he had been arrested and, if proven, probably would have resulted in a substantial prison sentence.

Detective Superintendent Martyn Lloyd-Evans and his team were confident that even if they were unable to prove that the gold neck-chain belonged to Morris, they would still be able to paint a picture of him as someone who was both violent and *capable* of committing murder.

An old acquaintance of Morris, 'Mr B' was serving a 12-year sentence in Swansea prison and, while Morris was awaiting trial, they shared a cell. As they exchanged stories, Morris told him about his affair with Mandy Power. When detectives interviewed 'Mr B' in the prison, he repeated to them what Morris had told him about his relationship with Power. In his statement, he added that Morris was a 'tidy' guy, which in South Walian parlance meant he was decent. 'Morris never looked for trouble but, if pushed, he could handle himself', detectives were told.

This, however, was not evidence which suited the police. Detectives returned to the prison to interview 'Mr B' a second time. On this occasion he said in his statement that Morris was a 'madman who always carried iron bars in his car and was always looking for trouble'. It was the polar opposite of his first statement. There can be no logical reason why he would have told them this unless the murder squad detectives had offered him a deal. Shortly after giving the police this new statement, 'Mr B' was released from prison before his due date. This suggests that such a deal had indeed been struck.

Further confirmation was provided by 'Mr B' himself. Immediately after his release, he had a change of heart and rang Morris' solicitor, David Hutchinson. He asked if he could arrange an appointment to make a new, third statement – basically the same as his first statement – confirming that Morris was not a man who looked for trouble, and that he did not carry iron bars in his car. The evidence 'Mr B' could have given in court was crucial to the defence, yet Hutchinson told him that there was no need to make another statement, and anyway it was too late. At this point Morris' trial had not yet begun and was, in fact, still several months away.

The Morris family believed that their telephones were being bugged after Dai Morris' arrest. This is routine police practice in cases of serious crime and often results in a suspect unwarily incriminating himself. At no time did Morris make any admissions when using a telephone to call friends and family which implicated him in the crime. During the entire time that Dai Morris was held on remand – from 20 March 2001 to 10 April 2002 when his trial began – he never once admitted responsibility for the Clydach murders. Neither has his stance on the question of his guilt changed since.

Morris had worn a heavy gold neck-chain for ten years. Yet, despite microscopic examination of the gold chain found at the crime scene, no DNA belonging to Morris could be found on it. While he was held in custody, Morris repeatedly insisted that the chain produced by the police did not belong to him, and he swore this on his children's lives.

In the meantime, as the investigation progressed and the search for hard evidence against Morris continued, the neck-chain was re-examined even more carefully than before. This time, under the blood on the chain, forensic scientists found a particle of brick dust, and a tiny speck of green paint that had adhered to the gold clasp. Returning to the Rhyddwen Road flat, forensic scientists resumed their search for evidence connecting Morris to the crime. Examining the kitchen cupboards more carefully, they found the same green paint that had been discovered on the gold neck-chain.

When confronted with this new evidence, Morris had little choice but to admit that the chain 'probably was his'. This was just four days away from the start of his trial. He confessed that one of his cousins, Eric Williams, had bought a replacement chain for him in a Swansea second-hand jewellery shop a few days after the murders. It was not even Morris' idea, he claimed. It was Mandy Jewell who had suggested to Eric Williams that he replace the chain, to avoid suspicion falling on him because Morris had told her he had lost it while he was working on one of Eric Williams' building sites.

For a brief moment it must have appeared to the detectives that they had Morris nailed. The chain, which he now accepted was probably his, seemed to place him at the scene of the murders on the night of the attack. It was evidence of the highest possible value, but the detectives' delight must have quickly turned sour when Morris gave them an explanation for its presence in the house. It was the same explanation he had given to Eric Williams on the day after the murders: he had left the chain at Power's home when he had had sex with her on the morning of Friday, 25 June.

Morris had begun working for Eric Williams on Monday, 28 June, the day after the murders, and had told him that he had 'screwed' Mandy Power the day before she was killed. This was a mistake on Morris' part because Friday 25 June was *two days* before the crime.

Williams had replied, 'You must be fucking joking'. Morris also told Williams that he had left his neck-chain at Mandy Power's home on a kitchen worktop by way of a promise to her that he would come back the following day. He said he could not tell the police this because his live-in girlfriend, Mandy Jewell, did not know anything about the relationship, and would cut his balls off if she did. How the neck-chain was later found on a bedroom floor at 9 Kelvin Road Morris could not explain. Eric Williams had bought him a new chain, and Morris had roughed it up in a cement mixer, hit it with a hammer and broken the clasp, to make it look as much as possible like his old chain.

Morris, however, also gave the police a revised version of events in another statement he made a day or so later, though it was broadly similar to his first statement. He told them he had been at 9 Kelvin Road the day before the murders. He claimed that he had gone to Mandy Power's home in the morning unbeknownst to his girlfriend. He had been fiddling with the broken clasp of the chain in the kitchen when Power had called him upstairs to her bedroom. He had placed the broken chain on a kitchen worktop before going upstairs. He said they had sex against the partition wall that separated her bedroom from her mother's double bedroom. This, he claimed, gave Power a 'buzz'. It was only afterwards – as he made his way by bus to his parents' home in Gendros – that he realised he had left the chain in Power's kitchen. At that point, it was too late to go back and retrieve it. At his parents' house, he found another gold chain which he also owned, and he put that on instead. He said it was smaller than the one he had left at Mandy Power's. Known as a Figaro-style chain, the design featured a recurring pattern of small, circular links and one elongated oval link. It was, Morris maintained, the chain he had worn in the New Inn on the night before the murders.

This presented the police with something of a dilemma. Morris had now given them two slightly differing accounts of how he had left his neck-chain in 9 Kelvin Road. But the differences were small and *might* be explained by lack of a clear memory owing to the passage of time, or for some other reason. The detectives must have been concerned that the sum total of evidence they possessed would be sufficient to take the case to trial, let alone secure a conviction. Thus, there was a serious possibility that, for a second time, a suspect for the murders would be freed. This was not a humiliation that South Wales Police was prepared to contemplate.

Any arguments raised by the defence about the quality of the police evidence would have to be demolished if Morris was to be convicted, and this was where Patrick Harrington QC, counsel for the prosecution, would come into his own. Described as 'a top silk' in *Chambers Guide to the Legal Profession*, Harrington was admired for achieving difficult convictions in high-profile cases. During his career, he had successfully prosecuted several complex murder cases and had earned a reputation for being a shrewd, competent and determined Crown prosecutor.

In *R* v. *David George Morris*, much of the prosecution's case rested on a most peculiar, but entirely legitimate, trial strategy which only a skilful and ingenious counsel could devise, let alone hope to pull off. It involved having to convince the jury that Dai Morris had never been involved in a sexual relationship with Mandy Power, when his confession to his cousin Eric Williams that he had been was what had got him into trouble in the first place.

If anyone could guarantee South Wales Police its conviction and weave a convincing case for the jury from so much innuendo and so little evidence – a broken gold neck-chain, various lies and no alibi – it was Patrick Harrington QC.

Part II

The 2002 trial of David George (Dai) Morris
at Swansea Crown Court

Chapter 13

Two men glared at one another across the crowded courtroom in Swansea Crown Court, each determined not to look away first. Detective Superintendent Martyn Lloyd-Evans held the unblinking stare of Dai Morris' elderly father Brian, who held Lloyd-Evans' steady gaze. Eventually, conscious of the attention they were attracting, Lloyd-Evans averted his eyes from the man he held in contempt. For his part, Brian Morris, satisfied that he had won this battle of wills at least, turned away from the detective he had grown to loathe. He then seated himself in the public gallery, next to his wife, Shirley, and Debra, their daughter, and waited for the trial of his son to begin. It was Wednesday, 10 April 2002. The trial had been scheduled to begin on Monday that week, but all courts throughout the United Kingdom were closed as a mark of respect for the funeral on Tuesday of the Queen Mother.

The trial, which was expected to last for three months, made headline news in Britain. The public gallery was packed with spectators, dozens of whom had queued for up to six hours in order to secure a seat, and forty members of the press. Many would-be spectators were turned away because there was simply no room for them all. Court administrators then took the unusual move of opening the upstairs gallery to provide extra seating. The families of the victims, including Mandy's older siblings, Margaret Jewell, Julie Evans, Sandra Jones and their younger brother, Robert Dawson, sat in a reserved section at the back of the court on the ground floor. From here, they had an unobstructed view of the dock and its hapless occupant.

As the legal teams took their places in court, it was notable that the prosecution fielded considerably more personnel than the defence. As is the custom, the defence team sat nearest to the jury. The barristers wore wigs and gowns while their instructing solicitors wore sober dark suits.

Prosecuting counsel Patrick Harrington and defence counsel Peter Rouch huddled together conspiratorially for a few moments before returning to their colleagues and outlining the content of their discussion in hushed tones. Earlier that morning, soon after Morris had arrived from Cardiff prison, Peter Rouch had conferred with him in the cells below the courtroom. It was their last conference before the trial. During their brief meeting, Dai Morris had confirmed that he was not going to change his plea to one of guilty. A change of plea often happens just before a criminal trial where the defendant thinks he has a weak case, in return for getting a lighter sentence. But Morris did not think he had a weak case, and he was not about to change his mind and plead guilty to a crime he swore he had not committed. This was the information that Peter Rouch had whispered to his opposite number, so that they both knew the state of play.

In addition to Patrick Harrington QC, the prosecution team comprised Tom Glanville Jones, head of Angel Chambers in Swansea, and barrister Jim Davis, also of Angel Chambers. Both were experienced and competent trial lawyers. The defence team comprised Peter Rouch QC, a Swansea barrister but who was then based in London, barrister Francis Jones of Iscoed Chambers in Swansea, and solicitor David Hutchinson. Peter Rouch had appeared in numerous cases, ranging from domestic murders to contract killings, and serious sexual offences to multiple murders. Rouch held a wealth of experience in cases such as this.

Queen's Counsel and junior counsel sat in the front row of the court facing the judge, while their instructing solicitors, together with their clerks, sat in the row behind, close enough to communicate verbally with counsel, though in hushed voices out of respect for the court and for privacy. Tension in the packed courtroom was palpable and security was tight. It became tighter still when a knife was discovered in one of the women's toilets. Neither the owner of the knife nor its purpose were ever established.

At 10.30 a.m. precisely, Dai Morris was led into the dock by uniformed security officers. Dressed in a dark suit, light-blue shirt and a blue tie, he stood and looked around nervously, searching the courtroom for anyone he knew. As he spotted his relatives and girlfriend Mandy Jewell in the public gallery, his eyes rested on them for just a moment. Later, as prosecuting counsel addressed the jury, Morris listened intently and scribbled notes. He continued to act in this way throughout the entire proceedings.

Silence descended on the courtroom as the trial judge appeared from his private chambers. The Honourable Mr Justice Butterfield scanned the sea of faces for a moment, but deliberately avoided catching the eye of the accused. He nodded his bewigged head slightly in the direction of the defence and prosecution lawyers, who responded by nodding back, and then lowered his frame onto his well-padded, red leather seat. The case of *R* v. *David George Morris* was about to begin.

The jurors, a panel of seven men and five women, were drawn from towns and villages up to twenty miles away because it was considered that many people living in the Swansea area would have a fairly good knowledge of the case, and might therefore have formed particular opinions before the hearing. The trial proper was preceded by five days of legal argument, during which time the jury was not required to be present. This was so that they would not be influenced by what they would otherwise hear.

What they would have heard was Peter Rouch alleging that a criminal conspiracy involving South Wales Police had taken place and that the conspirators included Detective Superintendent Martyn Lloyd-Evans, leader of the murder investigation. He alleged that police officers had 'deliberately set out to monitor confidential solicitor-client consultations at Morriston Police Station'. Referring directly to the bugging incident which had taken place on the day of Morris' arrest, Rouch said that detectives had 'made up or fabricated' evidence. 'The integrity of the entire investigation is open to question,' he said, and 'it amounts to an abuse of process that would allow the judge to stop proceedings'.

The defence produced an expert witness, who confirmed that the conversation Detective Inspector Ahmed had recorded on the Post-it notes did not conform to the usual rules of English grammar and could not, therefore, be an accurate record of what was said.

The judge rejected Rouch's argument to halt the trial. In his ruling, which took an hour to deliver, Mr Justice Butterfield said he was 'satisfied there had been no bad faith or serious failings that would render a fair trial impossible'. Explaining his decision, he said: 'A light in the interview room should have come on to indicate that monitoring was taking place….The fact that this did not happen was not deliberate, but was the result of inadvertent error.' The judge said: 'I'm satisfied there was at no stage any intention that police officers should overhear private and privileged conversations taking place between the defendant and his legal representative.'

Summing up, the judge ruled: 'I reject the suggestion that officers deliberately set up a monitoring system to hear private conversations. I reject that they deliberately manufactured a conversation attributed to the defendant and his solicitor.' Although the judge rejected the application by the defence to halt the trial at that stage, the prosecution did not refer to the Post-it note conversation at any time during the trial. Nevertheless, it was Round One to the prosecution.

Chapter 14

On Monday, 22 April 2002, the prosecution made its opening statement to the jury. Patrick Harrington QC painted a picture of the domestic bliss that Mandy Power and her family lived in, and then described with emotion how they were subjected to the most grotesque injuries at the hands of Dai Morris, who, he said, had bludgeoned them to death. The jurors would have to 'subdue their emotions' and prepare to be 'shocked and appalled' by the details of the killings. A vital clue – a broken gold neck-chain – was left at the scene of the crime where the most extreme violence had taken place. Harrington described how in numerous police interviews Morris had repeatedly denied that the chain was his, but, eventually, in the face of incontrovertible evidence, he had accepted that it probably was.

Harrington told the court about Mandy Power's relationship with married ex-policewoman Alison Lewis since late 1998, and how Lewis had 'tried to commit suicide' on hearing about the murders. But, in order to get the jurors on his side, Harrington was about to play his trump card – his description of the video footage of the crime scene taken immediately after the murders, which, the jurors were repeatedly reminded, was attributable solely to Dai Morris.

He recounted with passion and in graphic detail how 'the whole family had been slaughtered in their home, having been attacked with a long heavy pole.' The injuries 'were simply awful', Harrington said, pausing momentarily for the jury to take it all in. 'This was not merely murder, this was a massacre,' he told the visibly shocked men and women of the jury.

'For more than a year,' he said, 'the finger of suspicion pointed at three people – Alison Lewis, her police sergeant husband Stephen Lewis and his twin brother Stuart Lewis, a police inspector.' He then briefly explained why the police investigation had centred on the Lewises, and concluded with an apology: 'It was a matter of profound regret that a false finger of suspicion had been pointed [at the Lewises], especially in circumstances of a case such as this.'

The reason for this apology to the Lewises in open court was subsequently explained to the author by solicitor Simon Jowett, who acted for Dai Morris at a later date. He said that when prosecuting a murder case, it is vital that you do not allow any doubt to creep in. The prosecution's problem was that the police had investigated the Lewises for eighteen months, and then suddenly dropped the case owing to an insufficiency of evidence. The decision to drop the case was allegedly based on senior counsel's advice, even though Alison Lewis' DNA was found on Mandy Power's inner thigh and on a vibrator, and Nicola Williams, an eyewitness who had placed Stephen Lewis near the crime scene at the time of the murders. Simon Jowett said: 'We requested a copy of that advice numerous times, but it was never forthcoming. We assume it said there was not enough evidence to be sure of a conviction. If they'd been fair, they'd have explained it properly to the jury. But that would have made the Lewises suspects, allowing *doubt* to creep in, and the prosecution couldn't risk that happening. When Dai Morris appeared on the scene, he was an easier target altogether. They decided he was guilty and the entire focus of the case shifted to him. They built a case around him, even though his DNA and fingerprints were nowhere to be found in the house. After a year-long investigation, they were still unable to find any hard evidence against him. It was an intellectually dishonest prosecution, based on purely circumstantial evidence.'

In other words, the prosecution almost certainly apologised to the Lewises at the start of the trial, not because they believed they were innocent, but simply because they did not have sufficient evidence to be sure of convicting them. This simple ploy by Patrick Harrington QC left just one other possible candidate for the murders: Dai Morris.

Moving on to the investigation, Patrick Harrington explained how the police came to believe that Mandy Power was central to the crimes. After her divorce, he told them, she had enjoyed a number of sexual affairs with men, though at the time of her death she was in what he described as a 'settled and loving relationship' with former South Wales Police officer, rugby-playing Alison Lewis.

The stage being thus set and the principal characters introduced, Harrington then told the jury about the discovery of a broken gold neck-chain, covered in blood, which had been found on a bedroom floor where most of the violence had taken place. The police, he said, did not immediately realise the significance of the chain, but when the owner could not be identified, they reasoned that it must belong to the killer. Dai Morris had initially denied that the chain was his, admitting only that 'it probably was his', just four days before the trial, when faced with undeniable forensic evidence. In a simple message delivered to the jury with a logic that denied the possibility of an alternative, innocent explanation, Harrington said: 'Find the owner of the chain and you will find the killer.'

The prosecution case centred on the following assumptions: on three consecutive days leading up to the murders, Dai Morris, a violent thug, had bought drugs from a local dealer, Terrence Williams, in the form of amphetamines, popularly referred to as *speed*. These drugs, he said, make a person psychotic. On the afternoon of Saturday, 26 June and in the hours leading up to the murders, Morris was in the New Inn with his girlfriend, Mandy Jewell, her young daughter Emma, Janice Williams and Michael Randerson; later in the evening they were joined by Randerson's girlfriend, Fay Scott. By closing time, he had drunk at least seven pints of strong lager. Mr Harrington said the combined effect of the drugs and alcohol had made Morris angry and violent. In fact, in the pub he came close to violence in an argument with Adrian Davies, a local man also known as Sage.

While he was in the pub, Morris was allegedly heard openly expressing hostility to Mandy Power. Following an argument with his girlfriend, Mandy Jewell, she walked out on him and went home taking Emma with her. Sometime between 11.15 p.m. and 11.30 p.m., high on drink and drugs, Morris left the pub 'looking angry'. A man matching his description wearing a white V-neck T-shirt and blue jeans was seen walking towards Kelvin Road by witness Anthony Evans, who was looking out of his daughter's upstairs bedroom window. (Anthony Evans saw a man wearing jeans who looked like Morris, but Morris was wearing a track suit bottom.) Morris went to Mandy Power's home at 9 Kelvin Road, hoping to have sex with her. She refused and this incensed him, causing him to explode in a violent rage. He attacked her with a fibreglass pole, battering her to death. Doris Dawson, Emily and Katie witnessed the attack. They knew Dai Morris and could identify him, so he killed them too.

When Mandy Power was dead, Patrick Harrington told the jury, her body was stripped naked and, 'as a final act of desecration and humiliation', a vibrator was pushed into her vagina. He omitted to mention other anomalies such as the silver wrist watch placed on Mandy Power's wrist, the partially burned photograph of the children, and the engagement ring found on her dead mother's torso – perhaps because these acts did not support the theory of a raging drink- and drug-fuelled killer.

Afterwards, intending to avoid detection, Morris cleaned up the house, wiping away his fingerprints and DNA, removing all evidence that placed him at the crime scene. He then washed blood from his clothing in the upstairs bathroom, and either showered or had a bath to remove blood from his body. Finally, in an attempt to obliterate any remaining evidence, he set fire to the house.

But despite all Morris' efforts to forensically sanitise the crime scene, he inadvertently left behind something that revealed his identity. A heavy gold neck-chain with a broken clasp discovered on the bedroom floor at the spot where the most violent attack had taken place. It was the prosecution's case that, during the vicious attack, Mandy Power had pulled the chain from the murderer's neck. The chain belonged to Dai Morris and, the prosecution argued, it placed him at the crime scene at the time the murders were committed. Patrick Harrington described finding the neck-chain at the crime scene as 'a clinching piece of evidence'. After the murders, Harrington asserted, Morris realised that he had left the gold chain behind. Media publicity about the murders prompted him to obtain a similar gold chain which was bought for him. He deliberately hit it with a hammer and put it in a cement mixer, to make it look like his old one.

The accused's original story, Harrington said, was that, after leaving the pub, he had walked in the direction of his parents' home in Gendros, but then had 'wandered the lanes in the rain for the next four and a half hours' before returning to the flat he shared with Mandy Jewell.

Harrington then outlined the story that Mandy Power had made up about having cervical cancer – a story that was discovered to be a lie – and how this lie had spoiled her friendship with Mandy Jewell. Former South Wales policewoman Alison Lewis, Harrington told the court, lived under a cloud of suspicion, but she had an alibi, confirmed by her husband Stephen; that they were in bed together at the time of the murders.

Forensic scientists found that DNA from epithelial cells in vaginal fluids on the vibrator matched the DNA of Alison Lewis. They also found that the same DNA on swabs taken from Mandy Power's thighs, and on the vibrator that had been thrust into her, matched the DNA of Alison Lewis. The two women had been 'lovers in each other's arms, exchanging bodily fluids on two occasions shortly before the murders', Harrington said. The jury could therefore 'reject any suggestion that Mandy Power would have been interested in a casual fling with Morris. You must ask yourselves if you think it is even remotely possible that this mother of twin girls could have had anything to do with the murder of the woman she loved', he added.

It was also the prosecution's contention that Alison Lewis would not have had the slightest reason to wish to harm Mandy Power and her family. In his closing address to the jury, Patrick Harrington said that Dai Morris had lied 'at every stage and at every opportunity and on every topic. He knew the chain left at Kelvin Road was his, but in his interviews he swore on his children's lives that it was not.' The barrister said there would be evidence given by a neighbour in Kelvin Road, who would say that she saw Mandy Power leaving her home in a car driven by Alison Lewis on the morning Morris claimed that he had had sex with her. Alison Lewis's statement was that she was going to a gym in Pontardawe for a workout session, dropping Power off in Clydach village to do her shopping, which is where Morris claimed he had met her. The homes and cars of the Lewises had been searched and nothing incriminating was found in any of them, Mr Harrington said.

Harrington enumerated the events leading up to the night of the murders. By the time he concluded, he had left the jurors with a very clear image of Dai Morris: a mindless, violent, sex-crazed thug with a long criminal record, who was high on drink and drugs on the night in question, who not only *could*, but in fact *did*, commit murder.

As part of the prosecution's opening, Tuesday, 23 April was chosen as the day the jury would view forty minutes of video footage of the untouched crime scene on the day after the murders. Patrick Harrington warned them that some of the scenes they would see would be 'very distressing'. He described it as 'an orgy of savagery that cannot have taken very long'.

Patrick Harrington chose his words carefully and for their emotive effect upon the jury. While the crime was certainly shocking and violent in the extreme, it was important that the jury was given a balanced and fair view of the evidence. The terms 'massacre' and 'orgy of savagery' perhaps went beyond acceptable terminology and were highly prejudicial to the defendant.

The judge ordered the doors of the court to be locked as a precaution against anyone walking in unexpectedly and causing a distraction. The video opened with shots of Kelvin Road. An ordinary-looking semi-detached house came into view; the walls above the windows smoke-blackened, a blue tarpaulin covering part of the front. At the rear of the house, large white bed sheets on a washing line in the garden blew gently in the breeze. More outdoor views followed, and the camera zoomed in on Mandy Power's battered body lying under the blue tarpaulin, a resuscitation aid in her mouth. The camera turned to Emily, a resuscitation aid in her mouth also, and then to Katie.

As the camera moved inside the house, more shocking images appeared on screen, and Patrick Harrington's earlier description of the sickening violence inflicted on the four victims came vividly to life. The words he had used on that occasion had a profound impact on those who heard them: 'It would not have taken long for a powerful man to quell a woman, two little children and an invalid.'

One of the male jurors repeatedly wiped his hand across his

mouth in what might have been a nervous gesture, and glanced from time to time towards the back of the court where the victims' family was sitting. Other jury members displayed different reactions to the horrifying images unfolding before them and occasionally looked away from the screen or stared into their laps. For one of the jurors, a young man in his twenties, the stark reality was too much. About twenty minutes into the video, he fainted, falling onto a female juror sitting next to him. The judge ordered the video to be stopped. The trial was adjourned and the doors of the courtroom were pushed open. Several spectators in the public gallery abandoned their seats and fled the courtroom in tears. The juror was taken to Singleton Hospital, Swansea. By the following day, he had still not recovered sufficiently to continue as a jury member, and so the entire jury was discharged. The trial could have continued with one jury member less, but the judge decided that it was preferable to start again with a new jury.

On Thursday, 25 April a new jury was sworn in and the case began afresh. Since ten of the original jurors were selected a second time, they were obliged to listen to Patrick Harrington repeating the case for the Crown. They also had to view once again the horrific video that none of them would have wished to see the first time. This time the video ran non-stop for a full forty minutes.

Chapter 15

Over a five-day period commencing on Monday, 29 April, Patrick Harrington continued to mesmerise jurors and spectators alike as the first fifteen witnesses for the prosecution were called to give evidence.

The first of these witnesses was Sandra Jones, the youngest of Mandy Power's three older sisters. She gave the court details of Mandy's personal life: her failed marriage to Michael Power; her job as a nursing home care assistant; her friends and colourful lifestyle; sexual affairs with men, several of whom were married; and finally, her relationship with former South Wales policewoman Alison Lewis.

She said that on Saturday, 26 June 1999, she and her husband Ken returned from a week's holiday in Spain. It was their wedding anniversary and they had arranged to celebrate in Clydach's Sunnybank Club. Their son Stephen, a West Wales Dyfed Powys police constable, and his wife, Christine Jones, were going too, while Mandy Power minded their children.

Early the following morning Sandra told the court how she had she received a telephone call informing her about the tragedy, following which she and her husband rushed to Kelvin Road. They found the fire services already there. She then learned that her mother, sister and two nieces were all dead. Afterwards, although extremely distressed, she helped the police to identify a number of items recovered from the house, but when she was shown the gold chain, she did not recognise it.

Julie Evans, another of Mandy Power's older sisters, also told the court in cross-examination that Mandy had described Alison Lewis as 'possessive and jealous'. She added that she was prone to 'mood swings and her behaviour would be worse after drinking'. Julie Evans told the court that Alison Lewis could be deliberately hurtful and once said that she would not leave her

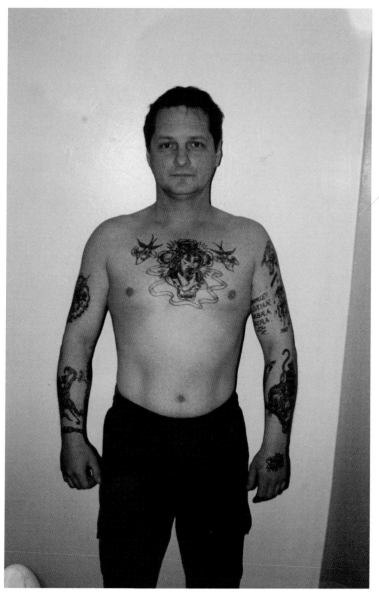
Dai Morris in a photograph taken by the police, which was used in court to show what 'he was really like'

Mandy Power

Doris Dawson, Mandy's mother and grandmother to the girls

Mandy and her daughters

Katie and Emily, aged 10 and 8

Mandy Jewell, Dai Morris' partner

Shirley Morris, Debra Morris and Brian Morris talk to the Swansea Evening Post after the first trial

Alison Lewis

Stephen Lewis (left)

mother 'in the care of someone like Mandy because Mandy did not look after her and feed her properly'. Evans had replied that 'Mandy looked after her mother well'. She added that whenever she went to 9 Kelvin Road and found Alison Lewis there, she would 'feel uncomfortable'.

Evans told the court that Alison had broken off the relationship when Mandy falsely told her that she had cervical cancer, but they had quickly got back together and 'seemed very close'. She also knew of Mandy's intimate relationship with former professional golfer Howard Florence, whom, she had heard, was intending to buy Mandy a ring.

Unfortunately, this latter aspect of her testimony was not expanded upon. How had Evans had come by this information, and, importantly, who else knew about it? All these potentially vital questions were never put to the witness.

Margaret Jewell also knew about her sister Mandy's relationship with Alison Lewis. She said that on 15 May 1999 Mandy and Alison Lewis had attended the opening of Gallivans Bar in Swansea, which Mrs Jewell ran. She told the court: 'Mandy and her lesbian lover, Alison Lewis, seemed to be getting on well.'

Police Constable Stephen Jones wept as he gave his evidence in the witness box. He and Mandy were both born in the same year – 1965 – and he said their relationship was more like that of a brother and sister than a nephew and an aunt. A few days before the murders, Stephen had called to 9 Kelvin Road and found Mandy in tears. She told him that she had just received a telephone call from Alison to say that Alison's husband Stephen knew about the affair and was making Alison choose between them. This evidence, confirming Stephen Lewis' knowledge of his wife's affair with Mandy Power, assumed crucial importance later on in the trial.

On the afternoon before the murders, Stephen Jones met Power at his parents' home in Clydach. She had offered to babysit his two children so that he and his wife, Christine, could attend his parents' wedding anniversary party in the Sunnybank Club that evening. Later that night, Stephen Jones and his wife returned home by taxi, arriving just before midnight. He paid the driver an extra sum, so that Mandy and her daughters could take the same taxi home. He broke down as he told the court: 'I kissed Mandy, thanked her for babysitting, and that was the last I saw of her.'

Giving evidence for the prosecution during the second week of the trial, Manon Cherry, a close friend and neighbour of Mandy Power, told the court that 'Alison Lewis dominated Mandy Power's life'. Cherry said that Power would often confide in her but had been 'almost too afraid' to admit that she was in a relationship with Lewis. She said Mandy called Lewis 'the love of her life'. However, some weeks before the murders, Power had told her she was 'sorting her life out'. She had been on a rollercoaster for quite some time but was now looking for a stable base, she said.

Recalling the morning of the murders, Cherry testified that she was awoken at about 4.30 a.m. by people in the street shouting about a fire. She went outside where she saw Alison Lewis standing amongst the crowd outside the house. Lewis spotted her, came over to her and buried her head in Cherry's shoulder. It was at this point that Cherry noticed that Lewis smelled of soap as if she had recently bathed or showered. 'She also seemed startled and jumpy', she told the court.

Manon Cherry said she knew all about the relationship between Mandy Power and Howard Florence, adding that Power had strong feelings for Florence and used to carry his photograph around with her. Florence often telephoned Mandy but 'Alison did not want Mandy speaking to Howard, and Mandy had to break off contact with him'. Alison Lewis was 'possessive and insanely jealous' of Howard Florence, she said.

Cherry said that Power had told her that when Lewis was premenstrual, she would become 'unbearable and unstable', to the extent that the lovers agreed not to see each other at these times because they would inevitably argue. Lewis had given Power a mobile phone so the two of them could keep in touch. Cherry described Lewis as 'controlling'. When they went to heterosexual functions together, Alison Lewis would become moody and they would always have to leave early. Power also told her that she thought Lewis had taken to spying on her. When she went to functions without Alison Lewis, she felt that Lewis was checking up on her by watching her clandestinely.

This allegation was given more credence later in the trial when witness Louise Pugh gave evidence that she had spotted a 'prowler' in the lane at the back of 9 Kelvin Road, though who this person might have been was never established.

Speaking with the author, Manon Cherry said Mandy Power was her best friend and that 'Mandy remembered little details about people which made them feel special.' She said that 'Alison Lewis was due to start her period at around the time of the murders.' At these times, she said, Mandy described her as 'evil'. Alison, she said, 'hated Mandy's children, especially Emily, but it was a mutual thing because Mandy's children hated Alison.'

Describing Mandy's relationship with Alison Lewis, Manon Cherry told the author, 'Alison was clever and obsessively jealous. She and Mandy were happy at first, but Alison drove all Mandy's friends away. The relationship was exiting for Mandy – it was different. Alison was playing Mandy like a mouse and Mandy was scared of Alison. On occasions I found her crying and shaking with fear.' Cherry said that Mandy complained that Alison wanted to control her. Sometimes Alison Lewis parked her car outside 9 Kelvin Road so that she could keep a watch on her. Cherry denied that, at this time, Alison Lewis and Mandy Power were the happiest they had ever been, describing Lewis' claim as 'completely untrue'.

Both Alison Lewis and Howard Florence wore gold neck-chains, said Cherry, and Lewis knew that Florence wore one. Speculating, she said that if Lewis had discovered a gold neck-chain in Power's home, she *might* have thought that it belonged to Florence and this thought would have incensed her.

This vital evidence was never brought up in court. Manon Cherry says she did not believe Dai Morris was guilty, and thought all the evidence pointed elsewhere. During her testimony, she felt she could not give vital evidence in the way she wanted to, or tell the court what she wanted to say. Discussing Dai Morris, Cherry said 'he was not a nice person,' and, 'it was in his nature to lie.' But she did not accept that he would have been able to clean away all evidence of his being in the house. 'Dai Morris didn't have a brain to clean up,' she said.

Robert Wachowski, who had enjoyed a brief sexual relationship with Mandy Power some months before the murders, told the court about how at 4.20 a.m. on Sunday, 27 June 1999, he heard loud noises and saw smoke coming from 9 Kelvin Road. He discovered the fire and had desperately tried to save Power and her family. After his relationship with Mandy Power had ended, their friendship continued and he learned from her that she had formed a physical relationship with Lewis. He told the court that Mandy had confided in him that 'Arguments in a gay relationship are worse than those in a heterosexual one.' In answer to Patrick Harrington's questioning, Wachowski replied: 'From all I heard from her, she was one hundred per cent committed to that relationship. She told me she had made her decision that she was gay and she was not interested in a heterosexual relationship when she was with Alison Lewis.'

A second video was played in court for the jury, this time a short interview with a young schoolgirl aged about ten. The judge explained that use of a video-link was standard practice when children gave evidence in criminal proceedings, and the child's name would not be revealed. The interview concerned the four-foot fibreglass pole – the murder weapon – at 9 Kelvin Road. The child said: 'I think I might have seen this in Katie and Emily's home.' She gave the date she had visited 9 Kelvin Road as some time in April 1999, and she told the detective that the pole had been 'lying against the wall in the girls' bedroom'.

Kimberley Wilson, a long-standing friend of Alison Lewis and also a lesbian, told the court that in June 1999 she had travelled to Ibiza hoping to get work as a barmaid. However, she did not like it there and decided to return home. She arrived back in Clydach two days before the murders, and on the night of Friday, 25 June she had stayed at 9 Kelvin Road. Mandy and the children were out for the night and only Doris Dawson was at home. Wilson slept in Power's bed and was woken the following morning at 9.00 a.m. when Michael Power dropped off Katie and Emily. A short time later, Mandy Power returned with Alison Lewis. Wilson told the court that Mandy 'seemed quiet, not her normal self'. Mandy told her that Alison Lewis had 'flipped' when she admitted that she had spoken to Howard Florence on her mobile phone.

Another witness called to give evidence by the prosecution was former Clydach resident Patricia Margaret Richards, who knew both the Power and Dawson families. She also knew Mandy Jewell and the defendant, David Morris, having met him when he had first moved to Craig Cefn Parc. About three weeks before the murders, Richards was walking her dogs up Rhyddwen Road when she heard shouting coming from Jewell's ground floor flat. She told the court that she heard Morris say: 'I don't like her – I don't like you having anything to do with her.' She said she believed that Morris was shouting at Mandy Jewell – and she thought he was referring to Mandy Power. She said, 'The whole thing was very angry.' In truth, Richards did not really know to whom Morris was referring; it could just have easily been next-door neighbour Janice Williams, who, according to Morris, frequently made a nuisance of herself. It was circumstantial evidence at best, put forward by the prosecution purely to establish Morris' supposed hatred of Mandy Power.

Donald Jones, formerly of Kelvin Road but at the time of the trial living in Llanelli, told the court how on the afternoon before the murders he had called to 9 Kelvin Road at 5 o'clock and had stayed for twenty minutes having a cup of tea with Mandy Power. In reply to his question about how her relationship with Lewis was going, Power said she was 'happier than she had ever been'. Under cross-examination by Peter Rouch, Jones said that some weeks before the murders he had seen a uniformed police officer leaving Mandy Power's home and getting into a police car. 'From the chevron-type markings on his uniform, I believe it was a sergeant.' He told the court that he thought this was strange because police cars were rarely seen in Kelvin Road.

Alison Sawyer, a Clydach bakery assistant and work colleague of Mandy Jewell, was questioned as to her recollections of a phone call, said to have been taken by her in the bakery on the Friday morning two days before the murders. Sawyer said she was unable to remember taking such a call, or indeed anything else that had happened that morning. Many months later, the story she gave to another court would change considerably.

Janice Williams was a key prosecution witness. She told the court that during the afternoon of the day before the murders, she and Michael Randerson were with Dai Morris and Mandy Jewell in the Masons Arms pub in Rhydypandy. Later they went to the New Inn pub in Craig Cefn Parc where they spent the evening together, sharing a table at the far end of the lounge bar. Shortly after they arrived, they were joined by Randerson's girlfriend, Fay Scott.

During the course of the evening, an argument broke out between Morris and Jewell and, Janice Williams claimed, it soon turned to the subject of Mandy Power. She had told detectives in yet another statement that 'Morris' eyes were wide and bulging' as he raved and cursed Mandy Power. This contradicted what she had said in other statements that were not put before the court. It was notable that no one else, either at the table or in the pub, mentioned Morris behaving or talking in this way. Janice Williams, it turned out, had given the police several statements, all of them different, and she had an axe to grind with Dai Morris. None of this was revealed to the court.

On Thursday, 2 May 2002, the murder weapon found on the landing in 9 Kelvin Road was shown to the jury for the first time. The four-foot fibreglass pole had been cut in half by forensic scientists so that they could subject it to a series of forensic tests in their search for DNA and trace evidence.

Glyn Hopkin, former landlord of the New Inn in Craig Cefn Parc, told the court that the pole had originally come from his pub and he had given it to his wife to protect herself whenever he was away from home. Contradicting Janice Williams' evidence given to the court earlier, Hopkin said that 'David Morris was in good spirits – there was no reason to believe otherwise. I could tell he had had a few pints, but he was in control of himself.' Hopkin had not heard any argument or raised voices from the group while they were in the pub. As Morris left the premises, he said goodnight to Hopkin. 'He appeared to be well in control of himself at this time,' Glyn Hopkin added.

Jayne Hopkin, wife of Glyn Hopkin, told the court that that day was the first time she had seen Morris in the pub. As he was leaving, he walked straight past her: 'It seemed he kind of marched out,' she said, adding 'his face had a menacing look on it'. She agreed, however, that Morris probably did not know who she was and, under cross-examination, she said she had 'only glimpsed him for a second as he left'.

Chapter 16

During the first weekend in May, just as the trial was entering its third week, a further setback occurred. One of the jurors, a middle-aged man, suffered a heart attack. Since the trial was already quite advanced, Mr Justice Butterfield announced that the hearing would continue with just eleven jurors.

The morning of Monday, 6 May found Alison Lewis in court as a witness for the prosecution. She was dressed in a dark suit with a light blue shirt. She stood quietly in the witness box, her hands resting on the top edge of the witness stand in front of her. Over a period of two days, she answered questions clearly, occasionally sipping water from a glass and, from time to time, running a finger just beneath her left eye. During the entire time she spent in the witness box, she rarely took her eyes off defence counsel Peter Rouch. Occasionally, she averted her gaze to take in the jury, and just once she looked towards the section of the public gallery where Dai Morris' family were gathered. Three times in the opening half-hour on her initial day in the witness box she was reduced to tears, and she continued to weep from time to time throughout the trial.

Patrick Harrington began his examination: 'Did you have anything to do with the death of your lover Mandy Power?'

'No I did not.'

'Did you have anything to do with the deaths of Katie, Emily or Doris Dawson?'

'No I did not.'

'What were your feelings for them?'

'I loved them all. South Wales Police wrongly branded me a murderer of four people I loved.'

Referring to her interrogations at the hands of South Wales Police detectives in July 2000, almost two years earlier, and with a voice trembling with emotion, she said: 'For as long as I live, I will never forget those four days. South Wales Police tortured me in my grief.'

In answer to a question about her relationship with her husband, Lewis replied that she was in love with Mandy Power and lived a double life with her husband. She had contemplated leaving him, saying that she would probably have moved back to her home town of Pontypridd. 'I only had sex with him when I had to,' she added. Her husband was anti-lesbian, she told the court. 'He said to me one day that lesbianism was like a cancer.' He never suspected she was gay, she claimed, and he knew nothing about her sexual orientation until the morning of the murders when her relationship with Power became generally known.

Sobbing as she spoke, Alison Lewis told the court that during her time in custody, detectives suggested that she had committed the murders alone. Later, they suggested that her husband Stephen was responsible. Finally, detectives suggested that they had acted together. 'They told me in graphic detail how I had beaten Mandy to death and how I had crushed Katie's skull using an iron bar. They tried to break me by using my grief, but the reason they did not break me was because I was telling the truth.'

Lewis told the court that the pole used as the murder weapon was stored not in the house, as a previous child witness had told the court, but under a tool shed in the garden. She denied that the bloody handprint on the living room floor was hers. It had been found on the carpet near the television set and it appeared to indicate that someone had been looking for – and perhaps had found – something they wanted. It was suggested to her that she had left her hand print on the carpet when she removed a video of the film *Armageddon* from the house. Neighbour and best friend of Mandy Power, Louise Pugh, would testify later that she had returned a copy of the rented film *Armageddon* on the Friday evening before the murders, pushing the video tape through Power's letter box. *Armageddon* had great significance for Lewis, because she and Power considered part of the soundtrack, 'I don't wanna miss a thing' sung by Aerosmith, to be their theme tune. During the murder investigation, police had found the empty cassette case in 9 Kelvin Road and the video cassette itself in Lewis' home. She had denied prosecuting counsel's suggestion that she had taken the video tape at the time of the murders.

Further significance was attached to Alison Lewis' DNA found on Mandy Power's thigh and also on the pink vibrator that had been thrust into her vagina. Asked to explain how it could have got there, Lewis told the court that she had not seen Power on the night of the murders, but said that they had had sex in her home in West Crossways early the previous morning. The pink vibrator thrust into Mandy Power's vagina was not the one they had used that morning. In that encounter, they had used a strap-on dildo that Mandy Power had brought with her. Lewis claimed that she had used the pink vibrator herself just once six months earlier, and she suggested that her dried bodily fluids might have 'flaked off' the pink vibrator and stuck to Mandy.

Lewis told the court that, at the time of the killings, she was at home in bed with her husband Stephen, having gone to bed 'tired drunk' following a barbeque at her home. She woke twice she said, once at about 1.00 a.m. and again at 4.30 a.m., to attend to one of her four-year-old daughters.

At times while giving evidence, Lewis seemed to be struggling to control her emotions. Occasionally, she took a step backwards, looked down at her feet and took several deep breaths. Twice during her first morning in the witness box, she asked for her glass of water to be refilled. She appeared to be wracked by grief.

Lewis told the court about a chain she had discovered under a pillow on Power's bed the previous December when they were having sex. It was in a jewellery case and looked new. Power told her that Howard Florence had bought it for her, which resulted in an argument between the two women. Power then changed her story and said she had bought the chain for her daughter Emily. After their argument, Lewis said she never saw it again.

Their relationship was, according to Lewis, 'deep and intense'. She said that during their lovemaking they used two types of vibrator: one of which Power called 'Fred' and kept in her bedside cabinet. The other was the strap-on device stored in a box with the words 'Mr Perfect' written on the side. The pink vibrator was left on top of the wardrobe.

In answer to Patrick Harrington's questions, Lewis told the court how she and Power had exchanged gifts. On Valentine's Day 1999 Lewis gave Power a silver wrist watch from Next – this was the watch that had been placed on Mandy Power's wrist after her death – and Lewis had received a silver wrist watch from Mandy in return. For Power's thirty-fourth birthday on 12 April 1999, Lewis gave her a ring which, she said, Power continued to wear. Alison Lewis' birthday was in September and she believed Mandy Power was planning a stay for them both in a hotel on the Gower Peninsula. She believed Power was also considering buying her a ring.

How sincere and committed Mandy Power *really* was to her lesbian lover is open to question. On the same day that Lewis and Power exchanged gifts, Power received Valentine's Day flowers from Howard Florence. And Mandy Power's telephone records, which were obtained only after the Swansea Crown Court trial ended, show that she rang Dai Morris repeatedly on St Valentine's Day. This was at a time when Morris was not living in the flat he shared with Mandy Jewell, but when he was living alone in a rented room at 607 Llangyfelach Road, Treboeth, the bolt-hole he went to following arguments with Jewell.

The court heard that the relationship between the two women had its share of ups and downs and they had already argued fiercely, separating twice. The first time involved a fourteen-day period in January 1999, when Power became jealous of Alison's relationship with an old flame, Meryl James. 'We got back together,' Lewis said, 'because I missed her – I missed the company and being with her.' The second time they split up was when Power had lied about having cervical cancer. Lewis even took her for treatment to Singleton Hospital in Swansea. She told the court: 'It turned out that she had done it because she felt insecure in our relationship and she had done it for attention.'

When Lewis confronted Power with the 'evidence', Mandy admitted that she had lied, following which the two women broke up. But the separation did not last for long and a week later they made up after Power repeatedly phoned Lewis. 'As soon as I saw her, I knew this was more than an affair and we got back together. I know I was married and was between two women but she seemed happy with me and I was happy and contented with her.' Lewis said: 'She [Mandy Power] said she would always be in my life and I would always be in hers.' At this point Lewis appeared to break down in tears. While Lewis did not clarify who the other woman in her life was at this time, all the evidence suggests she was referring to Meryl James.

The first, Alison Lewis testified, she heard about the murders was when she received a telephone call from Mandy Power's next-door neighbour, Christine Williams, just after 6.00 a.m. on the Sunday morning of the murders. Alison Lewis denied that she had been in Kelvin Road at the times alleged by several witnesses, claiming that the first time she went there was at around 9.00 a.m. with her husband Stephen.

Continuing to give her evidence, Lewis said: 'I have been as open and as honest as I could have possibly been. I have told the truth from day one.' She continued: 'I couldn't believe she had gone. I thought everyone had gone mad and I was the only sane one left.' She said of the days leading up to the murders, 'It was the happiest we had ever been.'

Patrick Harrington asked her: 'Have you sought any immunity as a condition of giving evidence?' Alison Lewis replied, 'No.'

'Have you been granted any immunity from prosecution?' Lewis claimed she had not and said: 'I came to court voluntarily.' Lewis' statement at this point was contrary to claims by the Morris family. They said that their solicitor David Hutchinson had told them that Alison Lewis *had* wanted immunity from prosecution as a condition of giving evidence for the Crown. (Witness immunity from prosecution occurs when a prosecutor grants immunity to a witness in exchange for testimony or production of other evidence. It is immunity because the prosecutor agrees not to prosecute the crime that the witness *might* have committed in exchange for the evidence given.) Hutchinson said that Lewis only reluctantly agreed to give her evidence without being given immunity following advice received from the Crown Prosecution Service and after she had discussed the implications with her solicitor. Whether or not this was true, immunity from prosecution is not, and should not be, construed as an evidence of guilt.

Lewis told the court about the effect her relationship with

Power had had on her marriage. Clutching a tissue passed to her by a court usher, she dabbed at her eyes from time to time, and compared herself to a wounded animal during her time in Cefn Coed Hospital. While she was there, the police had told her it would not be safe for her to return home, owing to the level of anger and animosity in the neighbourhood. When the time came for her to leave hospital, the police told her that her husband, Stephen, did not want her to return to the family home.

Melanie Coleman, a friend of Morris' wife Wendy, sitting in the public gallery close to the witness box told the author: 'I don't know why Alison Lewis kept wiping her eyes. I couldn't see any tears.'

Questioned about her alleged 'suicide attempt', Lewis told the court that she had no recollection of this.

During her examination by Patrick Harrington, Lewis gave the court some details about her background, including her martial arts training. This had involved the use of a bō, an instrument similar to, and about the same length as, the murder weapon. Lewis agreed that she was proficient in martial arts and said that in the past she had given demonstrations with a bō and was highly skilled in using it.

In the weeks before her death, Mandy Power had become 'more security-conscious, edgy and jumpy', Lewis told the court. When she asked her what was wrong, Power told her that she felt she was being watched by someone from the lane at the back of her garden. She said: 'To this day, I wish I had pressed her more and shown more interest in the fact that she had become edgy and started locking the front door, but I did not.'

Under cross-examination by Peter Rouch, Lewis admitted that no one could say where she was at the time of the Clydach murders because her husband was asleep. In reply to the suggestion that Stephen Lewis had been seen in Gellionnen Road, near 9 Kelvin Road, at about 2.20 a.m., she responded: 'When I woke at 4.30 a.m., there was no sign that he had left the bed.'

When it was put to Alison Lewis that she was 'insanely' jealous of Power's former lover, Howard Florence, Lewis admitted that she was jealous of him but denied that her jealousy was extreme. Asked how she would have responded to physical intimacy between Power and Florence, she replied: 'I wouldn't have been happy about it because I loved her. But if she wanted to be with someone else in a relationship, I would let her be. As long as Mandy was happy, I was happy.'

Alison Lewis told the court that 'being a lesbian was just an experiment at first for Mandy... but then she became fully gay and happy in our relationship.' Lewis also said that while Power made her happy, the double life she led with her husband made her depressed and drove her to occasionally take Prozac. About three weeks before the murders, she had begun using the drug regularly. When Peter Rouch QC asked her if she suffered from premenstrual tension and would become difficult with Power at such times, she denied that this was the case.

Cross-examined by the defence about possessing a key to 9 Kelvin Road, Lewis denied having one, but said she thought Power may have left a key under a flowerpot in the front garden. This was so that her next-door neighbour, Louise Pugh, could periodically look in on Mandy's mother, Doris Dawson.

Asked by prosecuting counsel about the last time she had washed herself before the murders, Lewis said she 'did not wash at all before leaving her home to go to Kelvin Road' with her husband Stephen Lewis on the morning of the murders. She claimed that her last bath had been taken at Mandy Power's home when she dropped her off on the Saturday morning.

No DNA was reported as having been found in the bath, although the scene of crimes investigator consulted by the author gave her opinion that DNA should have been present and detectable. Despite a written request for information directed to South Wales Police by the author on this specific point, they neither confirmed nor denied the presence of DNA in the bath or bathwater.

Peter Rouch reminded Lewis that in one of her police statements she had said of the killer or killers: 'I would have thought they would have to have had tremendous physical strength.' Questioned about her martial arts training, she observed: 'The faster you are, the more controlled you are, the better you are.' She said that in early 1999 she was weightlifting and circuit training at Pontardawe and Ystradgynlais leisure centres. She also 'went running' long distance. She agreed with Peter Rouch's suggestion that in June 1999 she would have been exceptionally strong. She trained harder than most men and was capable of lifting very heavy weights. At the time of the murders, she would have been able to bicep-curl 10kg in each arm, and bench press 60kg – extraordinarily heavy weights for a woman.

On the day that Alison Lewis' husband, South Wales Police sergeant Stephen Lewis, gave evidence, the public gallery was not as full as it had been earlier in the trial. A veteran of the courtroom and well used to facing shrewd questioning by counsel, Lewis appeared calm and controlled throughout and answered all questions put to him clearly and articulately.

Lewis told the court that he remained suspended from duty because of the gravity of the allegations, because of discrepancies between statements and interviews he had given, and because he and his brother Stuart had made certain allegations against police officers involved in the murder investigation.

He told the court that after learning of the killings in Kelvin Road, Alison became 'hysterical, like someone possessed'. He claimed he knew nothing of his wife's sexual relationship with Mandy Power, or her bisexuality, until that moment, and his life had collapsed around him on learning of her infidelity.

Watched closely by Patrick Harrington QC, Lewis firmly grasped an imaginary window frame as he explained how his wife had tried to throw herself out of a bedroom window in their home. Describing the morning of the murders as 'a traumatic time in which Alison was behaving in a bizarre manner', he told the court how his wife had told him that she had been having an affair with Power, but it had been her only lesbian relationship. He said she told him it had been 'a fling, an experiment or something like that'. Later, at Cefn Coed Hospital, she told him that it was a one-off affair and they could still save their marriage. Afterwards he found out that she had lied to him and it had not been her only lesbian relationship. 'That was the final nail in her coffin. I didn't want to live with her after that. She totally betrayed me. She made me look a laughing-stock in police circles.'

Occasionally rocking in the witness box, he told the court how in July 2000 he was arrested and interviewed by South

Wales Police on suspicion of involvement in the murders. 'I was on bail for six months and after that I was told there would be no charges against me.'

Stephen Lewis recalled his first meeting with Mandy Power at his twin daughters' third birthday in December 1998. He remembered her as 'happy and easy-going'. He said: 'She was a fun person, always cracking jokes.' After that he said he had met Power about half a dozen times and visited her home on three occasions. 'Sometimes', he said, his 'wife and the twins would stay overnight at [9] Kelvin Road.'

Lewis told the court about the barbeque they had had on the Friday evening before the murders. He and Mandy Power had spent some time talking about the problems she was having agreeing contact arrangements for the girls with her ex-husband Michael. Michael had 'given her grief' earlier that day 'and I gave her some advice', he said.

Lewis said that after he started his shift at Neath Police Station at 6 a.m. on Sunday, 27 June 1999, he had received a telephone call from a police officer colleague, Richard Burns, who was in Swansea. Burns told him about the fire in Kelvin Road and, from the description he gave, Lewis realised it was the home of Power and her family. He said the news left him in a state of shock because his own two children could have been sleeping there if he had been working nights. Burns also told him that Stuart Lewis had been one of the first people to arrive at the house after the fire was reported.

It was put to Stephen Lewis that in his interviews with the investigating team he had referred to a fight downstairs at the murder scene (between Mandy Power and her murderer). He replied: 'I was fed information from the word go about the murder scene and what happened there. Subsequently, those officers have denied telling me.' Whilst in police custody, Stephen Lewis was interviewed 34 times. 'In four days, I had seven hours' sleep. I was given medication by a police doctor to keep going. At the end of it I was a broken man.'

During the course of Peter Rouch's cross-examination of Stephen Lewis, it became clear, to the judge at least, that the defence QC was not pursuing an obvious and expected line of questioning. It was part of Dai Morris' defence that Stephen

Lewis was in some way involved in the murders. But instead of questioning Lewis about this, Rouch stopped short, and failed to challenge Lewis by asserting that he had actively participated in the murders.

Clearly concerned by the defence QC's unorthodox strategy, the judge asked Mr Rouch why he was not putting certain follow-up questions to the witness that he (the judge) expected him to ask.

'I cannot my Lord,' Mr Rouch replied.

At this point Mr Justice Butterfield intervened and told the court, 'It will be asserted by the defence that Stephen Lewis, Alison Lewis' husband, possibly assisted Alison Lewis by trying to destroy the scene of the murders.'

A statement was produced, signed by Morris, which included this paragraph:

It will be asserted by the Defence that:
a) The murders were probably carried out by Alison Lewis.
b) Stephen Lewis (Alison Lewis' husband) possibly assisted Alison Lewis by trying to destroy the scene of the murders.
c) Stuart Lewis (Stephen Lewis' twin brother) may possibly have thought that Alison Lewis was capable of carrying out the murders. This is evident from the evidence concerning his action at the scene and afterwards.

By way of background, Dai Morris' solicitor David Hutchinson was closely involved in preparing this very unusual statement. It would later be alleged that Hutchinson had struck an agreement with the Lewises that, in return for them agreeing to make no objection to Hutchinson representing Dai Morris in the murder trial, Hutchinson would make no direct attack on the Lewis brothers. This statement, which Hutchinson persuaded Morris to sign, meant that the hands of defence counsel Peter Rouch were effectively tied, and he could not question Lewis in a manner that might have pointed the finger of suspicion at him, and perhaps even change the eventual outcome of the trial. The fact that no direct challenge was made to either of the Lewis brothers strongly suggests that this allegation was true. (A transcript of the judgment at a later Appeal Court hearing confirmed that David Hutchinson had indeed struck a deal with the Lewises. In return for their making no objection to Hutchinson representing Dai Morris, he agreed not to directly accuse the Lewis brothers of the murders.)

A number of extracts from taped interviews with Stephen Lewis were then played in court. These contained several inconsistencies between the interviews and various witness statements he had made, and were the basis for his having been suspended for the previous two years. He had been 'trying to help the police', he claimed. 'You have to understand,' he pleaded, 'that I had found out a family friend and her family had been killed .... Then I found out my wife was having a lesbian affair and had had a series of lesbian affairs.'

Stephen Lewis denied that at 2.20 a.m. on 27 June 1999 he was seen in Gellionnen Road, Clydach, not far from the crime scene. He said he was at home in bed. He told the court that while he was held in custody, the police accused him of being in 9 Kelvin Road on the night of the murders. 'But this was not true,' he said. They also implied that he had started the fires in the house, 'but this was a fantasy', he had told them. When asked if he had ever threatened Mandy Power, he admitted warning her to stay away from his wife, but 'I said it in a taking the mickey way. It was not serious.'

Lewis admitted visiting 9 Kelvin Road occasionally but denied that he had ever gone there in a police car. Donald Jones had given evidence previously that he had seen a police officer in the uniform of a police sergeant leaving 9 Kelvin Road in a police car. The description he gave strongly suggested that the police officer he saw was Stephen Lewis.

Lewis told the court that before 27 June 1999 'life was fine. I loved my children and things were going great at work .... I had been recommended for a promotion assessment and I was confident about this. Alison and I were getting on fine and I had no reason to suppose her relationship with Mandy Power was anything other than a close friendship.'

Key witness Eric Williams, a retired fireman and part-time builder, gave his evidence in the third week of the trial. He said that on the Monday after the murders, he and Dai Morris, his second cousin, were laying a patio at a house in Sketty, Swansea.

It was while they were working together that Morris told him that two days before the murders he had had sex with Mandy Power. She had wanted to see him again and told him that she needed proof that he would come back the following day [Saturday]. 'He said he had given his gold neck-chain to Mandy Power.' Morris then told Williams that he had spent all day on Saturday with his partner Mandy Jewell and could not go to Kelvin Road to see Mandy Power and retrieve his gold neck-chain. Describing Morris' demeanour on the day after the murders, Williams said: 'He was his normal self. He wasn't like someone who had just gone out and committed a murder.'

Williams said he had seen Morris wearing a neck-chain before the killings but not afterwards. The chain discovered in 9 Kelvin Road subsequently featured in the national press and was shown on *Crimewatch*. But 'David didn't say the chain was his', Williams said.

Morris asked Williams to lend him money to buy a replacement chain. He told him that the police had asked him about his chain and he wanted one to show them. 'I agreed to it because I believed David to be innocent,' Williams said. 'I know David. He has got children of his own and I can't believe David could do something like that.' Within six days of the murder, Williams visited a jewellery shop in St David's Centre in Swansea, where he paid £170 for a gold chain similar to the one Morris had lost.

When asked why Morris had not purchased the chain himself, Williams answered: 'I believe the reason for that is if the police ever went around various jewellers to see if anyone had purchased a necklace, with a photo of David, then a member of staff might recognise him.' Williams explained how Morris 'took some dry cement and scuffed it up a bit to make it look older and he damaged the clasp'.

Called to give evidence for the prosecution, Kim Crowley, a friend of policewoman Deborah Powell, told the court that she had waited more than a year before passing Eric Williams' story on to the police. In November 1999, Crowley and her husband Michael asked Eric Williams to do some building work at her home. 'Williams turned up on site along with Dai Morris,' Crowley said. She found Morris 'to be a very quiet, unassuming person'. As the building work progressed, Williams told Kim Crowley what Morris had told him about his sexual encounter with Mandy Power. Williams told her that he saw no reason to withhold the information since Morris had not asked him to keep it a secret. In fact, Williams had already divulged what Morris had told him to two fire service colleagues and the steward of the Sketty Park Sports & Social Club.

Former Welsh Water worker and part-time builder's labourer Ronald Moss told the court that he and Dai Morris worked together for seven months from March 2000. In the summer of that year, Alison Lewis, her husband Stephen and her brother-in-law Stuart Lewis were arrested, and this generated much talk and speculation in pubs and clubs in and around Swansea, he said. At the time, both Morris and he were working for Eric Williams. At some stage, Williams told Moss that Morris had been involved with Mandy Power. Moss broached the subject with Morris and asked him if he had gone out with Mandy Power. Morris replied, 'Who's been gobbing off?' He then gave Moss 'a nasty look', the court was told. Moss had intended asking Morris about the gold neck-chain, but he thought better of it and kept his mouth shut. 'Sometimes,' said Moss, 'Mandy Jewell would phone him [Morris] to tell him the police had been up at the flat asking her questions over and over again. Morris would say: "'Why don't they leave her alone?'"

Moss told the court: 'He would talk about other things, but not about the chain, and I found this strange.' He said that Morris told him that he had been 'giving her one [having sex] for some months before the murders'. When they talked about the murders, Morris said that police officers had lit fires in the house to destroy DNA. At other times when the subject of the murders cropped up in conversation, Morris would just look away and stare into space, Moss claimed.

A video recording made in December 1998, six months before the murders, was played in court. It was filmed when Dai Morris and his employer at the time, former soldier Colin Williams of Treboeth, together with Eric Williams, Colin's twin brother, were all doing some work on a relative's house in Pentregethin Road in Swansea. The video film clearly showed Dai Morris wearing the gold neck-chain.

Colin Williams told the court that Dai Morris was his second cousin and he had employed Morris as a builder's labourer from the late 1990s until 24 June 1999 – three days before the murders. This was confirmed by Colin Williams' records. He described Morris as 'hard-working and conscientious with good physical strength'.

Colin Williams told the court that at some time or other Morris began renting a room at a property owned by him at 607 Llangyfelach Road in Treboeth. Morris had told him he wanted a bolthole to retreat to if he'd had an argument with Mandy Jewell.

Chapter 17

Fireman Neil MacPherson, who had fought the blaze at 9 Kelvin Road, told the court that in July 1999 he asked a former fire service colleague, Eric Williams, to do some building work for him at a residential property he owned in Swansea. Williams brought along Dai Morris. Over a period of two to three months while building work was going on, MacPherson and Williams discussed the Clydach murders on a number of occasions, often in the presence of Morris. During one or more of these conversations, Morris told MacPherson that he had had sex with Mandy Power a couple of days before the killings.

Police Constable Alison Crewe told the court that she was an Acting Sergeant at the time of the murders, and was one of a number of police officers summoned to Kelvin Road in the early hours of 27 June 1999. Firemen were already at the scene when they arrived. Crewe was the most senior officer present and she called Detective Inspector Stuart Lewis on her police radio, telling him he was urgently required. As soon as Lewis arrived, Crewe told him the casualties had deep cuts that were not consistent with a fire. He told her he would contact Major Crime [Support Unit] and arrange for a doctor to attend. Crewe then turned her attention to Sandra Jones and her husband Kenneth Jones, close relatives of the deceased who had just arrived in Kelvin Road, to inform them about the deaths. 'They were obviously very distressed,' she told the court. 'I told them to go home as there was nothing they could do.' But, as she was escorting them back to their car, Stuart Lewis went past her, saying he was leaving. 'I was surprised he left the scene so suddenly,' she said. 'I understood many things had to be done, but it was his decision that those things had to be done from the police station.' She said she thought the 'situation needed a senior officer or CID'.

Constable Geraint Usher gave evidence that he had returned

to Morriston Police Station in a police car with Stuart Lewis. At the police station he witnessed Lewis in the foyer talking on the public telephone. He said: 'It was clear he was talking about the incident. But I am not aware of who he was speaking to at the time.'

Key witness Sharon Jameson testified that on the evening before the murders, she had arrived at the New Inn at about 8.30 p.m. She stayed for the next three hours and claimed to have briefly seen Morris standing at the bar having a laugh and a joke with Janice Williams' father, Dai Sticks (he had once been a drummer in a group). The clothes he was wearing, she said, were identical to those worn by her partner, Ian Jameson – a white V-neck T-shirt and blue jeans. Morris 'appeared to be in a good mood', she said.

Jameson said she left the pub at about 11.30 p.m. to fetch a Chinese takeaway from Clydach just seconds after Morris had left. She confirmed that she did not see him on the road he would have taken if he had been walking towards Kelvin Road. This evidence is crucial and corroborates Morris' account that he did not take the Clydach Road, or go to Kelvin Road, after leaving the pub.

The statement upon which Sharon Jameson's evidence was based was dated 10 August 2001, more than two years after she claimed to have seen Morris standing by the bar. Morris later told the author that Sharon and Ian Jameson were part of the Craig Cefn Parc clique which despised him for reasons he never understood. She had claimed Morris was standing at the bar, whereas he was in fact sitting at a table some distance away in the crowded lounge bar. Dai Sticks, Janice Williams and the pub landlord all testified that at no time was Morris standing by the bar. Moreover, he was wearing the jogging pants Mandy Jewell had bought for him that day, not jeans. The clothes worn by Ian Jameson correspond more closely with Anthony Evans' description of a man he saw walking in the direction of Kelvin Road early the next morning. Did Sharon Jameson deliberately give false evidence against Dai Morris in order to help convict him, or, given the passage of time, did she simply confuse him with somebody else who was standing by the bar?

Eyewitness evidence can be notoriously unreliable and many cases have resulted in lengthy prison terms for persons who have been wrongly identified as the perpetrator of a crime. In cases where the identity of the defendant is at issue and the prosecution relies substantially on the correctness of the identification, the judge should warn the jury that it must exercise special caution before accepting this evidence. This is called a Turnbull direction (after a 1977 court case), which sets out important guidelines for judges to follow in cases of disputed identification evidence. It lists a number of factors that the judge must explain to the jury in order to reduce the chance of a mistake. No Turnbull direction was given in the trial of Dai Morris.

One of the New Inn patrons, Philip Turner, said he saw Morris wearing his gold neck-chain that evening, although he admitted he 'saw him for [only] a couple of seconds'. Turner made his statement on 27 March 2001, almost 21 months after his alleged sighting. He described the chain Morris was wearing as 'a thick gold chain, similar to the picture of the chain shown by the police'. At the time, the chain was also featured in hundreds of posters circulated by the police and displayed in shops, post offices, telephone kiosks and prominent public spaces in and around Swansea and the Swansea Valley.

Turner was a neighbour of Morris. He knew him well but did not like him. The feeling was mutual. Turner also knew that Morris habitually wore his gold chain. It was a short step from there to assume that Morris must have worn his heavy gold chain on the night of the murders. Again, it was Hobson's choice: the police had shown Turner just one chain, rather than a selection of chains to choose from, which they claimed Morris was wearing on the night before the murders.

Turner told the court that he lived near Morris in Craig Cefn Parc and often witnessed him fighting with his partner Mandy Jewell. He recounted one occasion when he heard Jewell screaming as she was 'being kicked down the street' by Morris. In an earlier statement that he gave to detectives, Turner said he had *never* seen Morris assault Jewell. When Peter Rouch cross-examined him about his contradictory statements, his only explanation was: 'Well, you haven't got to live next door to him.'

This feud meant that there was no love lost between the two

men who now faced each another across the courtroom. Dai Morris explained to the author the reason for their mutual dislike. He said that Craig Cefn Parc is a small valley village where the Welsh language is commonly spoken and everyone knows everyone else's business. A newcomer moving there might or might not be made to feel welcome. In Dai Morris' case, he had had an affair with Mandy Jewell, who was married to a local man, Andrew Jewell. The affair caused extreme resentment and ill feeling in the village towards Morris: Andrew Jewell was an employee of Philip Turner; Andrew Jewell and Philip Turner were also good friends and regularly frequented the New Inn together; Andrew Jewell's father was also a friend of Turner. When Morris moved in with Mandy Jewell, the three men took an even stronger dislike to him. The situation worsened after a friend of Dai Morris struck up a relationship with Philip Turner's sister and moved in with her, and subsequently let it slip that he [Morris] had a criminal record. From that moment on, Morris says, the village turned against him and did everything they could to make life difficult for him. Villagers talking in English in the village shop instantly changed to Welsh the moment he walked in. The van that Morris used for work was towed away after it broke down and Turner bragged in the pub that he had organised its removal. On another occasion, Turner blocked access to a common tarmacadam hardstanding between their two properties so that Morris was unable to use this when repairing cars for his friends.

On three occasions, the windows of the flat Morris shared with Mandy Jewell were smashed. The first time Morris and Jewell were in bed. He described the experience as 'terrifying'. On the second and third occasions when the windows were broken, Morris and Jewell were out. A neighbour, Kevin Ward, told them that Turner's wife had seen the person who had caused the damage. Mandy Jewell went to Turner's house to ask her who this person was, but Mrs Turner told Jewell to get off her doorstep and not to involve her.

On yet another occasion, Morris said Andrew Jewell and his father arrived at Mandy Jewell's flat and attacked him with a sledgehammer and a hatchet. Both men had been drinking and Morris managed to fight them off. He said: 'I never ever said anything to Turner. I never had an argument with him or anything, but for some reason, and I really don't know why, he really hated me.'

David Howell Thomas gave evidence that he was in the bar of the New Inn on the night before the murders. Morris, he said, was sitting at a table several feet away and was wearing a white T-shirt, blue denim jeans and a gold neck-chain. Thomas was a friend of Philip Turner and, like Andrew Jewell, he occasionally worked for Turner. Thomas' statement was given to the police many months after his brief sighting. He did not approach Morris at the table where he was sitting, nor did he get any closer to Morris than the bar, which is where Morris saw him standing. There was no particular reason why Thomas would have noticed Morris sitting at his table amongst a group of other drinkers in the crowded bar or whether he was wearing jeans or jogging bottoms. Nor was there any reason why he would have noted a gold neck-chain worn by any of the drinkers in the bar that night with sufficient recall of memory or clarity of sight to recall its every detail more than a year and a half later. Yet this is what the Crown Court jury was asked to believe.

There is another reason why Thomas' evidence may be doubted. He was short-sighted and, while he owned a pair of glasses, he didn't usually wear them – only putting them on whenever he needed to see things more than a few feet away. The distance between the witness box, where Thomas was standing, and the bench, from where Patrick Harrington addressed the court, was about the same as the distance between the bar in the New Inn and the table where Morris had been sitting on 26 June. During the course of cross-examining Thomas, Harrington held up a replica of the chain found at the crime scene and asked Thomas, 'Is this the same chain?'

Thomas squinted at the object being shown to him, then he reached into his pocket, took out his glasses and put them on. Even with the aid of his glasses, he still could not see clearly the gold neck-chain that Harrington was holding up in front of him. It was only when Harrington told Turner that it was identical to the chain found at the crime scene that Thomas agreed that he recognised it. Evidently, he did not.

Michael Randerson told the court that he had spent the evening before the murders in the New Inn with Janice Williams, her friend Mandy Jewell, Dai Morris and, later during the course of the evening, his girlfriend, Fay Scott. On 14 April 2001, 22 months after the murders, the police showed him a photograph of a gold chain. In his statement to the police, and also in court, Randerson identified the chain as the one Morris was wearing that night. He said: 'I am certain the chain Dai Morris had on in the New Inn is the same type and style as the one shown in the photograph, when compared with the chain worn ... on 26 June.'

Two days after Michael Randerson gave this incriminating evidence, trainee solicitor Gail Evans, an assistant to David Hutchinson, received a telephone call from Randerson's girlfriend, Fay Scott. According to a sworn statement made by Gail Evans for use in a later Appeal Court hearing,* she stated that Scott had told her that 'she had just read the newspapers, and particularly about the evidence that Mike Randerson had given. She was adamant that his evidence was not correct.' Part of Evans' statement read: 'She recalled that after he [Randerson] had been interviewed by the police early on in the case, he had been asked about a chain that Dai Morris was supposed to have had on in the pub on the night of the murders. She informed me that his account was all lies because after he had been interviewed, he had telephoned her to ask her whether or not DM was wearing a chain in the pub because he couldn't remember. She told him that she could not remember either.'

The police could have taken each witness to a jeweller's shop to see if they could identify the chain they said they saw Morris wearing that night, but they did not do this. The police had a photograph of five gold chains arranged next to one another for the purposes of identifying the neck-chain worn by Dai Morris. This photograph was not shown to any of the witnesses. None of the witnesses was able give the police a description of the chain supposedly worn by Morris on that night, until they were shown a photograph of a replica of the chain found at the crime scene and which had featured in the police publicity posters and in the national media.

* See statement of Gail Evans, page 255

Of the many customers in the lounge bar of the New Inn on the evening before the murders, just five gave evidence that Morris was wearing his trademark heavy gold neck-chain, rather than the smaller one he said he had worn, the only piece of hard evidence linking him to the crime. Of these, Janice Williams gave several conflicting statements; in one she said 'she could not remember if he was wearing a neck-chain or not'. Mike Randerson appears to have lied, Sharon Jameson's identification was doubtful at best, David Thomas had poor eyesight, Philip Turner was a close friend of Andrew Jewell, who Morris had cuckolded. Save for Randerson, the sighting of each of these witnesses was brief, or even fleeting.

Explaining the background to the various sightings, Morris told the author: 'All five witnesses in the pub who gave evidence against me hated me for one reason or another, and all of them were prepared to lie under oath to see me sent down. I was like public enemy number one as far as they were concerned. Well, that is how it felt.'

Police evidence-gathering methods after Morris' arrest fitted perfectly the accusation by civil rights campaigner Satish Sekar that South Wales Police detectives seemed to decide who was guilty, and then looked for the evidence needed in order to achieve a conviction. This certainly seemed to be the case for Dai Morris.

Police Constable Gareth Thomas told the court that he and Stephen Lewis worked the same shift in Neath Police Station and often travelled to work together. He told the court that on the morning of the murders he picked up Stephen Lewis at his West Crossways home, leaving there at 5.18 a.m. Describing Lewis' demeanour, Thomas said: 'He was as he is always, in a relaxed, normal mood. I can't recall anything untoward. He is one of the most professional police officers I have ever worked with. He is very enthusiastic.'

On Wednesday, 15 May, following a request by the jury, a site visit was arranged for them to view the scene of the murders and other locations mentioned in evidence given by witnesses. At

10.15 a.m. a convoy of vehicles left Swansea Crown Court heading for the Swansea Valley and Clydach. Police motor-cyclists escorted the convoy, which included a chauffeur-driven Mercedes carrying the judge and his clerk, a minibus with the jurors and ushers, a people carrier for the barristers and other legal personnel, a police car and a Land Rover.

Stopping first at the New Inn pub in Craig Cefn Parc, the jury members were taken inside to see the lounge and bar areas. Other locations visited included the shops in Sunnybank; shops near the Mond; the room at 607 Llangyfelach Road, some five miles from Clydach which Morris rented from his relative Colin Williams; and 11 Coedwig Place, Gendros, the home of Morris' parents. A lone policewoman stood guard by the front door of 9 Kelvin Road as the procession drew up and she remained there for the duration of the visit. Other police officers marshalled the crowds and directed traffic.

During the afternoon the jury spent fifteen minutes walking the short cut up a dirt track through the woods leading to Mountain Road in Craig Cefn Parc. This was the route Dai Morris said he took as he made his way home from the New Inn. Next, they visited the Rhyddwen Road ground floor flat that Morris shared with Mandy Jewell. According to the prosecution, a speck of green paint on the gold neck-chain left at the scene of the murders was indistinguishable from samples taken from a kitchen cupboard in the flat.

The tour concluded with a visit to 8 West Crossways in Pontardawe, the semi-detached two-storey former home of Alison and Stephen Lewis. Some jurors peered into the windows while others stared at the bedroom window eight to nine feet above their heads, from where, they had been told, Alison Lewis had to be physically restrained from leaping to her death.

Chapter 18

On Thursday, 16 May, Home Office pathologist Dr Deryk James, who had carried out postmortems on all four victims, began giving evidence in the trial. He told the court how he was called to 9 Kelvin Road shortly after the killings and saw the bodies of Mandy Power and her two daughters lying on the ground outside the house. He noted the 'obvious blunt head injuries' Mandy Power had sustained and the circular end of a pink plastic vibrator protruding from her vagina.

'There were also obvious blunt injuries to the face of Emily, who was partially clothed.' Katie, who was fully clothed, had sustained 'an obvious injury to the back of her head'. Dr James also saw the body of Mandy Power's mother, 80-year-old invalid Doris Dawson. She was lying on her bed with a partially burned duvet on top of her. Paper had been wrapped around her limbs and an attempt made to burn her corpse.

Looking at his notes, the doctor described in more detail the injuries sustained by the victims. Mandy Power, he said, had died from a blunt head injury when her skull was smashed with a rod-like implement. 'The skull injuries were particularly severe, the result of extremely hard blows.' Neck injuries she suffered showed there had also been an attempt to strangle her. Some of the injuries showed 'tramline bruising', suggesting they had been made by the same implement. On one part of her face there was an injury with a pattern like a Maltese Cross; this was caused when she came into contact with a similarly patterned knob on a chest of drawers in her mother's bedroom. 'Injuries to Mandy Power's wrists were the sort that resulted when someone was trying to ward off blows'. Dr James estimated that 'probably at least 15 blows' with a rod-like implement would have been needed to cause the injuries he described. Dr James was of the opinion that Mandy Power was dead by the time the fires were started because no smoke or carbon monoxide was detected in her airways.

Describing the injuries sustained by eight-year-old Emily Power, Dr James said her skull had been smashed by blows from a blunt instrument. 'We are looking at least seven or eight blows to the head, face, neck and chest areas,' he told the court. 'She would have been dead at the time the fire started.' Dr James said the child sustained 'no defence injuries – that is, injuries to the arms as though someone wants to ward off blows'. The absence of defence injuries, he told the court, is probably significant. 'She may well have been unconscious from the first blow which was across the face and was hard.' He said 'the pattern of injuries suggested a rod-like implement'.

Dr James told the court that Emily had a 15cm tramline bruise between her left shoulder and the midpoint of her chest. There was an 18cm by 9cm area of bruising between the front of her right shoulder and the base of her neck, and bruising to the left side of her neck as far as her left ear. She had an open wound on the left side of her face. There was also extensive fracturing of the upper part of her skull; her lower jaw was broken in four places, and her left cheekbone and eye socket were fractured. The child's upper chest area was bruised.

When questioned by Patrick Harrington as to the number of blows that would be necessary to inflict such extreme injuries, Dr James replied: 'There would need to be three to four blows to the back of the head and three to four blows to the face, neck and chest areas.' He gave the cause of Emily's death as blunt head injury.

'Katie', he said, 'suffered 22 separate external injuries'. He gave his opinion that she had been struck ten to fifteen blows. There were severe wounds to her scalp and extensive fracturing of her skull. Parts of her shoulder, wrist and hand showed bruising and grazing. 'There appeared to have been three blows,' the court heard. 'A cheekbone had been fractured along with a joint of the jaw, and a bone in the right hand. There was no significant carbon monoxide in her airways', which, Dr James considered, 'indicated that she also died before the fire started.' He added: 'It was an assault with a blunt instrument to the right side of the head where there was a very large laceration, a very severe skull and brain injury in keeping with a rod-like instrument which had been used to strike to the side of the head.' The cause of Katie's death was 'blunt head injury', he said.

'The injuries sustained by Mandy Power's mother, Doris Dawson, were consistent with her having been struck repeatedly with a rod-like instrument,' Dr James told the court. The 80-year-old invalid was struck five or six times, and was also dead before the fire started. Her body was charred from the mid-thighs to the face, and her right arm and hand were also charred, Dr James said.

Mrs Dawson had a 19cm ragged cut from the left side of her forehead to the right side of her chin, and a similar tear on the left cheek. A 23cm by 4cm bruise extended from the front of the left shoulder to the right breast. There was no skull fracture, but there was bruising to the left side of the scalp and to the left side of the face. Her left cheekbone had been crushed. The lower jaw and the margin of the eye socket were fractured. There was further fracturing to the bones of the middle of the face. Several ribs were broken, along with the voice box and a collarbone. There were no injuries consistent with Mrs Dawson trying to defend herself.

Dr James gave his opinion that Doris Dawson died of serious blunt head and chest injuries. The left side of her face had been crushed and she would have had difficulty breathing because blood was found in her airways. 'Her injuries were consistent with her having been struck repeatedly with a rod-like instrument,' he said.

Questioned by the judge about the amount of force required to inflict the injuries suffered by the victims, Dr James said, 'the force used would have had to be at the severe end of the spectrum'. Asked by Peter Rouch about the order in which the victims had died, Dr James was unhelpful, saying with regret that 'In this particular case I was not able to gauge the sequence of death.'

Dr James agreed that Mandy Power, her mother and daughters had been struck many times more than was necessary to cause their deaths. His reply suggested that the victims did not suffer such extensive brutality *just* as a means of silencing them, which Patrick Harrington had proposed, but for some other, as yet unknown, reason.

At the end of the fourth week of the trial, scene of crimes

investigator Detective Constable John Rees testified that when he and his colleagues entered 9 Kelvin Road soon after the murders, he found Mandy Power's skirt and tights in the hallway of the burned house, and he recovered a burnt white bra from the floor of Mandy Power's bedroom. This suggested that either Mandy Power had removed some of her clothing downstairs or her clothing had been forcibly taken from her in an attack which may have started downstairs.

Detective Constable Philip Bowen was called to give evidence and recalled interviews with Morris before he became a suspect. The first interview had taken place just two days after the murders. He said he saw no scratch marks on Morris' face. His testimony corroborated the evidence of several witnesses, including Jeff Jewell, Mandy Jewell's father, who also said he had no facial injuries. This seemed to indicate that either the memory of Morris' Rhyddwen Road neighbour Janice Williams (who gave several contradictory statements) were clouded, or she deliberately gave false evidence against Dai Morris in order to implicate him in the crime.

The final witness called to give evidence that week was forensic expert David White. He told the court that he was a civilian scene of crimes investigator with South Wales Police, and had arrived at the house shortly after the killings. On the first floor landing White found a four-foot pole that was later confirmed as the murder weapon. Among the items taken for analysis was a strap-on vibrator, which was recovered from an extensively burned hold-all in Mandy Power's bedroom, and the white T-shirt she was believed to have been wearing when she was killed.

White said that in the back bedroom the corpse of Doris Dawson was lying on the bed. When he examined her, he found an engagement ring lying 'isolated' in the middle of her torso. He took away the ring for forensic examination. He also noted that paper had been packed around the body.

In a subsequent visit to the house, White found a blood-stained white sock in Mandy Power's room which he also took away for forensic examination. And he removed a blood-stained heavy gold neck-chain found on the floor of Doris Dawson's bedroom.

In the fifth week of the trial, key forensic scientist Claire Galbraith was called to give evidence. Her opinion was that Doris Dawson was attacked while she was either sitting or lying in her bed. Katie Power was attacked and beaten on the landing and Emily Power attacked in the girls' bedroom. Galbraith believed Mandy Power was injured in her own bedroom before making her way into her mother's room. At this point she fell down and was beaten again and her head made contact with a chest of drawers.

It was Galbraith's opinion that Doris Dawson was probably the first of the murder victims to be killed. She reached this opinion on the basis that, while the pole had been used to beat the old lady to death, no blood or DNA belonging to her was found on it. But blood belonging to Mandy Power and the girls was found on the pole, so the pole had either been wiped clean for some reason after being used to kill the old lady, or Doris Dawson's blood and DNA had come off during the three attacks that followed.

During the assault on Doris Dawson, the pole smashed a ceiling light; this had resulted in a short circuit which plunged the house into darkness. In the downstairs lavatory detectives found a chair that had been used by someone to stand on while repairs to the fuse box were carried out to restore the electricity supply. Under cross-examination by counsel for the defence, Galbraith agreed that a television set found on a bed in the children's room could have been in this position when blood got on it and on a wall behind it.

Peter Rouch suggested that the television set had originally rested on the chair taken from the girls' bedroom, which had been brought to the downstairs lavatory. Galbraith said that if this was the case, the television set must have been lifted off it and the chair taken downstairs before Emily Power was attacked in the bedroom. Galbraith confirmed that the chair found in the downstairs lavatory at the house had no blood on it.

The significance of Claire Galbraith's expert evidence cannot be overstated. It not only corroborated her opinion as to the order of deaths, but it indicated that there was a considerable delay between the time of Doris Dawson's murder, and the attacks on the rest of the family. Even the approximate time when the electricity supply was interrupted can probably be ascertained. Neighbour Rosemary Jones testified later that when she looked across at 9 Kelvin Road at 12.30 a.m., the house was in darkness. This meant that the fuse had blown sometime *before* 12.30 a.m. – in other words, sometime before, or about the time Mandy and her daughters arrived home. But, even more importantly, it meant that the prosecution's proposed motive for the murders was almost certainly wrong.

The report of Glasgow-based pathologist Dr Peter Vanezis was read out to the jury. Dr Vanezis had been instructed by the prosecution to prepare a report following the postmortem examination of Mandy Power which had been conducted by Home Office pathologist Dr Deryk James. Part of Dr Vanezis' report read: 'Although Mandy Power had been subjected to a severe assault, it was notable that there were no injuries to her groin area.' He held the view that if the vibrator had been forcibly inserted 'during life', there would have been some injuries.

Dr Jonathan Whitaker, an expert in DNA profiling, confirmed that he could find no connection between Dai Morris and a large number of items removed from the house and subjected to forensic testing. Cross-examined by Peter Rouch, he said he could not find even a partial DNA profile relating to Morris on any of the items sent to him.

If builders' labourer Dai Morris, allegedly high on drink and drugs, really had wiped away all trace of his DNA and fingerprints in the house after committing the murders, and destroyed his DNA in the bath and bathwater also, it truly was a most remarkable clean-up operation. It was one which virtually all forensic experts insist could not happen.

Dr Michael Barber, a forensic scientist specialising in footmarks and fingerprints, took the stand. He had been asked by the prosecution to examine a piece of carpet from the living room at 9 Kelvin Road. On the exhibit sent to him at his London laboratory, he found three marks. One was a print made by footwear; the other two were handprints, he thought. Analysis of the prints indicated the presence of blood in all three. He carried out tests to see if the handprints could have been made by a hand inside a sports sock. Dr Barber confirmed that a hand shape would be visible even if a sock had been worn.

Cross-questioned by Peter Rouch, Dr Barber said that his tests 'resulted in marks that were indistinguishable from those found at the murder scene'. In his opinion, 'the two hand marks found on the living room carpet at [9] Kelvin Road could have been made either by a hand wet with blood, or by a hand inside a sports sock which was itself wet with blood'.

When opening his case for the prosecution, Patrick Harrington had told the court that a blood-stained sock found at the murder scene might have been used by the killer as a glove worn on the right hand. But, he added, handprints did not have anything like the status of fingerprints. He also told the court that, according to one expert, the handprint could have been made by the defendant Dai Morris.

Chepstow-based forensic scientist and DNA analysis expert Michael Appleby also told the court that he had examined hundreds of items removed from the murder scene. He confirmed that while he detected DNA from all four of the victims, he found no blood or cellular material on any of the items which belonged to the defendant. But cellular material found on one of Mandy Power's inner thighs could have come from bodily fluid or tissue emanating from Alison Lewis, he said.

Finally, Peter Rouch told the jury that Home Office scientists had examined hundreds of items removed from 9 Kelvin Road and had also carried out a detailed examination of the house. With the exception of the broken gold neck-chain lying in a pool of blood, no DNA, fingerprints or other trace evidence was found that linked Morris to the crime scene.

Chapter 19

Over a period of several days, beginning on Thursday, 23 May, the jury heard about Dai Morris' arrest and his subsequent seventeen interviews with the police. They read and heard extracts from statements given to detectives during these interviews, and they watched video recordings of his questioning by detectives. They also heard from other key witnesses, and from Detective Superintendent Martyn Lloyd-Evans, who led the murder investigation.

The jury heard that, dating from his first interview with Detective Sergeant Phillip Rees, Morris had repeatedly denied having anything to do with the Clydach murders. 'I did not go anywhere near that house that night. I am one hundred per cent positive I never went near the house that night.'

Regarding his relationship with Mandy Power, Morris said at first that they had had sex on only two occasions. The first time was at 607 Llangyfelach Road, Treboeth, the house owned by his cousin Colin Williams, from whom he rented a room. This happened, he said, after he had given Mandy Power a lift to Swansea. Mandy Power was his partner Mandy Jewell's best friend, so they were both left with a 'big guilt complex', he admitted.

Detective Sergeant Rees suggested to Morris that he had gone to 9 Kelvin Road after an argument in the New Inn with his girlfriend, Mandy Jewell, and a customer called Sage. According to witness Janice Williams, after Mandy Jewell had left the pub, Sage had called Jewell a 'slapper' in Dai Morris' presence without knowing that she was Morris' partner. Morris became annoyed at the slur and this had led to an angry dispute between the two men. Detective Sergeant Rees suggested to Morris that he then went to Mandy Power's home in order to ask her if she knew why Sage had made the insulting comment, and perhaps to find out if there was any truth in it. Morris denied this and said that he had not gone to Kelvin Road.

In his fifth interview on the day of his arrest, Morris was asked if he owned the heavy gold chain covered in blood that was found at the scene of the crime. He repeatedly denied ownership, saying: 'I swear to God it's not mine.' He later added: 'On my children's lives, that's not my chain. I'm positive my chain was never left at Mandy Power's.'

In his twelfth police interview in three days, Morris told detectives that the second time he and Mandy Power had had sex was four to five weeks before the murders. He said Mandy Power had been 'a terrible flirt'. They met near the shops in Sunnybank, Clydach and began chatting. He accompanied her back to 9 Kelvin Road and they went into the house through the rear patio doors. Morris said he was aware that Mandy's disabled mother, Doris Dawson, was in her bedroom and at first they had been 'kissing, touching and mucking about in the kitchen'. Then they went upstairs to her bedroom where they had sexual intercourse, with Mandy standing upright with her back against the wall. Mandy's mother was in bed in the next room. Katie and Emily were both at school. When asked by the detective if it had been risky to have sex when her mother was in the next room, Morris replied that Mandy got a 'buzz' from it. 'The element of risk got her going,' he said.

Morris said their sexual relationship might have gone on for years. 'But it was not something we wanted to get out [i.e. to become known] – we did not want to be together full time.' However, Morris agreed during his examination by Peter Rouch that he did not really know how Mandy Power felt about him. He said that when they had sex, 'it was straight and normal', with nothing kinky taking place involving vibrators.

He told the court that on Friday, 25 June, two days before the murders, he had thought of ringing Power to arrange to have sex with her the following morning, but in the end he did not do so.

Asked to describe Mandy Power, Morris told detectives that while she was having an affair with Howard Florence, she had asked to be introduced to his wife. 'She had a wicked sense of humour,' he said.

Morris told the detectives that he had met his partner, Mandy Jewell, in 1993 when they were introduced by a next-door neighbour. Morris was living in Swansea and had just split up with his wife, Wendy. About a month later, he moved in with Jewell at her council flat at 85 Rhyddwen Road. He described their relationship as volatile and admitted that he could be short-tempered, but they had had 'more good times than bad'. Jewell was Mandy Power's best friend, which was how he had got to know her, but describing Power as having 'been a bit of a girl for the boys', he said he did not approve of Jewell going out with her.

In one interview, the jury heard Detective Sergeant Rees suggest to Morris that he had noticed that his gold chain was missing when he arrived home and took off his blood-stained clothes to put them in the washing machine. The officer suggested that at this point Morris had begun to panic because he knew he would have to explain its disappearance. Detective Sergeant Rees claimed that Morris began to 'weave a web of deceit' as soon as he realised his gold chain had been left at the murder scene. This was why he had claimed to Eric Williams that he had had sex with Mandy Power on 25 June, two days before the murders. Morris denied this, adding that if he had committed the Clydach murders, there would be forensic evidence left behind to prove it; but there was none. Clothes and footwear taken from Morris, and other material removed from his apartment after his arrest, were examined microscopically for incriminating evidence. Apart from his broken gold neck-chain, for which he eventually provided a plausible explanation, no physical evidence was found linking Morris to the crime.

Morris' story was that the gold chain he was wearing in the New Inn on the night of the murders was not the same heavy gold chain with circular links that the police had found at the crime scene. It was a smaller Figaro-style chain with a recurring pattern of small circular links and one elongated oval link. He had collected this chain from his parents' home after he had left his broken gold neck-chain in Mandy Power's kitchen.

In one statement he told the police that he had broken his gold neck-chain at work, and put it in his pocket, and then had lost it when he was laying a patio at a house in Sketty in Swansea while working on a building project for his cousin Eric Williams.

In August 2001 a specialist team of police officers visited the home of Bernard Chaplin in Sketty, Swansea, where Morris had helped to lay the patio and where he said he had lost his gold chain. The officers, trained in search techniques, carefully removed the concrete slabs and then sieved stones and rubble underneath. They dug down as far as the subsoil and all the material they removed was stored in a skip, but no chain was found.

Morris later agreed that this claim was untrue. He said he became paranoid about the heavy gold chain in the weeks following the murders, because both he and Jewell felt people would be wondering where it was.

On the basis of Jewell's suggestion, and because Morris had told her he had lost his chain on a building site, he persuaded Eric Williams to buy him a replacement chain. Williams bought a replacement in a jeweller's shop in Swansea. Morris told detectives that this action was not to fool the police; rather, it was to fool everyone else. If he had wanted to fool the police, he would have bought a chain identical to the one he had lost in Sketty. He told detectives he was telling 'the total truth about the chain'.

Morris agreed that he and Jewell had told lies, but insisted he had not lied to cover up the murders. When interviewed as a witness soon after the murders, Morris said in his statement that he got home to Rhyddwen Road shortly after leaving the New Inn at closing time. However, in interviews conducted after his arrest he gave a different account, telling detectives that, after leaving the pub, he had decided to walk to his parents' home in Gendros. But when he got to Llangyfelach roundabout, he changed his mind and went home to Rhyddwen Road, arriving at about 4.00 a.m. He said that when he got to the flat, Jewell was in the kitchen but did not ask him why he had been out so late. He said it had been raining and his clothes were soaking wet. He took them off and put them in the washing machine, but could not remember if they were washed that day.

In an early interview, Morris told detectives that he had not mentioned his relationship with Power, either to Colin Williams or to Colin's twin brother, Eric, who had both employed him at various times. The only person he had mentioned it to, he said, was a friend called Martin Green. In another interview, the court heard Morris claim that if Jewell had discovered his relationship with Power, 'she would have hit the roof'. He said the reason he had not previously told the police about their sexual encounters was because he did not want his girlfriend to find out. This, he said, was the reason he had lied about his ownership of the gold neck-chain.

After the murders, he told detectives, Jewell was 'in a hell of a state'. She could not stop crying and went to stay with relatives in Yorkshire. He said that while his relationship with Jewell was volatile, there was nothing rocky about their sex life. 'It's one of the main things that keep us together, because even when we're rowing and arguing, the sex is still good.' The court heard Morris admitting to other sexual relationships while he was with Jewell. One of these was a woman called Connie from Gendros, while another woman was unnamed. He said that when Jewell found out about one of these relationships, she attacked him, hitting him on the head with a piece of wood.

Questioned about a time following the murders when he used his council flat in Arennig Road, he denied that he had ever burned clothing there. He told detectives he had once set fire to a newspaper which he had used as a torch while inspecting the attic.

The jury also heard Mandy Jewell's witness statement which she gave to the police in October 1999. She said that Morris was wearing his gold chain after the Clydach murders, but later she changed her mind and told detectives that she was not sure. Jewell felt she might become a suspect and wanted Morris to provide her with an alibi. That was why she falsely told the police she had opened the door to let him into their home at 12.30 a.m. on the night of the murders. He agreed to go along with her because 'the lie sounded better than the truth'. Later, she said, she wanted to tell the police the truth, but Morris stopped her, fearing they would be 'done' for perverting the course of justice.

Witness for the prosecution, convicted drug dealer Terrence Williams, who gave three different statements to detectives, told the court in his last statement that Morris had visited him at his Clydach home looking for amphetamines on three consecutive days leading up to the murders. Williams said that on each occasion Morris bought 1.5 to 2 grammes of amphetamine powder at a total cost of £30. 'I had never previously sold him amphetamines on three days one after the other,' he said. 'I did wonder why he wanted drugs three days running; it wasn't like Dai Morris.' Asked to comment on the effect the controlled drug might have, Williams replied: 'It speeds up your body and mind, keeping you awake and alert.' When Patrick Harrington asked him about any possible side-effects, Williams replied: 'If you don't sleep or eat, you get psychotic.'

Terrence Williams maintained that he sold drugs only to friends who were already users. He told the court that he himself had abused amphetamines for a number of years, sometimes taking up to 5 grammes a day. He described how he bought amphetamines 'from people in the supply chain' before cutting and mixing it with glucose. But when he sold it on, it was still potent: 'it would still have an effect.'

Williams noted that Morris always dressed casually and wore a heavy gold chain. In the week before the Clydach murders, he saw Morris three times, first on 24 June when Morris called at his home and purchased £10 worth of amphetamines. He said, 'There was no conversation about what he wanted it for and I gathered it was for personal use.' He knew that Morris used to inject the drug because he had seen him doing it in the past. Morris turned up again at Williams' home on Friday, 25 June and on Saturday, 26 June, buying £10 worth of amphetamines on each occasion. 'Again I understood it was for his own personal use,' Williams said. When asked by Patrick Harrington whether the amount bought by Morris represented a lot or a little, Williams replied: 'It depends on how much you take.'

Whether or not Terrence Williams could be regarded as a reliable witness is open to question. As a small-time drug dealer well known to the police, he may have been susceptible to pressure from the detectives investigating the case. Three different statements he gave seem to confirm this. Evidence that Morris had taken drugs in addition to alcohol before the murders would boost the prosecution case enormously. It stretches credulity to believe that Williams would have gone to the police voluntarily to give them the minutiae of his drug deals with Morris.

When questioned on his use of amphetamines, Morris

agreed that he used them from time to time because they gave him energy. However, he categorically denied buying drugs from Williams in the three days leading up to the murders.

Terrence Williams' wife, Beverley, claimed that Morris came to their home at around 9.30 a.m. on the [Sunday] morning of the murders to buy cannabis resin. She said her husband was out fishing at the time and Morris seemed 'agitated' when she could not give him the drug. She gave him a lift to a shop, where he bought two bottles of cider. (Morris denied that a meeting at 9.30 a.m. ever took place, or that Beverley Williams gave him a lift to a shop to buy cider. It should be noted that U.K. licencing laws at this time prohibited the sale of alcohol in Wales before 11.00 a.m.) She claimed to have noticed a scratch on the side of his nose, and that he was not wearing the gold chain he usually wore.

Beverley Williams' claim of a facial injury was subsequently contradicted by Mandy Jewell's father-in-law, Jeff Jewell, and also by the police detectives who interviewed Morris two days after the murders. None of them saw scratch marks on Morris' nose. These claims of scratches to Morris' face by his neighbour Janice Williams and by Beverley Williams may have been fabricated after they were visited by South Wales Police detectives seeking to build their case against Morris.

On Wednesday, 29 May, during the sixth week of the trial, forensic scientist and chartered chemist Robert Bell was called as a prosecution witness. He told the court that he had discovered a green spot on the neck-chain, which he identified as paint. He also found what he thought was brick dust on the chain. After analysing paint on the chain, he examined parts of kitchen units removed from Mandy Jewell's flat. He found a layer of green paint sandwiched between a layer of grey paint and another layer of pinkish-fawn paint on the units. The green paint there was the same as the green paint he had found on the gold chain. It was the same colour, had the same organic resin, the same inorganic filler, and was chemically indistinguishable from paint on the units in Mandy Jewell's kitchen.

Prosecuting counsel Patrick Harrington told the court that

just four days before the trial was due to begin, and only when faced with the incontrovertible forensic evidence of expert prosecution witness Robert Bell, Morris had admitted that the broken gold neck-chain was 'probably his'.

Robert Bell gave evidence about the cause and effect of the fires at 9 Kelvin Road. He told the court that four separate fires had been started; one in Doris Dawson's upstairs bedroom, one in Mandy Power's upstairs bedroom, another in the ground-floor kitchen and the fourth fire in the ground-floor front room or lounge. The last of these fires had damaged a lace-like table-cloth on a small round table where a photograph of Katie and Emily was found, charred around the edges. The small tablecloth and the photograph on top were the only items burned in the lounge. In Bell's opinion, the tablecloth would have burned for just a few minutes before going out. He could not, however, say when the fire had started.

In Doris Dawson's bedroom, there was fire damage to both the bed and the bedding. Paper had been packed around the corpse of the frail old lady which was then set alight. This fire caused contact burns to her mid-thighs, her face and her right arm and hand, but it had also gone out of its own accord before the fire services arrived. Bell believed 'the close weave of some of the bedclothes may have helped to stifle the fire', which he thought had merely smouldered for a half hour or so.

A third fire, started in Mandy Power's bedroom, Bell said, damaged her bed, bedding, the carpet, a box in which a vibrator had been kept, some clothes and a bedside cabinet. He thought that this fire had been burning for 'something in the order of two hours, possibly even longer' and producing a great deal of smoke, but very little flame.

The fourth fire in the kitchen, Bell said, was of a totally different sort; a fast fire producing high temperatures. By the time the fire services arrived, it had almost burned through the ceiling to the bathroom located immediately above. This fire, he suggested, could have spread to the rest of the house, causing more extensive damage, perhaps even destroying the entire property, if the fire services had not arrived in time.

It was Bell's opinion that the upstairs fires were probably started first; the one in Mandy Power's bedroom at about 2.30

a.m. The kitchen fire, he believed, had been started at about 3.50 a.m.

Bell said he was troubled by something: police enquiries established that the photograph of Katie and Emily was not normally kept on the small round table in the lounge. Therefore, he reasoned, it had been placed there deliberately and the killer had attempted to burn it by setting fire to the lace tablecloth upon which it had been placed. He said in answer to Peter Rouch's cross-examination: 'I have spent many hours puzzling why it was set on fire and I have no logical explanation.' But, he said, it suggested some emotional reaction by the killer.

Robert Bell also examined a bloody handprint left on the carpet in the lounge near the television set. 'A large number of hands could have made such a mark,' he said. He was unable to say if a male or female had left the mark, and a random sample taken from 420 people showed that 10 per cent of them could have made the mark. Questioned on this point by Patrick Harrington, Bell said: 'There is no possible way the hand of David Morris could be eliminated from having made the mark on the carpet.'

Recalled to the witness box the following week, and cross-examined on the point, Bell agreed that he could not exclude Alison Lewis as being the person who left the mark either. 'However,' he said, 'the handprint of Morris was a very much better fit than that of Mrs Lewis.'

Bell's opinion was disputed later in the trial by two experts, Peter Swann and Allan Ford, called by the defence. Both these expert witnesses were far more experienced in the identification of handprints than Bell, and their professional credentials and evidence should have carried more weight. Under cross-examination, Bell admitted: 'It was not possible to attribute the carpet mark to any specific individual.' He repeated, 'A number of hands could have made it.' Bell also admitted that, although he had been a forensic scientist for more than forty years, this was the first case in which he had been involved where he had had to compare handprints. He denied defence suggestions that outlines prepared for the trial were imprecise and inaccurate. The two far more highly qualified and experienced handprint experts would later testify that Bell's handprint outlines were indeed wrong.

Questioned about the possibility of a forced entry at 9 Kelvin Road, Bell said there was no sign of a forced entry at the house before neighbours' attempts to gain entry at the time of the fire, and when the door was finally kicked in by firemen. This confirmed earlier speculation that the murderer had either been let into the house, or possessed a key.

Neath solicitor Joanne Anthony, a friend of Alison and Stephen Lewis, told the court that she had visited Alison Lewis in Cefn Coed Hospital. She watched as Lewis suddenly became violent, striking out with her arms, legs and head, taking up to eight members of staff to restrain her. 'She would suddenly lash out and we had to hold her on the bed to stop her [from] hurting herself,' Anthony said. 'After a while she would subside and we would be able to carry on with our conversation.' Anthony agreed with Peter Rouch under cross-examination that Alison Lewis was extremely fit: 'She trained to the absolute limit of her endurance and her fitness and strength were comparable with that of most men,' she said. Joanne Anthony had helped to restrain Lewis during one of her attacks. She described how Lewis' eyes took on a faraway look and they could see her 'boiling up again' before exploding into another vitriolic attack. 'This happened several times while we there and we had to hold her down,' she told the court.

Victoria Anthony, Joanne Anthony's daughter, gave evidence that she knew Alison and Stephen Lewis through babysitting their twin daughters from time to time. She and her mother had gone to the Lewis' home on the morning of Saturday, 26 June where they found Alison Lewis in a very distressed state. Lewis was having 'conversations' with Mandy Power, she said, as though Mandy was in the room with them.

In his evidence, Detective Chief Inspector Chris Coutts, deputy senior investigating officer (formerly senior investigating officer in 'The Cardiff Three' case), told the court that Alison Lewis came under the most intense scrutiny in the wake of the murders. 'No avenues were left unexplored,' he said. 'All police requests relating to searches and other aspects of the investigation were complied with by the Lewises. 'It's safe to say that they opened their lives to us and acceded to any requests we made.'

Detective Chief Inspector Coutts told Peter Rouch in cross-examination that Stephen Lewis had cooperated with inquiry officers. The search of his home 'was conducted with his consent and the police objectives were achieved.' However, Coutts' evidence conflicted with information passed to the Morris family by Dai Morris' solicitor David Hutchinson, who told them that Stephen Lewis initially gave his consent for his home to be searched, but then became uncooperative and withdrew his permission. Hutchinson's account of events, as relayed to the Morris family, was corroborated by Detective Constable John House, one of two police officers assigned to search Stephen and Alison Lewis' house following the murders. The officers did not have a search warrant, he said, but Stephen Lewis had given his permission for a search to be carried out. He described Stephen Lewis as unhelpful in the inquiry. 'He was cooperative but very awkward,' he said.

On Friday, 7 June, the last day of the prosecution's case, Alison Lewis was unexpectedly recalled to the court to face further questioning. When asked by Patrick Harrington whether or not she had claimed immunity from prosecution as a condition of giving evidence in the trial, she told the jury she had never sought immunity from prosecution. 'I didn't want to look as if I had anything to hide, or to look as if I was keeping anything away from people, and I felt if I had immunity from prosecution, it would make my evidence pointless and worthless.' Morris' solicitor David Hutchinson, however, had already told the Morris family that Alison Lewis agreed only reluctantly to waive her claim to immunity.

When asked by Peter Rouch if she had telephoned Mandy Power the night before she was killed, to say she would be calling around to Kelvin Road later, Alison Lewis replied that she had not. She was then asked if she had gone to Kelvin Road and taken the video of the rented film *Armageddon*. She denied this and said that she had had the video at her home for several weeks.

As Lewis stepped down from the witness box, one of the

jurors handed a note to the court usher which the usher passed to the judge. The note contained a request from the jurors to see a video or live demonstration illustrating how an expert would wield a *bō*, the pole-like weapon with dimensions similar to the fibreglass pole used in the murders. Mr Justice Butterfield told the jurors they 'were not required to act like detectives'. Rather, 'it was their duty simply to assess the evidence presented by the prosecution and the defence. The prosecution was not proposing to put forward a video or a live demonstration of a *bō* being used, and the defence evidence had not yet begun,' he said.

The jurors also asked to view the route between Lewis' home at 8 West Crossways, Pontardawe, and Gellionnen Road, which led up from Lone Road past the junction with Kelvin Road. But the judge denied this request, saying that 'instead of a site visit, the court would arrange for a video to be made of the route'.

By Friday, 7 June 2002, Dai Morris had been on trial for nine weeks. Patrick Harrington had called 84 witnesses to give evidence and had read statements from 64 others. Detective Chief Inspector Chris Coutts had outlined the grand scale of the investigation – not merely as interesting fact, but to impress upon the minds of the jury how much time and effort had been expended in bringing the accused before the court.

By contrast, the case for the defence, led by Peter Rouch, took just one week. Only 19 witnesses were called, while statements were read out from two more. Of these witnesses, two were members of Dai Morris' immediate family: his father, Brian, and his mother, Shirley. Morris' sister Debra was inexplicably not called as a defence witness, even though she knew Mandy Power and was aware of her brother's sexual relationship with her. Power, she told the author, frequently called Morris a 'Chippendale', likening him to members of the well-known male touring dance group, famed for their attractive looks and sculpted bodies. Other witnesses called by the defence included Morris' girlfriend, Mandy Jewell, and his cousin Eric Williams.

Peter Rouch would attempt to redress the imbalance in due course, but it would be an uphill task. His instructing solicitor, David Hutchinson, continued to act for the Lewis twins, taking their phone calls and entertaining them in his office. In addition, he had prohibited Rouch from questioning the Lewis brothers on their possible involvement in the murders. Hutchinson's unethical relationship with the Lewises inevitably affected his handling of Morris' defence and made it certain that Dai Morris would not get a fair trial.

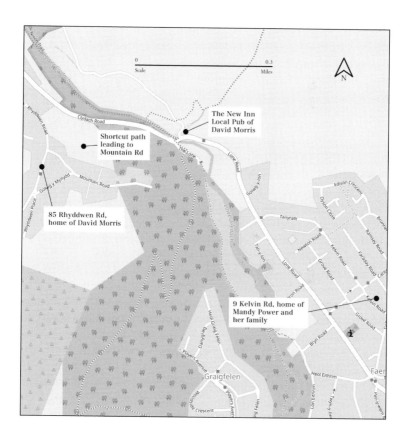

Chapter 20

David George Morris, aka Dai Morris, was born on 5 May 1962 and was 38 years old on the day of his arrest. He was at various times described as a builder's labourer, a scrap metal merchant, a mechanic and a dealer in second-hand cars. While he could turn his hand to many different types of work, his preferred trade was that of a plasterer. The only son of Brian and Shirley Morris, both Welsh, his parents had lived since 1995 in Coedwig Place in Gendros. Morris enjoyed a close relationship with his younger married sister, Debra Thomas.

Described by his schoolteachers as 'remedial', Morris was in fact dyslexic. Perhaps it was this condition, for which he had attended a special school twice weekly when he was a child, which caused him frustration, manifesting itself in unpredictability and aggressiveness. As a youngster he often got into fights and frequently caused trouble. This trend continued as he became older and by his mid-thirties he had acquired almost two dozen convictions, some for robbery and violence. One of his convictions involved a woman whose handbag he had tried to grab, causing her to fall across the bonnet of a car, an offence for which he received a four-year prison term. After Morris served his sentence, he realised that prison life was not for him and he decided to go straight, getting into trouble only occasionally for minor driving offences.

Now, five years after being released from prison, he was back in court again, this time beginning the sixth week of his trial for the murder of Mandy Power and her family.

Peter Rouch rose and asked his first question: 'Did you kill Mandy Power, Katie Power, Emily Power and Doris Dawson?'

David Morris, his hands resting on the top of the bench in front of him, replied in a clear, but distinctive Swansea accent: 'No, sir.'

Peter Rouch then asked Morris a series of questions about

his personal life. Most of his replies were punctuated with the word 'sir'.

Members of the jury watched intently, some leaning forward so as to catch Morris' every word, while others sat back and scribbled notes on their pads. Members of the packed public gallery and upper tier also leaned forward, their ears straining for every verbal exchange.

Carefully guided through his story by Peter Rouch, Morris said he first met Mandy Power soon after meeting Mandy Jewell. The two women had lived near each other in Pendre, Clydach and were close friends. He began a sexual relationship with Mandy Power in 1998 and they had had sex on six or seven occasions, the last time being two days before the murders. He told the court that the first time anything happened between them that was 'other than purely friendly' was in May or June 1998 when Mandy Power had joined Morris and Jewell for a meal at the flat he shared with Mandy Jewell. He told the jury that Mandy Power was joking and flirting with him.

After the meal, he gave her a lift back to her home. A few streets away from Kelvin Road, he stopped the car and they began kissing. Then they made arrangements to meet the following day. As planned, he picked her up at a bus stop and drove to the remote Gellionnen and Graig Unitarian Chapel on Gellionnen mountain, known locally as the 'White Chapel', owing to the colour of its outer walls. This isolated building stands on open moorland about halfway between Pontardawe and Craig Cefn Parc. Here they had sex in his car and afterwards he dropped Mandy Power off at the same bus stop. This was the first of at least three visits they made to this location for sex. He said: 'We got on but the relationship was just a sexual one. It wasn't as if we were partners or anything like that. It was just sex.'

Rouch probed Morris' earlier life and the court heard that he had met his girlfriend Mandy Jewell in 1995. Jewell was from the Halifax area of Yorkshire. Morris soon moved in with Jewell and her young daughter, Emma, at her council flat in Craig Cefn Parc. He did not socialise much in the village. If he went out, 'it would usually be to Swansea,' he said.

Morris also had accommodation at 607 Llangyfelach Road in Treboeth, he told the court, and would sometimes stay there if he and Jewell had argued. Yet another address he used was a council flat which he rented in Arennig Road in Penlan, Swansea. He took on the tenancy of this property some time after the murders to use as a bolt-hole when he felt the need to be on his own.

Describing his relationship with Jewell, Morris said: 'Me and Mandy had a very volatile relationship. We could get on for a week or two and then have a big argument and I'd leave.' At these times Morris returned either to his parents' home or to his rented room in Llangyfelach Road.

When Peter Rouch questioned Morris about the gold neck-chain covered in blood which had been found at the crime scene, he formally confirmed that the chain belonged to him. He said the clasp had broken on 24 June while he was carrying trees on a site. The following day, he went out to price a replacement clasp and met Mandy Power in Clydach village centre. They went back to her house at 9 Kelvin Road and had sex in her bedroom with Mandy Power standing against the bedroom wall.

It was only some time later, after he had left the house and was travelling to his parents' home, that he realised he had left the chain on a kitchen work top in 9 Kelvin Road. By then it was too late to go back to get it. He had no idea how the broken gold chain had come to be found upstairs covered in blood after the murders.

Morris admitted that he lied repeatedly to the police about his ownership of the neck-chain. He also lied about the last time he had had sex with Mandy Power, claiming in one statement that it was three to four weeks before her death. He told the court, 'I was trying to distance myself. I did not want them [the police] to think I was there on 25 June.' He explained that one reason he had denied that the gold chain was his was to stop his girlfriend Mandy Jewell finding out that he had been seeing her best friend. He said he got scared when newspaper articles suggested that the chain must have been 'torn from the killer's neck'.

Morris said that when he went to his parents' home on 25 June, he put on a smaller gold chain with circular links that he also owned. This, he said, was the chain he was wearing in the New Inn on the evening before the murders, but it was under his

T-shirt and could not be seen. While they were in the pub, he had a row with Mandy Jewell and did not want to go home to the flat. Instead, he decided to walk to his parents' home in Gendros; this was quite a long walk. But when he reached Llangyfelach round-about, he changed his mind and went home to the flat he shared with Jewell in the village of Craig Cefn Parc.

Some time afterwards Morris obtained a replacement chain to match the one he had left in Mandy Power's kitchen. His cousin Eric Williams went to a jeweller's shop in St David's Centre in Swansea to buy one for him. Elaborating on his admission to Eric Williams about his ownership of the gold chain and the fact that he had had sex with Power on the Friday morning before her murder, Morris said, 'I told him I had left my chain there but I said I did not mind because it gave me an excuse to see her again.'

Asked about the telephone call he had made from Morriston Police Station after his arrest when he was overheard to say angrily, 'Eric, I'll never forget what you've done', he explained that it referred to the fact that Williams had been interviewed by police a few weeks before his arrest on 20 March 2001 but he had not told Morris about this.

At the end of Morris' evidence, Peter Rouch finished as he had begun, by asking him, 'Did you murder Mandy Power or any member of her family?' Dai Morris' reply was a simple 'No'.

Morris was cross-examined by the prosecution about the lies he had told in police interviews about his ownership of the gold chain. 'It's not my chain. I swear to God. On my children's lives, that's not my chain,' he had told detectives. But he told the court by way of explanation: 'When you are scared as that, you will say anything.'

Earlier the previous year he had signed a statement denying that the chain was his and had asserted that the lack of his DNA on the neck-chain confirmed this.* However, he had decided to

---

* The scene of crimes investigator consulted by the author agreed. She said that if the chain had been worn by Morris for ten years, as he claimed, his DNA should have been both present and detectable in every link of the chain. In fact, she said that even if the chain had been worn for just five minutes, enough epithelial skin cells would have sloughed off to provide a sufficient sample for effective testing. If DNA was not found, she suggested either that the forensic examination was sloppy, or the chain had been forensically cleaned, or another similar chain might have been substituted for the original.

tell the truth a few weeks before the trial began. He said he knew he had left his chain at 9 Kelvin Road on the Friday before the killings, but had no idea how it had come to be found at the point where Mandy Power was beaten to death.

Questioning Morris about the clothes he usually wore, Patrick Harrington suggested that he was more at home in jeans and a T-shirt than in the suit, shirt and tie he was wearing in court. He passed to the members of the jury a photograph of Morris taken in police custody. The photograph showed him bare-chested and heavily tattooed, the implication being that this was the real Dai Morris and not the rather more conservative figure standing in the dock. It was highly prejudicial and yet another tactic in the prosecution's strategy to paint Morris as a thug who was capable of murder.

In his answers to Patrick Harrington's relentless questioning, Morris denied that he had gone to 9 Kelvin Road and killed Mandy Power and her family after she refused to have sex with him. He disagreed with Harrington's suggestion that life for Mandy Power in June 1999 was very different from the way it had been in the previous year, in that she was now in a 'settled relationship and her sexuality was very different'. Morris responded: 'But I don't think she was a lesbian. She was just trying it out. I think she was just experimenting.'

Admitting that he had last had sex with Mandy Power two days before she was murdered, Morris added that if he had turned up at her home late at night [on Saturday, 26 June], she would have 'looked at me stupid'. This is because Mandy Power's children would have been there. Katie and Emily were friends with Jewell's daughter Emma, and Mandy Jewell would have found out about his visit.

Responding to claims made by drug dealer Terrence Williams that Morris had bought amphetamines from him, Morris denied that he had bought drugs from Williams on the three days leading up to the murders (and was not, therefore, high on drugs as the prosecution had alleged). He could not give the court any reason why Williams should have lied about selling him drugs, though he was adamant that he had not bought any drugs at this time. 'Terry and I were not good friends; he was my supplier,' he said.

Asked about witnesses who claimed to have seen him wearing a gold chain at the New Inn, he replied that the chain he had worn that night was not the chain found at 9 Kelvin Road after the killings. He said it was a chain he owned which he had collected from his parents' home after leaving his broken chain in Mandy Power's home. The chain was smaller and *could not be seen* under his T-shirt. The chain found at the crime scene had curved links, whereas the new chain incorporated a pattern of small circular links.

Morris denied Harrington's suggestion that by calling Janice Williams, one of the witnesses in the pub, 'an alcoholic', Morris was attempting to blacken her character. 'It was significant,' replied Morris, 'that only Janice Williams had said I had left the pub with a strange look on my face.' (This was not quite correct. The New Inn landlord's wife, Jayne, described Morris as having a 'menacing look' on his face, though she admitted that she had caught only a glimpse of him as he was leaving.)

Morris said he got cross with Jewell in the pub, calling her 'anti-social' because she did not want people to come back to their flat for more drinks. After he left the pub, he went home by a short cut through the woods, but when he arrived at the flat, he changed his mind about going in. Instead, he decided to walk to his parents' home. At Llangyfelach roundabout he had a change of heart, turned around and walked back to Mandy Jewell's flat. 'I was feeling sorry for myself,' he said. 'But when I sobered up, I realised the argument was my fault because I should not have embarrassed her.'

When asked by the prosecution about the gold chain, which Morris now admitted was his, he replied that he did consider telling the police that the chain was his, but that would not have been easy because he would have had to tell his girlfriend he had been having an affair with her best friend and this would have broken her heart. He had recognised his chain when it was shown on a televised police appeal for information about the murders.

Late in the afternoon on the day he finished giving his evidence in court, Morris was returned to Cardiff prison from where he rang Mandy Jewell. He was concerned that she would discover from looking at Ceefax (the BBC teletext information service which was covering the trial) the precise number of times he had had sex with Mandy Power. The following day, under cross-examination by Patrick Harrington about this telephone call, Morris said that up to that point Mandy Jewell had not known the number of times he and Mandy Power had had sex. His phone call had ended abruptly after just five minutes when Jewell screamed and shouted at him that she was not supposed to be talking to him.

On Wednesday, 12 June Patrick Harrington made an application to Mr Justice Butterfield, *in camera*, to disclose Morris' previous convictions to the jury. The judge ruled in Patrick Harrington's favour, and the jury subsequently learned that Morris had acquired almost two dozen previous convictions. The offences dated back to the 1980s and included robbery, conspiracy to rob in 1987, burglary, using threatening behaviour, offences involving the theft of motor vehicles, and driving while disqualified.

Patrick Harrington put it to Morris: 'You are a man capable of violence, aren't you?' Morris replied: 'No, no more than anybody else.' Harrington continued: 'You have been to court many times before.' In reply, Morris nodded slowly, just once. 'You have convictions for violence – one for hitting somebody over the head with a piece of wood frame,' Harrington continued. Morris agreed that the incident had taken place during a fight in a street, but claimed he had only 'given as good as he got'. Harrington carried on, listing Morris' catalogue of crimes, including his conviction for attempting to steal a woman's handbag, and a conviction for threatening behaviour when he allegedly attacked someone in a pub. Morris denied that he had attacked anyone, but acknowledged that he was arrested, after the police were called.

The purpose of these disclosures was to demonstrate to the jury that the defendant was capable of inflicting the dreadful injuries suffered by the Kelvin Road murder victims. While it was not evidence that he was the murderer, its persuasive effect was immense, and was likely to have made a significant impact upon the jurors.

Brian and Shirley Morris told the court about their son's stormy relationship with Mandy Jewell, confirming how, from to time, he would turn up at their home after having a row with her. 'He would just turn up if they had had an argument,' Brian Morris said, adding that he did not appreciate being woken up by his son, sometimes at 2.00 a.m., 3.00 a.m. or even 4.00 a.m., but he would always let him in and give him the use of a box room. 'He had a key but he lost it,' said Mr Morris. The significance of this evidence was that it demonstrated that Morris was in the habit of walking to his parents' home in Gendros, usually arriving during the early hours of the morning. So his decision to make this journey on the night of the murders was not out of the ordinary.

The public gallery was packed when Mandy Jewell was called to the witness box on Wednesday, 12 June, day three of the defence case. The divorced mother of a young daughter, Emma aged eight, Jewell was working as a counter assistant at Eynon's bakery in Clydach at the time of the murders. She had met Mandy Power when they lived near each other in Pendre at a time when they were both pregnant – she with Emma, Mandy Power with Emily. They remained close friends until May 1999 when Jewell discovered that Power had lied to her about having cancer. 'I was really scared for her; I thought she was dying', she said.

The day before the murders, Mandy Jewell and Emma had gone shopping in Swansea and she had bought Dai Morris some new clothes. Later that afternoon, Emma went to a friend's birthday party while Jewell and Morris decided to go for a drink – first to the Masons Arms in Rhydypandy, then afterwards to the New Inn in Craig Cefn Parc. Morris wore the new clothes she had bought him: Adidas tracksuit bottoms and a white T-shirt. When questioned by Peter Rouch about whether or not Morris was wearing his gold chain, Jewell replied that she could not remember.

The jury heard her describe a quarrel with Morris in the pub on the evening before the murders in which he had called her 'an anti-social cow'. Jewell made no mention of Morris making any criticism of Mandy Power. She said that she had left Morris at the pub and returned home with her daughter at about 9.00 p.m.

They watched television for a while; she made supper for Emma, and shortly afterwards they went to bed, Emma sleeping by her side. 'Emma sleeps with me if Dai is not in, or if I am annoyed with him,' she explained.

The next morning Mandy Jewell was awoken early by their dogs making a noise in the kitchen. She did not know what time it was. She thought at first it was a neighbour, but when she went downstairs she found Morris outside the flat. Opening the door to let him in, she noticed that he was wearing the brand-new Adidas tracksuit bottoms and white T-shirt she had bought him the previous day – the same clothes he had been wearing in the pub.

Asked by Peter Rouch to describe Morris' demeanour when he came in, she replied: 'He was alright. His clothes were wet but there was no blood on them.' She began to suspect that something had been going on between Morris and Power only after Morris' arrest. She had been living with Morris 'virtually full time' but nothing had made her suspect that anything had been going on between Mandy Power and Morris before the killings.

Jewell told the court that she lied to the police, and encouraged Morris to lie also, because she feared she would be made a suspect in the murder investigation. She had told detectives that Morris arrived home about half an hour after she had gone to bed. 'I thought I needed an alibi,' she said. After the murders, her neighbour Janice Williams had 'been going on about everyone needing an alibi'. At some time before the murders, Jewell had fallen out with Mandy Power over the lie that Power had cancer. Jewell said the police had asked her about the row and she was afraid they would regard her as a suspect.

According to Jewell, it was not until the trial that she discovered that the gold chain found at 9 Kelvin Road belonged to Morris. She said: 'He did not say before his trial began that the chain found covered in blood was his.'

Jewell confirmed that after Morris' arrest, he telephoned her and said: 'You opened the door to me, you twat.' This was a reference, she said, to his returning home in the early hours on the morning of the murders. As the conversation continued, she asked him about his relationship with Mandy Power and demanded to know what had been going on. She told Peter Rouch in her examination how she had got up early on the morning of the murders and found Morris on her doorstep 'rain-soaked'. But under Patrick Harrington's cross-examination, Jewell admitted that she had not got out of bed at all. She said that until the start of the trial she had always believed the truth to be that Morris had lost his chain while working with his cousin Eric Williams. She denied a suggestion by the prosecution that she was prepared to say anything that she thought would help Morris.

At 7.00 a.m. on the morning of the murders, she told the court, she received a telephone call at her home. The caller was Alison Lewis. Jewell knew Lewis well because of her relationship with Mandy Power. It was in this call from Alison Lewis that Mandy Jewell learned about the deaths. There had been 'a terrible accident', Lewis told her.

Referring to the witness statement she had given to detectives at an early stage in the investigation, they had suggested that leaving her home and going to stay with her mother so soon after the murders made her look suspicious. Mandy Jewell told the officers she would have no loyalties to Morris if she thought he had been involved in the killings. 'If I knew anything about it, I would tell you,' she told detectives. 'My daughter Emma is the most important person in my life and I would not risk losing Emma for him, especially if he had done something like that.'

When Patrick Harrington questioned Jewell about Morris' claim to have had a sexual relationship with Mandy Power, she fought back tears as she told him that she had learned only after she had read media reports of the trial that week that Morris had been involved in a sexual relationship with Mandy Power for a year.

Mandy Jewell's former father-in-law, Jeff Jewell, took the stand and told the court that on the evening before the murders he went to the New Inn to watch the Wales v. South Africa rugby match. He saw Morris and his former daughter-in-law in the pub. Later, he had dropped her and his grand-daughter home in a taxi.

He said the first he had heard about the murders was when he spoke to the chef at the New Inn early on the following

Sunday morning. He immediately went to tell Mandy the news, arriving at her home at about 9.00 a.m. When she answered the door, he saw Morris standing behind her. The prosecution case was that Morris had a scratch on his nose, but when counsel for the defence questioned Jewell about this, he replied: 'I did not see any mark on him at all.'

Marketing manager Timothy Cherry of 16 Kelvin Road testified that he and his wife, Manon, returned very late from a visit to relatives on the night of Saturday, 26 June. He said his wife noticed 'there weren't any lights on in Mandy Power's house.' At about 4.30 a.m. they were woken by shouting because of the fire at 9 Kelvin Road. Timothy Cherry knew Power and was aware that she was involved in a relationship with Alison Lewis. At 6.00 a.m. he saw Alison Lewis in her casual clothes walking along the pavement in Kelvin Road and watched as she spoke to his wife. He said she [Lewis] seemed upset and troubled, but also quite controlled.

Rosemary Jones, who lived almost directly opposite Mandy Power's house, told the court that when she looked out of her window at 12.30 a.m., there were no lights on in number 9, so she thought no one was in. 'She [Mandy Power] had two young children and they always had a light on. I thought it was very unusual because the place was in darkness.'

At about 12.45 a.m. on 26 June, Jones heard a diesel-engine car pull up outside. A moment later she heard the vehicle drive off. Then heard the sounds of someone mounting the steps to Mandy Power's house, and the front door handle being turned. Seconds later, the front room light came on and then the landing light. 'I saw the profile of somebody's head through the frosted glass window in the front door,' Rosemary Jones said. She then went back to bed where she slept until being awoken by shouting outside.

This testimony given by Mrs Jones, which suggested that the murderer had been driven to the house by an accomplice, did not fit in with the prosecution's theory that the killer – in their eyes, Morris – had walked to 9 Kelvin Road and committed the murders acting alone. Little weight was attached to this crucial evidence either during the trial or at the judge's summing up, even though Mrs Jones' evidence was corroborated by her son.

Former police officer Mick Finn was called as an expert witness on the fifth day of the defence case. Finn is one of the world's leading experts on martial arts, having studied the discipline since 1955 both in Britain and Japan. The holder of 40 black belts in ten martial arts, he has taught and advised British and American police forces on various arrest methods. He has also lectured on the subject at several universities, including Cambridge. He is often called to give expert evidence in both civil and criminal cases involving martial arts and the misuse of weapons and violence. No one is more qualified to give evidence in this field than Mick Finn.

Giving his evidence, Finn told the court that he had examined pictures of the murder weapon, along with a video of the crime scene. He had read the postmortem reports, knew the dimensions of 9 Kelvin Road, and had seen photographs of the fatal injuries inflicted on the victims. He told the court that the dimensions of the murder weapon meant that it resembled a weapon used in martial arts known as a *jō*, a pole-like weapon about four feet long. A *bō*, he told the court, was a similar weapon but was about six feet in length. 'Someone who was trained in the use of a *bō* would be able to use those techniques with a *jō*,' he told the court. 'With a *jō*, both ends of the weapon are used, but, with a *bō*, the striking tended to be with one end.'

Finn said control and accuracy were crucial in martial arts, and practitioners would learn and know that there were a number of vital 'striking' areas on the human body. He told how, after studying pathology reports, he had drawn a diagram of the injuries inflicted on Mandy Power and the other victims, and had compared these to the 'vital points' shown on a martial arts chart. After examining the injuries collectively, his view was that they had a consistency, suggesting that the killer had knowledge of martial arts *and* the vital striking areas. In his opinion, the injuries could have been inflicted only by someone specially trained in the use of weapons, either a police officer or a martial arts exponent. Finn did not agree with prosecuting counsel's suggestion that the injuries could have been caused by someone with no specialist training. Based on his own experience, coupled with nine years working as a police officer, Finn told the court that people who did not have such knowledge tended to deliver blows that were wild and random.

'The head injuries suffered by the four deceased showed a consistency of target,' he said. He felt there had been a degree of control in the execution of these injuries, and it was significant that there was no carry-through to other parts of the body. 'There are indications here that the person who inflicted these injuries had had some martial arts training.' While standing in the witness box, Finn gave a demonstration with a four-foot broom handle, showing how the instrument could be used as a weapon by performing a series of high-speed manoeuvres. 'It was significant that there were no marks from the murder weapon on the walls or ceiling,' Finn said. 'This shows it had been wielded with a degree of control. An expert would be able to wield a *bō* in a confined space. You can get a lot of power in a very short distance,' he said.

Cross-examined by Patrick Harrington, Finn said he did not know that Morris was 'used to wielding a sledgehammer in confined spaces' as a builder's labourer. Harrington suggested: 'While these injuries might be consistent with having been inflicted by a person with martial arts training, they could equally have been inflicted by a person without it.'

But Mick Finn rebutted Harrington's suggestion: 'No, I don't agree with that,' he said. He was adamant: the injuries inflicted on the victims could have been inflicted only by someone with police or martial arts training.

Chapter 21

On day five of the defence case, former police superintendent and Home Office advisor Peter Swann, an expert in fingerprints and handprints, told the court that no fingerprints belonging to Dai Morris had been found anywhere in the house. Neither did he believe that the bloody handprint found on the living room carpet belonged to Morris. 'It doesn't fit at all,' he said.

Swann told the court that he had 45 years' experience of analysing fingerprints and handprints, and had given evidence in hundreds of trials, both in Britain and abroad. He was therefore much more highly qualified to form an opinion as to who had made the handprint on the living room carpet than expert witness Robert Bell, who had given his opinion earlier. Swann had examined the handprint on a piece of carpet taken by police to his office in Wakefield. Afterwards, he visited Morris in Swansea prison (where he was held until his trial started and was then moved to Cardiff prison), where he took a number of impressions of Morris' left hand. Morris' hand was inked and he was asked to press it on a different section of the same carpet, kneeling down to comply with Swann's request. After examining the marks, Swann said: 'It is possible to exclude him as being the person who could have left that mark.'

Swann went further, telling the jurors that while the handprint did not belong to Morris, it could have belonged to Alison Lewis. As part of his investigation, Swann had tested an outline of Alison Lewis' hand against the bloody carpet mark and said he could not discount it as having been made by her left hand. 'It's a much closer fit,' he said.

Commenting on the drawing of the carpet print that expert witness for the prosecution Robert Bell had produced for comparative purposes, Swann was critical. He said: 'I don't think the orientations of Mr Bell's sketch are correct.'

New Scotland Yard fingerprint expert Allan Ford, with thirty years of practical experience behind him, but acting as a private consultant at the time of the trial, was also called to give evidence for the defence. Mr Ford, too, had examined the handprint and, after conducting his own independent research, said that he agreed with Mr Swann's findings; that the bloody handprint found on the carpet in the living room did not belong to Morris.

Handprint of
David Morris' (dark)

Handprint found
on carpet (light)

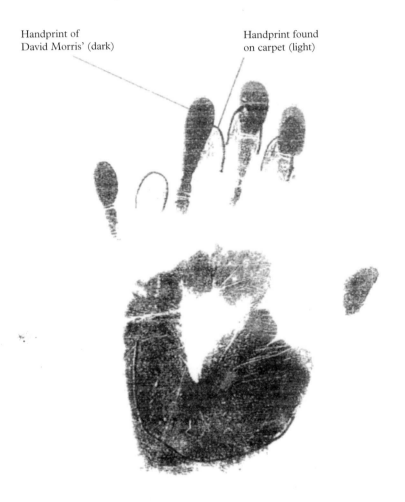

Comparison of handprint of David George Morris
with handprint on carpet

The next witness, Amanda Jones of West Crossways, Pontardawe, a former next-door neighbour of Alison and Stephen Lewis, told the court that on the night before the murders, she and her husband David were invited to a barbeque at the Lewises. When they arrived, Stephen Lewis was drinking cider but his wife was not drinking. Also present at the gathering were Alison Lewis' brother Paul Powell and his wife Sandra.

'At about 10.00 p.m., Alison Lewis suddenly fell asleep. She was not drunk,' Mrs Jones said. Soon afterwards, Lewis woke up and then she and Stephen Lewis said they were going to bed. David and Amanda Jones continued chatting to the Powells for a short time, and then they all went home.

Mrs Jones told the court that the Lewises gave 'every impression of being a happily married couple'. After the Lewises split up in July 1999, David and Amanda decided to support Stephen Lewis in the custody battle for the children.* This was because he assumed responsibility for the children after the murders, whereas Alison 'used to go out a lot'. Even so, Mrs Jones said that she 'felt uneasy' about living next door to Stephen Lewis after the murders.

The two Clydach taxi drivers, Beverley Lewis and Carol Ann Isaac, were called to give evidence for the defence. They both knew Mandy Power well from taking her shopping and driving her children to school every day. They also knew Alison Lewis, and had driven her home from 9 Kelvin Road from time to time. In addition, a few weeks before the murders, Mandy Power and Alison Lewis had joined Carol Ann at her fiftieth birthday party in the Carpenters Arms in Clydach.

Isaac told the court: 'Early on the morning of the murders I was in bed with Beverley at my council-owned flat in Morriston. Our mobile phones were turned off, so we could get an uninterrupted night's sleep. At 6.00 a.m. I heard the sound of someone knocking on our ground floor bedroom window. It was Beverley's mother, Lorna Lewis, and Beryl Hawkins, the owners of Clydach Cabs. They told us there had been a fire at Mandy's – they had

---

* In 2000 Alison Lewis won sole custody of the children following a two-day contested hearing.

heard the news from controllers as they arrived at work early that morning – and they thought the children had died.'

Isaac continued: 'We arrived at Kelvin Road at between 6.30 and 6.45 a.m. There was just a single fire engine outside and one police constable. It did not look like a crime scene. We thought it was just a fire. We called to the home of Christine Williams, who lived to the immediate right of number 9, and Beverley asked her what was going on. She replied, "They all died in the fire," then she invited us in. Sitting on a chair in Christine Williams' living room was Alison Lewis. She was wearing a white T-shirt, white shorts and trainers. Her hair was wet. She smelled very fresh. It was as if she had just come out of the shower or bath. Beverley went over to her, put her arm round her and told her how sorry she was. Her attitude was normal and she was calm throughout. I thought it was very strange.' In a later part of her testimony, Isaac added that Alison Lewis 'was not crying, was not as upset as she ought to have been'.

Beverley Lewis' testimony told the court the same story. She had been in bed with Isaac when they were roused by her mother, Lorna, and Beryl Hawkins. They drove to Kelvin Road and then she and Isaac went into the home of Christine Williams where they saw Alison Lewis sitting on a chair in the living room. 'She was dressed in a white T-shirt, white shorts and trainers', Beverley told the court. Her hair looked wet. Christine Williams confirmed, in reply to Beverley's question, that the family had all died in the fire. Beverley described Lewis' demeanour as 'calm' but she thought that 'she was not that upset'. She went over to Lewis and put her arm round her shoulders to comfort her and told her she was sorry for her loss. She also noted that Lewis smelled fresh, as though she had just showered or bathed.

The penultimate witness for the defence was the next door neighbour of Mandy Power, teenager Louise Pugh. In her examination she told the court that on the evening of the 25 June she returned a borrowed video tape of the Bruce Willis film *Armageddon*, by posting it through the letter box of Mandy Power's home. The cover was found at 9 Kelvin Road after the fire, while the film itself was later discovered in a police search of Alison Lewis' home in Pontardawe.

According to prosecuting counsel, Pugh had not mentioned the *Armageddon* video to the police in her earlier interviews. Patrick Harrington suggested that Pugh was trying to build a case against Alison Lewis. Louise Pugh denied this and said she had had too much to think about at the time.

Pugh also told the court that a few weeks before the murders she had seen Stephen Lewis at 9 Kelvin Road, just as it was getting dark. 'I heard banging,' she said. 'I thought it was my door and opened it but there was no one there. Then I heard shouting. Stephen Lewis said: "If you do not keep away from my wife, I will kill you." He was standing on the top of the steps pointing his finger. He said it very aggressively.'

Pugh added that there had been another incident a few weeks previously, when she had seen someone standing in Mandy Power's garden after dark looking in at the window. 'It looked like a man and he was wearing a black jacket.' She said it was the type of jacket that police officers usually wear.

Harrington asked her: 'You did not like Alison getting involved in a lesbian relationship with Mandy.'

Pugh replied: 'I did not mind. It was Mandy's choice. I love her for what she is, not what her sexuality is.'

Harrington continued: 'In your statement you say Stephen Lewis shouted, "Keep away from my wife."'

Pugh added: '...or I will kill you.'

'That is not in your statement,' Patrick Harrington said.

In Stephen Lewis' first statement to the police, he had denied ever threatening to kill Mandy Power, only to change his statement the very next day by admitting that he had. Then he added that he had said it as a joke. The suggestion by the prosecution was that Louise Pugh had fabricated evidence to suit the case for the defence. Clearly she had not.

Shortly after 4.00 p.m. on 19 June 2002 the proceedings came to an abrupt halt. As Patrick Harrington continued to cross-examine the teenager, Louise Pugh became upset and told him: 'Do not try to undermine me. I do not like it. You were not there. I am going.' She then left the witness box and stormed out of the courtroom shouting: 'You are a bunch of twats.'

The following day Pugh returned to the court. She said, 'I'm sorry about that. I didn't swear at the barrister. I told him not to undermine me.'

During cross-examination, Pugh told the court that she and Mandy Power had been very good friends and were 'like sisters'. In her statement she said: 'Mandy would confide everything in me. Our relationship was very close.' She was aware of Mandy's sexual relationships with several men, but said she 'did not have feelings for men anymore and did not need another man'.

The last witness to give evidence on the seventh and final day of the defence case was Clydach resident Nicola Williams. She related how she had seen a man walking in the direction of Kelvin Road at 2.20 a.m. on the morning of the murders, and subsequently helped the police compose an e-fit image of him. The court heard that she attended a video identity parade more than a year later in which she unhesitatingly picked out the man she believed she had seen: it was Stephen Lewis, Alison Lewis' husband.

When asked by Peter Rouch how positive she was that the man she had picked out was the same man she had seen near the scene of the murders, Nicola Williams replied: 'At the time I remember being pretty certain.'

The prosecution claimed that Williams was mistaken, and had changed the time of her sighting in statements to the police. 'I don't think I did,' she said. 'After hearing what happened the next day, it just stuck in my mind, his face.'

Harrington suggested that she may have seen Lewis at Pontardawe Leisure Centre where they were both members. 'Not to my recollection,' she replied. She agreed that when she first gave police a description of the man she had seen, she estimated him as being between five feet eight inches and five feet ten inches tall.

'Now you are saying he was six feet tall,' Harrington challenged, to which she responded: 'I'm not very good with heights.'

When Nicola Williams was asked what the weather was like when she had seen the man, she said, 'Fine, dry and clear'. Other witnesses, Harrington told her, gave evidence that it had been raining. To this, she replied: 'It was not raining in Clydach at the time I was driving through it.' A meteorological office report, subsequently obtained, confirmed that the weather in South Wales in the early hours of 27 June 1999 was 'variable, raining on and off'.

What the jury was not told at any stage of the proceedings was that Stephen and Stuart Lewis were biologically identical twins. They differed only slightly in appearance. Stephen had an alibi for the time of the murders, whereas Stuart did not. Furthermore, Stuart looked even more like Nicola Williams' e-fit image than Stephen did. Nicola Williams was never given an opportunity to identify Stuart Lewis.

Despite the fact that Stuart Lewis was the first senior police officer to arrive at the scene of the murders, the prosecution did not call him to give evidence. Incredibly, the defence did not object to this decisive omission which left a series of essential questions unasked about Lewis' movements at the time of the murders, and those in the aftermath of the fire. This was a blatantly obvious omission by the defence, and one that would become the subject of judicial criticism at a later stage.

Chapter 22

In his closing speech, delivered on Wednesday, 19 June, Patrick Harrington told the jury that 'a week from now marks the third anniversary of the deaths of two little girls and their mother and grandmother'. By that date, the jury would have spent 'the best part of three months investigating these awful crimes'. They would then 'have to undertake the most important exercise of anybody who has ever been involved in this case'. They would have to decide 'and let the world know whether or not Morris was guilty of four counts of murder.'

'It is possible,' he added, 'that the jury already has strong views and are close to deciding the answer to this important question. The case is one that had been bound to prompt everybody to have opinions.'

Harrington said the jury had heard every word said in court and seen every piece of evidence, and had come to the trial 'uncontaminated by preconceptions'. He said 'there are stark issues in the case and the jury will have to deal with fundamental questions. One question is the identity of the killer. Was it Dai Morris, or might it have been Alison Lewis?'

Patrick Harrington's question to the jury was perhaps unfair. Their sworn duty was to try Dai Morris. They were not there to try Alison Lewis: she was not on trial.

Harrington continued: 'The defence has always alleged that the killer was probably Alison Lewis and has produced evidence to support this contention, but the finger of suspicion that has been pointed at Alison Lewis and her husband Stephen Lewis is a false one.' Harrington emphasised the importance of drawing a contrast between what was known about Alison Lewis in the lead-up to the murders, and what was known about Dai Morris.

Harrington painted a picture of domestic harmony before that fateful night. 'Mrs Lewis was happy and contented and closer to Mandy Power than she had ever been', he said. 'Those who spoke of their relationship described it as a loving and caring one.' He avoided all reference to witnesses who had testified to Alison Lewis' jealousy, her possessive and controlling nature, and that she had raged at Mandy Power on the day before the murders.

'On the evening of 26 June 1999, Mrs Lewis went to bed at approximately the same time as her husband, and she stayed at home throughout the night,' Harrington told the jury. 'It was significant that after the revelation came about the tragic death of her lover, Mrs Lewis was so distraught she tried to jump from an upstairs window at her home. Please always remember that when Alison Lewis chose a career, she chose to join the police and serve the public and uphold the law.'

The purer Alison Lewis was portrayed in Harrington's description of her, the more sullied the image of Dai Morris appeared.

Harrington reminded the jurors that on the night of the murders Morris was in the New Inn wearing a heavy gold chain and he had drunk significant amounts of alcohol. He had also taken amphetamines in large quantities recently, and drink was known to make him angry and violent. Indeed, he argued with his girlfriend and had been aggressive towards another customer before he left the pub.

Harrington suggested that he 'perhaps harboured a desire to have sex with Mandy Power, whom he knew lived close by. The next day Morris was not wearing his gold chain and was drinking on the steps of Jewell's council flat,' Harrington told the court. 'From that day on he began a campaign of lies which he has continued since he left the witness box in this court.'

'It was significant,' Harrington added, 'that Mrs Lewis was the mother of little girls, twin daughters born in December 1995. Whatever views anyone might take on her morality and sexuality, she is a loving mother,' he told the jury.

Patrick Harrington had used Alison Lewis' status as a mother and a bereaved lover to win the jury's sympathy, and had successfully portrayed Dai Morris as a lying, selfish, violent man with no regard for his family or the truth. Had the trial not been characterised by emotion and prejudice, the only evidence in the prosecution's case would have been the gold neck-chain found at the scene, evidence which, given Morris' intimate relationship with Power, was circumstantial at best.

David Morris had 'lied, lied and lied' in trying to conceal the fact that he was guilty of the Clydach murders,' Harrington contended. It was significant that Morris had told lies 'at every stage, at every opportunity, and on every topic. He was prepared to 'swear on his children's lives as he was lying his head off in a series of police interviews,' he added.

The prosecution barrister highlighted the difference in mood between Dai Morris and Alison Lewis on the eve of the murders, relying extensively on the uncorroborated and doubtful testimony of Janice Williams. Mrs Lewis had begun her day with a 'steamy sex session' with her lover and finished it with a family barbeque at home. David Morris, by contrast, drank seven pints of lager in a pub and described Mandy Power as 'evil' in the hours before she was brutally murdered.

'Mrs Lewis had been in a relationship outside the bond of matrimony, but neither the police nor the defence had been able to prove that she lied about a single thing,' he told the jury. But testimony given by Alison Lewis during the trial had been challenged by several reliable witnesses on a number of occasions. One of these concerned her denial about being in Kelvin Road early on the morning of the murders, while in another she testified that Stephen Lewis knew nothing about her sexual orientation until the morning of the murders. A telephone call Alison Lewis made to Mandy Power shortly before her death confirmed that he did know.

Nevertheless, Patrick Harrington concluded, 'The jury would never know exactly what happened at the murder scene,' he said, 'but if the victims could speak from beyond the grave, their voices would say "Dai Morris did it."'

Peter Rouch QC countered Harrington's pathos with a plea for reason. 'We do not need to overdramatise matters by references such as voices beyond the grave,' he told the court in his closing speech. 'The case has all the drama it needs – drama is implicit in it.' He said: 'The prosecution had done its best to whitewash the Lewises, making a public apology to them at the start of the case and noting how cooperative the two have been. It points to another or others having been involved, and some of it to persons who can be identified. By that, I mean Alison Lewis and Stephen Lewis. My client is no angel – he has had fights and he has stolen property. But this case is not about somebody who has a fight in a pub. This is wholly out of the ordinary. The case against David Morris is flawed and absurd.'

Rouch continued: 'Evidence from witnesses, who claimed the accused was wearing the gold chain found at the murder scene, on the night of the killings, is totally unsafe.' He told the jurors that 'David Morris could not have left his chain at Kelvin Road at the time of the murders and is not guilty of all four murder charges'. Rouch was using substance not spin in his analysis of the evidence against Morris.

Rouch made it clear that the prosecution was using nothing more substantial than character assassination and circumstantial evidence to convince the jury of the defendant's guilt. He claimed that the prosecution had been struggling to think of a motive for the murders and told the jury: 'Some cases cry out for a motive, they scream out for a motive, and this is one of them. The injuries sustained were really unbelievable. It was not just a case of killing. It was the continuation of violence.'

Rouch was implying that there must have been a compelling reason for someone to have launched such a violent attack, and to have used far more force than was necessary to kill the victims. The cornerstone of his defence was that Morris had no such motive. 'What it comes down to is this: there is no reason at all why Dai Morris should have attacked any of the victims.'

And that was the sum total of Peter Rouch's closing address for the defence. He had done his best to repair Morris' tattered character in the eyes of the jury, to portray him as a flawed man, but one with no reason to violently bludgeon Mandy Power and her family to death, one with no motive to commit such terrible crimes.

Rouch had tried to introduce an element of doubt – that somehow Alison Lewis may have been involved; though Hutchinson's agreement with the Lewis brothers prevented him from suggesting that they were in any way responsible for the deaths – so his closing arguments lacked the substance and punch needed to convince the jury.

Following Peter Rouch's closing address, the case was adjourned.

On Monday, 24 June, in the last week of a trial lasting almost three months, Mr Justice Butterfield began his summing-up. He told the jurors that if they excluded the possibility of a chance intruder or another acquaintance of the victims, then either the defendant David Morris, Alison Lewis or Stephen Lewis had to be the killer. As Patrick Harrington had suggested to the jury earlier, the judge was also directing the jury to choose between Dai Morris and Alison Lewis.

He reminded the jury that Morris' gold chain was found covered in the victim Mandy Power's blood, and that the defence had sought to show that the probable killers were Alison Lewis and Stephen Lewis. The judge told the jury that the former Welsh women's rugby international Alison Lewis had been forced to leave the police force in 1991 because of the trauma she had suffered after a man had gassed himself in his car. 'One of her last duties was to take the hosepipe used in the suicide to the Coroner's Court. She couldn't stomach it,' he said.

'The killer at Kelvin Road exploded into violence,' the judge said, 'and with the upstairs awash with blood and with bits of flesh, bone and teeth scattered around, wrapped the limbs of Doris Dawson in paper and moved the bodies of Mandy and the children. Whoever did it must have had the capability and the stomach for the gruesome activities.'

Referring to Nicola Williams' identification of Stephen Lewis and the e-fit image composed by police as a result of the description she had given, the judge directed the jury to disregard this evidence because Stephen Lewis had an alibi: he was in bed with his wife at the time of the murders.*

The Lewises' alibis were given the judicial seal of approval and were therefore watertight. Nicola Williams' eyewitness evidence was ignored and could not be used to suggest that the alibis were false. In directing the jury to exclude Nicola Williams'

---

* At this critical juncture, it is important to note that no criticism was made, either at that time, or later, of the judge's conduct at the trial or of his detailed and comprehensive summing-up.

evidence, Mr Justice Butterfield reduced considerably the prospects for the defence to prove that both or either of the Lewises had lied. Even more astonishingly, the jurors were not told that the e-fit image also resembled Stephen Lewis' identical twin brother, Stuart, who was never required to appear in an identity parade. Surely, this piece of testimony should have been included as potentially exculpatory evidence.

Continuing his address, Mr Justice Butterfield said: 'You'd need a heart of stone not to be affected by the photographs of the injuries to the victims. And anyone seeing them may feel anger and outrage, particularly at the humiliation heaped on the victims even after death. You may feel sympathy for the defendant's parents caught up in the allegations against their son. But you must put aside those feelings because emotion and prejudice have no place in a criminal trial. We look for cool heads.'

For a second time, the judge directed the jury that the murderer was one of three people in the courtroom: Alison Lewis, Stephen Lewis or Dai Morris. Of these three, the jury had to choose between two: Alison Lewis and Dai Morris. According to the judge, one of these possessed a great propensity for violence, and he then recapped Morris' string of criminal convictions. And in order to drive home his point, he repeated how Alison Lewis had been forced to resign from the police force following a suicide, because 'she didn't have the stomach for these things'.

Late on Wednesday morning, 26 June, the judge finished his summing-up and at lunchtime the jurors retired to review the evidence and consider their verdict.

The next day, Thursday, 27 June, marked the third anniversary of the murders and while the jurors continued their deliberations throughout the day, fresh floral tributes arrived at 9 Kelvin Road: two bunches of yellow and purple flowers were tied to the front gate, in memory of the four tragic victims.

Chapter 23

By mid-afternoon on Friday, 28 June 2002, following fourteen hours of intense deliberations over three days, eleven ordinary citizens, their lives changed for ever by their harrowing eleven-week ordeal, returned from the jury room and took their places on the bench. Chatter and clamour in the packed public gallery quickly died away to a pin-drop silence.

Outside the court building, news of the jurors' return spread swiftly through the crowd, as heads lifted and eyes turned in the direction of the doorway from where the announcement was expected to be made. Around 100 members of the international press corps, including seven television crews, prepared themselves to report on the finale of this headline-making murder trial.

At 3.38 p.m., the first of four guilty verdicts was read out. It was unanimous. A loud cry of 'Yes' rang out in unison from relatives of the murder victims, while incredulous shouts of 'No,' sounded from the public gallery. Journalists clutching notebooks rushed from the courtroom to send their copy to the news desks. Outside, shouts of 'guilty' spread like wildfire through the crowd. Shocked members of Dai Morris' family yelled abuse at the judge, at the jury and at anyone in their way; others fled the courtroom deeply distressed and in floods of tears.

When relative calm was restored, Mr Justice Butterfield gravely addressed Dai Morris, who was still standing in the dock. 'These were horrific murders committed with great savagery in which you inflicted appalling injuries on four innocent and defenceless victims. You have shown not a trace of compassion or sympathy for the terrible suffering you inflicted. The sentence of the court is life imprisonment on each count.'

Still stunned following the jury's verdict, even if the surprise failed to register on his face, the convicted prisoner turned and left the dock. He was led down the narrow stairway to the small holding cell in the basement where he contemplated the reality of his sentence – a lifetime behind bars.

The judge then addressed the relatives of the victims: 'It is abundantly plain that the Dawson family is close-knit and a family which has suffered grievously as a result of these tragic, senseless and brutal killings.' He expressed his hope that the conclusion of the trial 'would help in some way to assuage the grief suffered by them'.

Brian Morris emerged from the courtroom looking defiant and irate; his wife Shirley was red-eyed and pale. Their daughter Debra was crying bitterly as she followed them out. They gathered with their wider family in the foyer immediately outside the courtroom as Brian angrily defended his son. 'David is innocent and knew nothing about the murders. This is just the start and we are going to fight this ourselves now as much as we can.'

Shirley Morris, looking shaken and tearful, had more to say in her son's defence and told reporters in a diminutive voice that faltered with emotion, 'He's an innocent man. My son is innocent. He never done this. This is an unfair justice. They got the wrong man and they know it. They know they have.'

Debra, still tearful but determined, was even more forceful in supporting her brother. Stunned by the guilty verdict, which she had clearly not expected, she told reporters: 'I'm in shock. I'm totally shocked. I'll fight for him – everything I can. I'll fight for him.' Then, with a belief borne of blind certainty, she added: 'My brother is innocent.'

In response to questions about threats received by the family, Debra replied that there had been no threats since Dai Morris was charged with the murders. She said: 'Nothing at all – all we've had is support. All the way along is support.'

Morris' brother-in-law, Neil Thomas, expressed his confidence that Morris would cope with life in prison, even though he had appeared in the dock nursing a black eye during the early days of the trial, the result of a revenge attack by an inmate in Cardiff prison. He said: 'I think he'll be alright. Inside – he's a sensible boy. He doesn't know anything about Kelvin Road. He had nothing at all to do with it. He's not a bad boy.'

Less than an hour after the verdict was delivered, the Morris family and their supporters appeared on the steps of the court and announced that they would carry on the fight. They confidently predicted 'Justice will prevail'.

Replying to questions from the press, Shirley Morris said the family had received tremendous support throughout the trial: 'We couldn't have asked for better. The people in the gallery all were there to support him,' she said. 'And even [the people] outside. This is not British justice.' She told reporters that Morris would lodge an appeal.

Debra Thomas later read a statement in which she said the family could not understand how a guilty verdict had been reached.

At 4.04 p.m., less than 30 minutes after passing sentence, Mr Justice Butterfield left the court building. He sped away in the same chauffeur-driven Mercedes he had used to visit Clydach six weeks earlier. Now he was accompanied by a police motorcycle escort, sirens blaring, heading in the direction of the official judges' accommodation on Fairwood Common in the Gower peninsula.

Five minutes later, Michael Power left the court building with his partner, Sara Williams. He told the waiting reporters that he had 'nothing to say', and hurried away. Later that week, he released a statement in which he thanked South Wales Police and in particular those officers involved in the investigation. He described the last three agonising years before concluding: 'Perhaps now I will be able to put Katie and Emily to rest in peace.'

Michael Power was followed from the court building by Alison Lewis, who stood at the top of the steps to read out a prepared statement, which was met with some jeers and boos of derision. Between sobs, she said: 'I am pleased with the verdict. Justice has finally been achieved. While standing trial for murder, the judicial system afforded David Morris the luxury of being innocent until proven guilty. Throughout the trial period, my rights as an innocent person were neither given nor respected, as David Morris' defence team did their utmost to make me look guilty by implication and insinuation. I have felt the loss of Mandy, Katie, Emily and Doris more than anyone will ever know. However, I have never lost sight of the pain Mandy's family must have suffered, and still are suffering, and I wish them the strength to move forward in an attempt to rebuild their lives, as my family and myself now have to work at rebuilding ours.'

Closely behind Alison Lewis, the brother and sisters of Mandy Power emerged into bright sunlight and they also halted on the steps of the court building. All wearing violet ribbons of remembrance, the sisters struggled to hold back their tears as their brother, Robert Dawson, read out a prepared statement on behalf of the family. It reflected the pain the family had lived through since the night of the murders and the mental anguish they had endured every day since.

> It has been three long and difficult years since Mam, Mandy, Katie and Emily were so cruelly taken from us, and today we know that the evil person responsible for this will spend the rest of his life behind bars. But this will never be enough for the sense of pain and loss that we feel every day, nor for the sheer hell and fear our family went through that terrible night. So many lives have been devastated by the horror of that night and by the lies and deceit that have that so prolonged today's conclusion. We are deeply grateful to those who with great courage have come forward with vital information that has helped the police in this difficult case. We can never thank the police enough for the help and support they have given to us throughout this case, especially our liaison officer and victim support. Perhaps now we can begin to come to terms with our loss, although our lives will never be the same. We hope the media will recognise our need for privacy and time to do that. This trial has been an extremely testing time for us.

As Dai Morris was driven away in a blacked-out, unmarked police van flanked by police motorcycles and four police cars, his supporters cheered and one shouted: 'The wrong one went in the van.'

Mandy Jewell had bravely decided to stand by her boyfriend of eight years, despite his having had a year-long sexual relationship with her best friend. Ashen-faced and looking tired, she told reporters: 'He may have gone behind my back and slept with Mandy, but that does not make him a killer. I have not even talked to David about his fling with Mandy. I am more concerned that an innocent man is banged up in jail for a crime I am one hundred per cent convinced he did not do. Yes, David had a temper, but he would never lift a finger to his kids.'

The next day, Mandy Jewell had a series of panic attacks. She then overdosed on beta-blockers and was rushed to hospital. She denied that it was a suicide attempt and, upon leaving hospital, she and her daughter Emma returned temporarily to her parents' home in Halifax.

Speaking at Swansea Central Police Station, and accompanied by his deputy, Detective Chief Inspector Chris Coutts, senior investigating officer Detective Superintendent Martyn Lloyd-Evans refused to answer detailed questions about the murder investigation, but instead read a statement: 'The verdict today brings to a close the largest murder investigation ever undertaken by South Wales Police, and our thoughts are with the family and friends of Doris, Mandy, Katie and Emily. Their strength and support has been an inspiration to the investigating team and I hope today's verdict will give them some reassurance, and enable them to start looking to the future and rebuilding their lives. Throughout the investigation, South Wales Police has not only had the support of the family and friends, but also of the close-knit community around them, and I would like to thank everyone who came forward offering information, especially those witnesses who gave evidence at the trial.'

Without another word and ignoring reporters' further questions, Lloyd-Evans collected his papers and left the conference room.

Speaking to BBC Wales' *Week In, Week Out* programme, Sandra Jones described the pain she and her family were going through: It's like a living hell for us. We will always suffer. We always will.' She added: 'we will never see our loved ones again. It's ruined our lives. Nothing will ever be the same.'

Commenting on his sister's several affairs, Mandy Power's brother Robert Dawson said: 'They can print what they like, but that wasn't Mandy.' He added, 'They never knew her. That's one of the hardest parts of it. The press can print what they like.'

Swansea Councillor Roger Smith, speaking with evident relief after the verdict, said: 'I sincerely hope now that the families and parties that have suffered great distress and trauma can now try to rebuild their lives. We as a community must support all of them and hope this will be the end of this most dreadful part of Clydach's history.'

Clydach councillor Sylvia Lewis expressed her delight at the outcome of the trial and was confident that the verdict was the right one. She said: 'When he [Dai Morris] was arrested for murder, it was like a cloud lifting over the community. People have been petrified of him for a long time and he was the sort of person you feared could literally get away with murder. People were very afraid of what he might do and avoided confrontation in any shape or form. It was just self-preservation.'

Councillor Lewis had unwittingly hit upon the real reason behind Dai Morris' conviction. In the absence of a suspect whom the South Wales Police force was prepared to charge, they had chosen a man on the fringes of society whom nobody would question was capable of committing such a violent crime. They had removed from the streets a man widely considered to be something of a thug and, with the possible exception of Mandy Jewell, his former wife Wendy, his children, immediate family and a handful of supporters, he was someone they were all glad to see the back of.

This view was unwittingly endorsed by Mike Randerson, who had given evidence against Dai Morris in the trial. Appearing to speak on behalf of other Craig Cefn Parc villagers, he told reporters: 'It was frustrating and it was annoying because [within days of the murders] most of us were pretty well convinced that it was Dai Morris and yet they just didn't seem to have any interest at all.'

Yet this was the same Mike Randerson who, immediately after he had testified that he had seen Morris wearing his gold neck-chain on the night before the murders, rang his girlfriend to ask her if he *was* wearing a chain because he couldn't remember. In the absence of hard evidence, Mike Randerson at least appears to have made up his mind from the outset that Dai

Morris was guilty of the murders. This was purely on the basis of his personal hatred of him, and suspicion that he was the *type* of person who could have committed the crime. Morris was indeed a victim of extreme prejudice.

It was Round 2 to the prosecution.

Chapter 24

While the outcome of the trial was greeted with delight and relief in some quarters, it was met with suspicion and outright hostility in others. The jury's unanimous verdict did little to stifle speculation that someone other than Dai Morris was responsible for the murders. In particular, attention focused on the supposed forensic clean-up operation in which, it was alleged, Morris had wiped away all trace of his DNA and fingerprints.

The people of Clydach had followed the case keenly, and were both stunned and confused by the verdict. Repeating what many others were thinking, one local person told the *South Wales Evening Post*: 'There was conflicting evidence and I was rather surprised by the verdict. He lied and lied, and there was the evidence of the necklace, but there was no evidence against him.'

Other villagers held similar views on the judgment. Roger Simmonds of Ffynnon Wen, Clydach commented: 'I am not totally convinced. I think there is a lot of things we don't know. It's purely hearsay.' Another villager told reporters: 'I don't think we know everything about the case and are not in a position to pass judgment.' One man who had known Morris since his schooldays said, '… there was no way he was intelligent enough to clean up the crime scene.' Clydach resident Emma Gribble said: 'Everyone is saying it should not end here. I hope it does go on because I am sure there is more to it. This is not going to be the end.'

Emma Gribble was right. This was the start of a four-year campaign by Morris' family and their supporters to have the guilty verdict overturned. On Monday, 1 July, just three days after the guilty verdict was delivered, Wendy Morris, former wife of Dai Morris and mother of his three children, launched a petition to clear his name. Speaking to reporters at her home in Penlan, Swansea, she confidently declared: 'He is not a murderer. I am absolutely positive. I've seen him in drink and drugs and he is not that sort of person.' She told the media gathered at her home that she, her family and friends had 'raised a 200-signature petition asking for a retrial. We've already got 200 signatures on the petition and we're not going to give up to prove he is innocent.'

Some took the protest even further, and voiced their disgust that the Lewises had not been convicted. Protest banners with the slogan 'Killer Walks Free' were hung from bridges over busy main roads in Dyfatty and Ravenhill in Swansea. Posters protesting Morris' innocence were affixed to lampposts; graffiti were painted on walls to garner support for a second trial, and a website was launched which gave further details about the appeal.

Wendy Morris' campaign for a second trial continued to gather momentum. It gained supporters from outside the family who visited pubs in Clydach to collect more signatures. The petition now had the names of 350 supporters. Speaking on behalf of the community, Councillor Sylvia Lewis said Morris' supporters had no business being in Clydach, describing their visit as an 'insult' to the families of the victims. She told reporters: 'It is sad they were in this village trying to drum up support – stay away from Clydach. Let us get back on track. They were apparently on licensed premises, looking for people who had had a drink, asking them to sign a petition. It is an insult to everyone living in the village.'

After two councillors received several complaints about the protest, council workmen in Swansea were ordered to remove the offending banners from the bridges over the main roads. In direct response to the 'Dai Morris is Innocent' campaign, some Clydach residents started their own poster campaign called 'Support for the Victims' Families', but it was short-lived and quickly died out.

Swansea Valley Councillor Ioan Richard, speaking on 9 July 2002, called for an end to the campaign. He said: 'If the Morris family are blinded with family loyalty to attempt to go to an appeal, then I respect their emotions. But I ask them to leave it to the lawyers and not to gossip, banners and lies. Sadly, there are far too many people out there talking about this case when they have no idea of what happened in the trial or what has gone on in this village. Two neighbours fled away from living in the village in fear of their lives after crossing Morris. And a third was absolutely desperate for a transfer away from Morris. I know, because as a councillor I helped them fill in housing transfer application forms to the council. The reasons given were absolute terror of Morris' frenzied temper. People were regularly complaining of his intimidatory attitude and of the occasions when his coldness would erupt into a red-hot frenzy of violence. I can sympathise a little bit with Morris' close family, as the relatives of mass murderers can go into denial. But disgusting gossip is splitting the community of Clydach.'

Councillor Richard was clearly keen to see a troublemaker off the streets, and was not open to the possibility that Morris had been sent to prison as a result of an unsafe conviction.

And yet, regardless of the notable lack of hard evidence presented at the trial by the prosecution, and a divergence of opinion among members of the public regarding Dai Morris' guilt, the fact remains that he was convicted of the murders by the unanimous decision of a jury of his peers – a randomly selected group, comprising eleven ordinary citizens, sworn to do their duty – upon hearing all the evidence presented to them in court over a period of almost three months. If they were satisfied that Dai Morris was guilty of the crimes, why were so many other people uneasy about the verdict?

A close examination of witness statements shows that the story Morris eventually told about his relationship with Mandy Power had not been developed and refined throughout the investigation. It was virtually identical to the account he gave to Eric Williams on the day after the murders. Morris' story about his sexual relationship with Mandy Power and his explanation as to how the broken gold neck-chain came to be in her home at the time of killings never changed significantly from day one.

Many people felt that the decision of the jury was inconsistent with the evidence presented at the trial. There was something that didn't quite add up. There were just too many unanswered questions and the shadow of doubt continued to hang over the jury's decision like a dark cloud. These questions were, and still are, the subject of discussion in pubs and clubs throughout Wales, and remain unanswered to this day. Some of these questions are as follows:

1. What was contained in the forensic report delivered to Detective Superintendent Martyn Lloyd-Evans three weeks after the murders which he was so reluctant to make public, and which gave rise to speculation that the murderer was 'forensically aware'?

2. Had Dai Morris really wiped away all traces of his DNA and fingerprints at the crime scene, or was he simply never there?

3. Where was Detective Inspector Stuart Lewis between midnight and 3.00 a.m. on the morning of the murders? Why did he leave Kelvin Road so soon after arriving and to whom did he speak in his untraceable telephone call from Morriston Police Station?

4. Why did Detective Superintendent Martyn Lloyd-Evans fail to release Nicola Williams' e-fit image for more than a year? This image resembled South Wales Police officers Stephen Lewis and Stuart Lewis.

5. Why did South Wales Police arrange for Stephen Lewis to participate in the video identity parade when the man in Nicola Williams' e-fit image looked more like Stuart Lewis, who had no alibi for the time of the murders?

6. Why were South Wales Police so reluctant to act against the Lewises? It took them more than a year after the killings before the three were arrested, yet much of the evidence gathered in the first few weeks of the investigation appeared to implicate them in the crime.

7. What was in prosecuting counsel's advice, leading to the Lewises' release, which was never made available to the defence, despite protocols on disclosure that it should have been?

8. Why did the prosecution insist that Mandy Power was the first victim to be killed when the best forensic evidence suggested that she was not?

9. How did a forensic examination of the gold neck-chain reveal a microscopic speck of green paint but, allegedly, no DNA?

10. Were South Wales Police completely honest in the course of their investigation, or were they holding back certain facts?

These are just some of the questions that have been discussed for well over a decade and a half and have yet to be satisfactorily answered.

Chapter 25

If Dai Morris was indeed innocent – as he, his family and supporters claimed, and which the banners strung from bridges, and posters plastered on walls in Swansea declared – how did one of the best criminal justice systems in the world let him down? Why did it allow him to be convicted, and where had it all gone so terribly wrong?

There were three entirely separate factors that ensured a guilty verdict. Any one of them could have been fatal to Morris' case. That there were so many elements combined made his case, in my view, unwinnable from the start.

The conflict of interest

David Hutchinson should not have acted as Dai Morris' solicitor. Not only had Hutchinson acted for the Lewis twins for several months while South Wales Police investigated them in connection with the crimes, but he continued to represent the brothers in their civil claims against South Wales Police *after* their criminal cases were dropped and at a time when he was acting for Dai Morris.

To make matters worse, Hutchinson effectively tied the hands of defence QC Peter Rouch, by agreeing with the Lewis brothers that, in return for their allowing him to represent Morris, the defence would make no direct attack upon them by suggesting they had been involved in the murders.

Since Hutchinson represented Morris from the time of his arrest, and Morris claimed that the Lewises were responsible for the murders, Hutchinson had a clear conflict of interest, which made it impossible for him to do his best for two parties with opposing interests.

The South Wales Police investigation

Morris was as good as convicted from the moment Police Constable Deborah Powell told the murder investigation team Eric Williams' story about Morris having sex with Mandy Power just before the murders and leaving behind his gold neck-chain.

Whether guilty of the murders or not, Morris was the ideal person to take the blame. He had a long criminal record, some of it for violence. He was despised by neighbours and villagers in the small, close-knit community where he lived. These were some of the very people who would testify against him at his trial. The neck-chain found at the crime scene connected him to the murders and, best of all as far as South Wales Police were concerned, he had no alibi for the time of the attacks. He was the perfect fall guy. All South Wales Police had to do was to come up with enough evidence linking him to the crime to be sure of a conviction.

But there was no other evidence. Forensic experts who carried out a detailed investigation in the house could find no DNA or fingerprints belonging to Dai Morris. Neither could they find any trace of the victims' blood at his flat, or in any other property he used. The unlikely suggestion that he had destroyed all trace of his DNA and fingerprints became a legend. The bloody handprint found on the downstairs carpet near the television in 9 Kelvin Road did not match Morris' handprint: two leading expert witnesses called by the defence said it could not have been made by him.

Against this negative background, the police were forced to rely on other tactics, including character assassination and circumstantial evidence, in order to convict Dai Morris.

During the hunt for evidence to convict him, South Wales Police detectives searched for evidence to fit the crime, rather than letting the evidence lead them to the criminal. In the past, the force was widely condemned for this illegal and unethical practice which had led directly to numerous cases of wrongful imprisonment. Where evidence did not fit in these cases, detectives made it fit. Where there was no evidence, they fabricated evidence. Where witnesses gave testimony which did not suit the prosecution case, they persuaded or intimidated the witness into changing their evidence, or into admitting that they had been mistaken. In some cases, they encouraged them not to attend court at all. Certain witnesses were badgered into giving false evidence, while other witnesses were almost certainly bribed; all this with the sole aim of securing a conviction.

One such witness was Nicola Williams, who should have been given the opportunity much earlier to positively identify the man she had seen on the night of the murders near Kelvin Road. But South Wales Police did not appear to want their police officers Stephen Lewis or Stuart Lewis exposed to the risk of a formal identification. Detectives visited Nicola Williams and pleaded with her to change her testimony, begging her to make a new statement in which she would admit that she had been mistaken in her identification. This she refused to do.

When this approach failed, the job of persuading Nicola Williams that she was mistaken was handed over to the prosecution team. In court, she stuck doggedly to her story that Sergeant Stephen Lewis was the man she had seen. The trial judge, Mr Justice Butterfield, reminded jurors that Sergeant Lewis had an alibi for the night of the murders. 'He was in bed with his wife,' he said. This comment reduced the value of Nicola Williams' evidence to zero. Nicola Williams was never given the opportunity of identifying Stuart Lewis who had no alibi for the time of the murders.

In the case of taxi drivers Carol Ann Isaac and Beverley Lewis, the police adopted a harder line. When the two women persisted in their claims that they had seen and spoken to Alison Lewis in the home of Christine Williams, Mandy Power's next-door neighbour, early on the morning of the fire, Alison Lewis denied this meeting had taken place. Carol Ann Isaac's and Beverley Lewis' claims were corroborated by two other witnesses, Timothy and Manon Cherry, who testified that they too had seen Alison Lewis in Kelvin Road early on that morning. The two taxi drivers were arrested and threatened with the charge of perverting the course of justice. When interviewed for this book, Isaac told the author: 'I know what I saw. I had no reason to lie.'

Others witnesses were induced into giving incriminating statements. 'Mr B', who shared a cell with Dai Morris while Morris was awaiting trial, may have had his sentence reduced by giving detectives a statement testifying to Morris' violent character and alarming practice of carrying around with him in his car an iron bar which he kept 'in case of trouble'.

Drug dealer Terrence Williams, who testified that Morris took large quantities of speed on three consecutive days before the murders, gave investigating detectives three different statements before they were satisfied that he had finally 'got it right'.

And Janice Williams, Morris' next door neighbour with a score to settle, gave several conflicting statements, but only those which demonstrated Morris' supposed hostility towards the victim, Mandy Power, were given in court.

The prosecution case

The prosecution team's case was based on two main premises: the first was that Dai Morris had never had a sexual relationship with Mandy Power; the second was that he murdered Mandy Power because she refused to have sex with him. Then he murdered Doris Dawson and Mandy's daughters, Katie and Emily, because they were witnesses to his crime.

Establishing that Dai Morris had *not* had an affair with Mandy Power was crucially important to the prosecution case. If Morris had had an affair with Mandy Power, there could have been a perfectly innocent explanation for his gold neck-chain being found in the house. It was essential for the prosecution to demolish Morris' claims of an affair with Mandy Power, to the satisfaction of the jury. Despite all the evidence that Morris *was* having an affair with Power, the prosecution managed to persuade the jury that he was not.

The second leg of the prosecution's argument was that Mandy Power was the first of the four victims to be killed because she refused to have sex with him. It was essential that the jury believed that this was how the crime had unfolded. Claire Galbraith, the forensic scientist appointed by the government to investigate the crime, spent weeks examining the evidence, including the murder weapon. In her evidence to the court, she said that Doris Dawson was the first to be killed. Galbraith's testimony was of great importance because it meant that the prosecution's theory that Dai Morris had killed Mandy Power because she refused to have sex with him, must almost certainly have been wrong.

And then there was the matter of direct evidence in the form of DNA which belonged to Alison Lewis. This was discovered on one of Mandy Power's thighs and also on her pink vibrator. According to the evidence given by several witnesses, including Alison Lewis herself, the DNA would *not* have been on Mandy Power's body if she had showered the day before she was killed. A forensic study commissioned by *The Observer* newspaper some time after the trial highlighted a possible inconsistency in Alison Lewis' evidence. In his article on Sunday, 23 November 2003, journalist David Rose wrote:

> She [Alison Lewis] told the court she had not seen Power on the night of the murders, although they had sex early the previous morning.
>
> Yet samples taken from Mandy Power's inner thighs found traces of Alison's DNA, suggesting they might have had a more recent [sexual] contact. Several witnesses also said Mandy, who had the skin complaint psoriasis, bathed often, and a relative who saw her the evening before she died said she was freshly showered. The prosecution agreed that washing would have removed Alison's DNA, but explained its presence by the fact that a vibrator was found inside her [Mandy's] body. Alison Lewis claimed that she had used this particular vibrator herself just once, six months earlier. The prosecution said the remains of Alison's dried bodily fluids might have 'flaked off' the vibrator and stuck to Mandy.
>
> An analysis carried out by the Manchester-based forensic science consultancy Hayward Associates confirmed that Alison Lewis' DNA could not have stayed on the vibrator for six months if it had been washed, or if Power had repeatedly used the vibrator in the meantime.
>
> So did Power use the vibrator regularly? The only evidence comes from Lewis' own testimony. She told the court that Mandy frequently said she was using it as they talked on the phone. Alison Lewis told *The Observer*: 'I never actually saw her using it. She only ever told me she was using it on the phone. I don't know if she actually was.

Another issue involved the prosecution's claim that 'neither the police nor the defence had been able to prove that she [Alison

Lewis] lied about a single thing.' This was not correct. The defence team had actually managed to show several inconsistencies in Alison Lewis' testimony, including her denial that she was in Kelvin Road early on the morning of the murders. Four independent witnesses contradicted Lewis' evidence on this crucial point.

At the start of the trial Mr Patrick Harrington apologised to the Lewises for having the 'finger of suspicion' pointed at them and expressed his regret that they were suspected of involvement in the first place. 'Quite simply,' he said, 'we were looking at the wrong people.'

But there had been sufficient evidence to arrest the Lewises on suspicion of their involvement in the murders, if not enough evidence to charge them.

Moreover, Stuart Lewis was charged with serious disciplinary offences. These had been dropped by the time of the trial, but he did not have the exemplary record that was claimed for him in court. The Lewises were presented to the jury as 'clean' characters when they were nothing of the sort. This left the jury with just one possible candidate for the murders – a man with a history of violence, who had no alibi for the time of the crime, and whose broken gold neck-chain was found at the scene – David George Morris.

Part III

The 2006 trial of David George (Dai) Morris
at Newport Crown Court

Chapter 26

Even before they left the courtroom on Friday, 28 June 2002, the Morris family was already planning an appeal. They shouted their intention to the throng of press and TV news reporters gathered below the steps of the court, anxious to record their reactions to the sensational verdict. In his small basement cell, Morris numbly awaited the arrival of his legal team. It did not take him long to figure out that David Hutchinson was responsible for his conviction. And South Wales Police had chalked up another miscarriage of justice.

Later that same afternoon Morris was taken to H.M. Prison Wakefield in Yorkshire, the largest maximum security prison in Western Europe. Within a week David Hutchinson had been ignominiously fired as Morris' solicitor. Danny Simpson, a high-profile Yorkshire solicitor, was then instructed to act for Morris and his files were transferred from Swansea to Simpson's law practice in Sheffield. He, together with leading criminal barrister Courtenay Griffiths QC, spent several months reviewing Morris' case. They discovered serious failings on the part of David Hutchinson, and decided there were sufficient grounds to lodge an appeal against Morris' conviction.

But the wheels of justice grind slowly and, even at that stage, it would take many months for Morris' appeal to be heard. During this time, Simpson and his legal team were obliged to investigate in minute detail the huge, almost overwhelming, mountain of evidence that had accumulated in the lead-up to the trial.

While Simpson and his team were preparing the case for hearing, the relentless campaign by the Morris family, led by Dai Morris' sister Debra Thomas, continued. An independent investigation carried out by BBC's *Panorama* resulted in a documentary called *Fair Cops* being broadcast on national television on 21 October 2003. The programme declared: 'For

South Wales Police this was the murder from hell – not just because one of their own officers was a suspect, but because they were under intense pressure to get this case right after a series of miscarriages of justice going right back to the 1980s. Innocent people had spent years in jail while killers walked free.' A trailer for the programme said: 'In the summer of last year, David Morris, a labourer with a criminal record for drunkenness and violence, was jailed for life for the Clydach murders. But there was no forensic evidence linking him to the crime, and his family protest that this is the latest in a long line of miscarriages of justice in South Wales.'

Panorama accused South Wales Police of failing to investigate the case properly. Researchers discovered similarities between Morris' case and earlier miscarriages of justice, which, according to the documentary, carried 'disturbing echoes of past wrongdoing by South Wales Police'. The BBC's inquiry also uncovered a number of serious failures on the part of the police, including vital witness statements that had not been acted upon.

Programme researchers discovered that in a pre-trial hearing, the trial judge had been shown a photomontage of Nicola Williams' e-fit picture, with a photograph of Stephen Lewis next to it. But forensics expert Ashley Windsor, who was asked by *Panorama* to examine the two images, said that the photograph of Stephen Lewis was distorted. He remarked: 'It's very significant because the faces look completely different and I know this one [the photograph of Stephen Lewis] is not a true representation of how the person looked.'

Once again, the spectre of past miscarriages of justice involving wrongdoing by South Wales Police reared its head, since they appeared to have manipulated the evidence yet again to swing the trial in favour of the prosecution.

Solicitor Danny Simpson based Morris' appeal on two grounds: first, that he did not get a fair trial; second, that his conviction was unsafe. Issues were raised supporting the Morris family's view that David Hutchinson had contravened Law Society rules on conflict of interest. Furthermore, he had acted in a way that was detrimental to Morris' best interests. Hutchinson had represented two parties: the Lewis twins and Dai Morris. Morris had claimed from the outset that the Lewises were responsible for the murders. Hutchinson would not, and could not, do his best for both parties given their diametrically opposed positions; it was a situation he should have avoided by ceasing to act for one or even for both parties.

The appeal hearing at Cardiff Court of Appeal began on Monday, 14 February 2005. By now, Courtenay Griffiths QC had been replaced by Michael Mansfield QC, one of the country's leading barristers. Mr Mansfield had been involved in a number of prominent cases. These included his representation of the families of two victims shot dead in the Bloody Sunday incident in Derry in 1972, those wrongfully convicted of the IRA's Guildford and Birmingham pub bombings, and Mohamed Al Fayed in the inquest of Diana, Princess of Wales.

During hearings in February and April, which were attended by members of the extended Power family and members of Dai Morris's family, the three appeal court judges, headed by Lord Justice Pill, heard arguments from Michael Mansfield QC and from Patrick Harrington QC.

Michael Mansfield's argument concerned Morris' solicitor David Hutchinson's failure to properly represent Morris. The grounds of appeal claimed that Hutchinson's connection with Stephen Lewis affected the fairness of the trial and, therefore, the safety of the conviction; in addition, Hutchinson had failed to present evidence that would have been favourable to Morris' case. Mansfield told the court that it was inexplicable why Stuart Lewis did not give evidence at the 2002 murder trial. He said it may have been because prosecuting counsel did not wish to call him. If he had, Lewis' disciplinary report would have to be shown to the court. This would have disclosed serious disciplinary proceedings against Stuart Lewis. Hutchinson should have called Lewis to give evidence and disclose the disciplinary report to the court, but he failed to do so.

David Hutchinson denied the conflict of interest allegation, stating that he was careful to ensure that Morris was happy that he continue acting for him, even though he had already represented the Lewis brothers. He had also checked his position with the Law Society's ethics department. By the time Morris was charged, Hutchinson said he had stopped acting for the Lewises.

This claim was untrue.

Trainee solicitor Gail Evans, who worked for Hutchinson, gave a sworn statement in which she said that David Hutchinson continued to accept telephone calls from the Lewises, and entertained them in his offices long after his association with Dai Morris began. Peter Rouch QC also denied that there was a conflict of interest. He said Hutchinson had made all the evidence available to the jury.

Patrick Harrington opposed the application to appeal the case, claiming that 'Morris' convictions were safe'. He said: '[The jury] had the advantage of a comprehensive and utterly fair summing-up and they were given every assistance in defence counsel's speech.'

Rejecting the arguments of QCs Peter Rouch and Patrick Harrington, the three judges accepted Michael Mansfield's contention finding in favour of Dai Morris. They agreed that he had not had a fair trial because of a conflict of interest involving one of his legal team. As Lord Justice Pill declared his finding, a delighted Dai Morris mouthed a silent 'Yes'. Morris' convictions from 2002 were then quashed, or set aside as if it had never existed. A second trial was ordered to take place, the arraignment (plea) to be heard within two months. In October of that year, a hearing date was to be scheduled in Newport Crown Court. Morris was further remanded in custody pending the new trial.

Concluding, Lord Justice Pill awarded the prosecution its costs in the Swansea Crown Court trial and those in the Appeal Court hearing against David Hutchinson personally. As the announcement was made and the enormity of the likely amount involved dawned, Hutchinson's mouth dropped open and his face drained of colour. The costs far exceeded one million pounds; a sum way beyond his means. The forewarnings of the two Swansea lawyers in Bristol four years earlier had finally become a reality and, by ignoring them, it had cost Hutchinson his career.

This ruling provided the Morris family with the opportunity to right the wrongs of the past, to put forward a proper defence in the next trial, and to challenge and destroy the prosecution case.

Finally, the Morris family had an opportunity to engage lawyers with no hidden agenda who would be expected to fight tooth and nail for the truth, for justice, and above all, for freedom for David Morris.

While it was Round 3 to the defence, the family were guarded in their optimism. Debra Thomas, for one, had little faith in a judicial system that had already put her brother away for more than four years, and she had no faith in South Wales Police, whom, she believed, would do whatever it took to ensure that he stayed behind bars.

Chapter 27

In October 2005, a date was set for the new trial of David George Morris in Newport Crown Court. Scheduled to start in April 2006, it was expected to last for forty days. Mr Mansfield was unable to represent Dai Morris because he was to represent a plaintiff at a hearing in the European Court of Human Rights in The Hague, and another barrister, Gareth Rees QC, was instructed instead.

Patrick Harrington QC, on the other hand, was available, and so the brief for the prosecution was delivered to him. Mr Harrington not only had a keen understanding of the many complex issues involved, he also knew the weak points in the prosecution's case which would need to be shored up, and the strong points in the defence case that would have to be countered and defeated. Harrington had the advantage of knowing what both prosecution and defence witnesses would say in the witness box, and, significantly, the further evidence required to make his case watertight. By the time the trial started in April 2006, no one was better prepared than Patrick Harrington QC, and no one was more confident of winning.

Just three years earlier, at the age of forty-six, Welsh junior barrister Gareth Rees had become a QC. Most of his career at the bar had been spent defending fraud and corruption cases, financial and commercial crime. Mr Rees is today considered to be one of the leading lawyers in the United Kingdom, but in 2006 he accepted the legally aided brief for the defence of Dai Morris in what would be his first murder trial.

Mr Harrington had once described the case as having a 'unique and complex background'. Not only was it complicated and confusing; the logistics were simply staggering, with the legal teams on both sides expected to wade through 4,596 witness statements, 1,547 messages received from members of the public at the police incident room, and 15 million words of testimony and other evidence contained in the 300-plus lever arch files. It was clearly a huge amount of information to take in and a very difficult case with which to come to grips.*

In order to help them make their case even more forcefully than they had at Swansea Crown Court in 2002, the prosecution team may have considered that they needed additional evidence to reinforce their case and, this time, more prosecution-friendly witnesses.

South Wales Police detectives visited several witnesses who had given evidence in the first Crown Court trial. They tried to persuade some of them to change their testimony in order to make their evidence more favourable to the prosecution. If they were unwilling to co-operate, or could not be persuaded, intimidated or bribed, it was suggested to them that they need not turn up at court.

One of these witnesses was Mrs Rosemary Jones, who lived opposite 9 Kelvin Road. In the first trial, she gave evidence that at the critical time she heard a diesel car pull up outside the house and drive off. She then heard the steps of 9 Kelvin Road being climbed and the front door handle turned. She saw lights come on inside the house and the silhouette of a person through the frosted pane of glass in the front door. She told the author that detectives had visited her and 'tried to put words in my mouth by saying that the person I saw was a different height to the person I actually saw', thus making it appear more likely to be Dai Morris. She refused to cooperate, telling the detectives that she was 'not prepared to lie'. Mrs Jones was not called upon by the prosecution to give evidence in the second trial.

A prisoner serving time with Dai Morris, now in Long Lartin Prison near Evesham in Worcestershire, told a disturbing story.

---

* Writing in an online forum, *The Justice Gap*, Brian Thornton said: 'The case is big – more than 300 lever arch files – and utterly complex. When it first arrived at Winchester University in December 2009, I was utterly defeated by the scale of it. The first few months were spent just trying to organise the files and the students. We made little or no impact in those early days and I felt completely out of my depth.' See: http://thejusticegap.com/2014/11/clydach-murders-five-years-working-hopeless-case/ Nb. By way of comparison, the English version of the King James Bible contains approximately 780,000 words. Therefore, the written evidence at this time was roughly equivalent to more than almost twenty bibles.

David Tucker said in a handwritten statement, dated 13 October 2006,★ that he was fighting to have his case reviewed, and his freedom depended on a statement being provided for him by a police officer, Detective Constable Jo Fletcher. Fletcher, he said, was evasive and dragging her feet about giving him her statement. Early in 2006 Tucker was called into a prison office where a police liaison officer offered him a deal: if Tucker gave South Wales Police detectives a statement that Dai Morris had confessed to the Clydach murders, the murder squad detectives would ensure that he got the statement he wanted from Fletcher. He then gave an outline of the statement they wanted Tucker to make.

Tucker's statement at this point reads as follows: 'I asked him why him and South Wales Murder Squad were going to all this trouble to get a jail cell confession. I also asked if the case was weak against Morris. He [the police liaison officer] looked grim when he replied to me. He said in a low voice "It was easier to convict Morris than two police officers." I said what are you on about. He said "South Wales Murder Squad spent over 18 months gathering evidence against a woman police officer and her partner, but Morris's name come up, due to a chain he had left behind at an earlier time than when the murders happened, so they used him as the fall guy to avoid a scandal in the police force." He then winked and said "Forget about Morris and what's what in the case, just do your part and you'll get your statement which will help you prove your innocence and get you back home."

Subsequently Tucker provided the required confession in a written statement to South Wales Police detectives in a tape-recorded and filmed interview at Worcester Police Station.

But Tucker had reservations about making the false statement and when asked at the end of the interview if he had anything else to add, he said he deliberately replied: 'I couldn't have done better myself,' or words to that effect.

Afterwards David Tucker was transferred to HM Prison Birmingham where he had second thoughts and told Principal Officer Jones of K-Wing to: 'Contact South Wales Murder Squad as I don't want any part of helping them to lock up a innocent man.'

★ See statement of David Tucker, page 256

He concluded his signed statement thus: 'I want this on record so David Morris is aware of how far the prison and police are prepared to go in keeping him in custody to avoid the scandal of two police officers being convicted for the murders, also the implications of the cover up and substantial amount of compensation police would have to pay Morris.'

It is assumed that South Wales Murder Squad got the message because David Tucker was never summoned to the Newport Crown Court as a witness for the prosecution, nor was his statement read out in court. It is not known if he ever received the exonerating statement he needed from Detective Constable Jo Fletcher and whether or not he gained his freedom.

On Thursday, 18 May 2006 the trial of David George Morris began at Newport Crown Court in a national blaze of publicity similar to that seen in the 2002 trial. Once again, the prosecution team was gathered under the leadership of veteran lawyer Mr Patrick Harrington QC. Mr Gareth Rees QC led the team for Morris' defence. Mr Patrick Harrington's seniority, experience in criminal trials and familiarity with the case gave him a major advantage over Mr Gareth Rees, his relatively junior and inexperienced murder trial opponent. The jury of six men and six women would sit through the same ordeal as their predecessors for three months.

The prosecution case was a virtual carbon copy of the first trial. One of the firemen called to give evidence in both trials described the second trial as 'a formality'. He felt the lawyers were only going through the motions and the outcome would inevitably be the same. In both his opening address to the jury and during the second trial itself, Patrick Harrington repeated the same account he had given at the first trial. 'Three generations of one family were brutally put to death, we say by the defendant, who exploded into an uncontrollable rage. This was likely to have been a spurned sexual advance. This was not merely a murder,' he added; 'this was a massacre.'

Harrington described Morris as a violent thug with a history of 'violence against women'. Once again, he repeated his story to the jury that the Lewises had been wrongly suspected of involvement in the murders which was very much regretted, describing the accusations as 'the false finger of suspicion'. The barrister talked about the gold neck-chain covered in blood which he declared 'may be the clinching piece of evidence in this case' and about the witnesses who had seen Morris wearing the chain 'in a public house a 14-minute walk away from Kelvin Road in the hours leading up to the killings'.

When questioned by detectives, Morris had lied repeatedly by denying that the chain was his. It was not until five days before the first trial started, when he was faced with irrefutable proof, that he accepted that the chain probably was his. 'That was a blatant lie which goes straight to the core of this case', Mr Harrington said.

It was all fine rhetoric designed to impress the jury, and it had an undeniable logic in that all the pieces of the jigsaw seemed to dovetail perfectly. But, looked at rather more closely, the pieces did not fit together at all. The prosecution's theory flew in the face of the forensic evidence: there was no substance to the suggestion that Morris attacked Mandy Power because she refused to have sex with him, or that he killed her first, and they had still not come up with a plausible motive for the crime.

This time, Morris' legal team was fresh; they had no hidden agenda or misplaced loyalties, and they were expected to expose the flaws in the prosecution case. The witnesses called, and the issues raised during the trial should have given the defence team the opportunity to create sufficient doubt in the minds of the jury for them to deliver a not guilty verdict.

Patrick Harrington led key prosecution witness Alison Lewis through her story. She told the court that Mandy Power 'had a personality you instantly liked'. Describing her sex life with Power, she said: 'If we met ten times, we would end up in bed on nine of those occasions.' The relationship was, she said, 'very intense'. When asked to describe her relationship with Power's children, Lewis appeared to become upset. She dabbed her eyes with a tissue and requested a break to compose herself. Resuming her testimony, she replied: 'I got on well with the children. They were lovely kids.'

Alison Lewis went on to describe her sporting background, her interest in martial arts, how and when she met Mandy Power and the manner in which their relationship had developed, quickly becoming sexual. She denied that she had killed Mandy Power and her family, repeating the familiar line: 'The only thing I am guilty of is not being there to protect her when she needed me.'

Lewis admitted that she had acted in a 'mean and spiteful way' towards her husband over the affair and had treated him with 'selfish contempt' by bringing Mandy Power back to the home she shared with him, for sex.

Under cross-examination, Alison Lewis told Gareth Rees: 'I'd have given my life to protect them and that's the truth.' She agreed she could be jealous but said it was 'no more than anyone else in a relationship'.

When asked if she had been to Ms Power's house in Kelvin Road, Clydach, in the early hours of Sunday, 27 June 1999, Lewis seemed to break down as she denied the allegation, saying her only guilt was that while Mandy Power and her family were fighting for their lives, she was in bed asleep with her husband. She added that she was tired of being made a 'scapegoat for the murders'. However, four witnesses testified that they saw Alison Lewis in Kelvin Road during the early hours of the morning of 27 June 1999 and their evidence contradicted the evidence Lewis had given from the witness box.

Kimberley Wilson, a friend of both Alison Lewis and Mandy Power, was in 9 Kelvin Road on Saturday morning, 26 June when Lewis and Power arrived back from an overnight stay in the Lewis family home. Wilson repeated that Lewis had flipped earlier that morning upon hearing of Mandy's telephone conversation with Howard Florence. And Alison Lewis had claimed to have taken a bath in 9 Kelvin Road on the Saturday morning. Whether or not this claim was true was never established.

The importance of this point was that no DNA was *reported* as having been found in the bath used by the murderer after the killings, to wash away blood. The scene of crimes investigator consulted by the author said that DNA should have been both present and detectable. But if Alison Lewis's DNA *had* been found in the bath, and if she had explained its presence to investigating detectives by saying she had taken a bath there on the Saturday morning, the police could not then use this evidence against her to suggest that it was she who had bathed after the killings.

Sharon Jameson, who was in the New Inn on the night before the murders, told the court that she had seen Morris that night standing at the bar wearing his gold neck-chain. No challenge was made by the defence about the fact that Jameson and her husband were known to dislike Morris.* Furthermore, it was well established that at no time that evening was Morris standing at the bar. Once again, the judge omitted to give the jury the essential Turnbull direction which he was required to do, warning them of the need to take special care in accepting this disputed identification evidence.

Other key witnesses, Philip Turner and David Thomas, two drinkers in the pub that night, also swore that they saw Morris wearing the gold neck-chain found at the murder scene. Turner's evidence was not challenged, even though it was well known that there was no love lost between the two men and, indeed, there was a history of conflict between them. Like many other residents living in the small mountain village, Turner, would have been glad to be rid of a neighbour he detested. David Thomas was a friend of Philip Turner who also hated Morris. But, as he demonstrated clearly in the earlier Swansea Crown Court trial, he would not have been able to see clearly the chain Morris was wearing that night, even with his glasses on.

Once again Michael Randerson repeated the evidence he had given at the first trial: that Morris was wearing his trademark gold neck-chain in the New Inn on the night before the murders. This, despite his admission to his girlfriend Fay Scott that he could not remember whether or not Morris was wearing his gold neck-chain that night. Scott had duly passed this information on to David Hutchinson's assistant, Gail Evans, and this evidence was now in the possession of Morris' defence team. Scott could have been called to rebut Randerson's damning testimony, but the defence, astonishingly, decided not to call her.

On Thursday, 6 July Morris appeared in the dock. Led through his story by Gareth Rees, Morris told the court how he had bumped into Mandy Power in Clydach village on the morning of Friday, 25 June and they had gone back to her house for sex.

* See statement of David Tucker, page 256

While Power was upstairs, Morris stayed in the kitchen fiddling with his gold neck-chain which he said he had broken two days before. When Power called him upstairs, he left the chain on a kitchen worktop.

After he left 9 Kelvin Road for his parents' home in Gendros, Morris realised that he had left behind his gold neck-chain, but by this point he was on the bus, and it was too late to go back and retrieve it. At his parents' home, he put on another chain that he owned – a smaller gold neck-chain with circular links – this was the chain he said he had worn in the New Inn on the night before the murders. He admitted that he had lied repeatedly about his ownership of the gold chain found at the crime scene because he did not want to implicate himself in the murders, and he especially did not want his partner, Mandy Jewell, to find out about his sexual relationship with Power. 'It would break her heart,' he added.

Oddly, Stuart Lewis was not called to give evidence in either trial and, to this day, he remains a shadowy figure in the murders, somehow involved in all key events, yet never questioned as a potential murder suspect. Michael Mansfield had already criticised David Hutchinson for not calling Stuart Lewis to give evidence, during the Appeal Court hearing in Cardiff, when he told the judges, 'it was inexplicable why Stuart Lewis did not give evidence at the 2002 murder trial.' Now it had happened again. Morris' new defence team could and perhaps should have called Stuart Lewis to give evidence about the disciplinary proceedings and his movements that night, but it was their decision not to do so. Another opportunity to get to the truth was lost.

Another important witness the defence decided not to challenge was Clydach bakery assistant Alison Sawyer. Sawyer was a work colleague of Mandy Jewell at the time of the murders. In Sawyer's evidence at the first trial, she said she could not recall anything significant that had happened on the morning of Friday, 25 June 1999. Now, seven years later, following a visit from South Wales Police detectives, her memory returned, and she told the court that she did, after all, recall receiving a telephone call on the Friday morning before the murders. She remembered clearly the time it was made; that it was she who had answered the phone; that the caller was Dai Morris and that he had asked to speak to Mandy Jewell. Remarkably, she even remembered the duration of the call – 15 minutes. The detectives produced a telephone statement for June 1999 which showed that a call had been made from Jewell's flat to the bakery on the Friday morning.

This evidence, they said, established that Dai Morris had been at home in Jewell's flat on Friday for the whole morning, which was when he had made the calls, and not at Mandy Power's home having sex with her, as he claimed. He could not, therefore, have left his gold chain in 9 Kelvin Road on that Friday morning.

Dai Morris' explanation was that on the Friday before the murders, Mandy Jewell went to work as usual in the Clydach bakery. Since he was then unemployed, he walked Jewell's daughter, Emma, to school. Then he returned to Clydach village intending to get his broken gold neck-chain repaired. On his way to the jewellers' shop, he met Mandy Power, who had been dropped off in the village by Alison Lewis. She took him back to 9 Kelvin Road for sex. Afterwards he left and caught the bus to his parents' home.

Meanwhile, Mandy Jewell left work early because she was feeling unwell, and returned to her flat. She decided not to return to work and rang her workplace, spoke to the bakery shop assistant, Alison Sawyer, and told her that she would not be returning to work that day. This was the telephone call Patrick Harrington claimed Dai Morris had made. Then Jewell rang Morris' parents' home in Gendros, spoke to his mother, Shirley, asking her if she knew where Morris was. Shirley said she did not know. When Morris arrived at his parents' home soon afterwards, Shirley told him about the telephone call she had received from Mandy Jewell. Morris immediately rang Jewell to tell her where he was.

All these telephone calls were logged on various telephone statements and they fully supported Morris' version of events. This, however, was not evidence that suited the detectives' purposes. While the entry on the telephone statement showing the call from the flat to the bakery was clearly shown, the other telephone call to Morris' parents' home and the call from there to Jewell's flat were redacted. This telephone statement, deliberately altered by detectives, was used by the prosecution to show that Dai Morris' version of events was untrue.

By failing to counter this critical claim by the prosecution, the defence allowed the altered telephone record to stand instead of explaining how, instead, it supported Morris' case. Neither was the evidence given by Alison Sawyer challenged. Once again a story of dreadful fiction became accepted fact.

In his summing-up at the 2002 trial, Mr Justice Butterfield told the jury that if they thought Morris was lying when he said he [Morris] and Power were having a relationship, this would be important in reaching their verdict. The guilty verdict delivered soon after this direction was given clearly showed that the jury preferred the prosecution's suggestion that there was no sexual relationship between Mandy Power and Dai Morris.

In 2003, the year following the Swansea Crown Court trial, new evidence came to light which strongly suggested that Morris and Power were indeed having a sexual relationship. While the prosecution vigorously claimed that Mandy Power had no contact with Dai Morris, her telephone statements showed that on Valentine's Day in 1999 she rang him repeatedly. Furthermore, he was not at that time in the flat he shared with Mandy Jewell, but was staying on his own in his room in Llangyfelach Road.

The defence could have used this telephone record as evidence to prove that an intimate relationship existed between Mandy Power and Dai Morris. But they decided not to produce it, even though its evidential value was enormous and would have strengthened the defence case immeasurably. Debra Thomas could have been called to give evidence regarding her knowledge of the sexual relationship between her brother and Mandy Power. But, regrettably, the defence did not call her to give this crucial evidence.

Moreover, almost the first words spoken to Morris by his mother Shirley after his arrest were: 'But we all knew you were having an affair with her.' To which he had replied, 'They [the police] are not supposed to know that.' All this evidence, including Morris' knowledge of Mandy Power's shyness in the bedroom, demonstrated that he and Mandy Power certainly were involved in an ongoing sexual relationship.

This evidence in Morris' favour was contained somewhere in the hundreds of lever arch files, but it was never produced to the court. Perhaps the defence never found it, or maybe they did but failed to recognise its probative value. Whatever the truth of the matter, it was never brought to the attention of the court, and, as a consequence, the jury was not aware of the possibility that Dai Morris and Mandy Power could have been sexually involved, and they could make their decision only on the basis that they were not.

When I first began conducting research into the Clydach murders, I was hampered by the lack of accessible documentary material to work from. The original 2002 court transcripts had, amazingly, been destroyed; South Wales Police had refused point-blank to deal with my enquiries; legal teams on both sides were reluctant to become involved or to answer my questions, and so I was left with newspaper reports, transcripts of radio and TV broadcasts, journalists' trial notes, and mostly fading memories of family members, friends and neighbours with which to reconstruct this verifiable account.

While researching the retrial, I found a BBC News report dated 6 June 2006 on the internet which truly astonished me. It concerned a brief statement given by Stephen Lewis in his court testimony, the day after his wife Alison gave hers. It demonstrated clearly that Alison Lewis had misled the police in her statements and had perjured herself from the witness box.[*]

In the first trial in 2002, four witnesses said they had seen Alison Lewis in 7 Kelvin Road, and in Kelvin Road itself, between 6.00 and 6.45 a.m. on the morning of the murders.

Alison Lewis denied their accounts and swore that the first time she had gone there on that day was at around 9.00 a.m. when she was accompanied by her husband. Referring to their testimony, prosecuting counsel asserted that the witnesses were lying or mistaken. In a comment during his summing-up, the prosecution claimed the defence was 'unable to prove that Alison Lewis had lied about a single thing'. Now, in the 2006

[*] http://news.bbc.co.uk/2/hi/uk_news/wales/5053088.stm

retrial, Alison Lewis' claim was exposed for the untruth it was, and of all people, by her own husband. The following account recaps part of the evidence given by Stephen Lewis at Newport Crown Court on Tuesday, 6 June 2006.

Stephen Lewis knew Mandy Power because of her friendship with his then wife Alison. He said he went to bed early on the night of 26 June, because he had to be up for his early shift. He told the court that he slept all night, waking at 5.00 a.m. the next morning and left the house for Neath Police Station at 5.18 a.m. When he arrived at the police station at around 6.00 a.m. he telephoned a work colleague who asked him if he had heard about the fire.

A tape was played to the jury of that telephone conversation, which ran as follows:

> Colleague (C): 'Have you heard about the fire?'
> Stephen Lewis (SL): 'No.'
> C: 'Four dead.'
> SL: 'Where?'
> C: 'Kelvin Road.'
> SL: 'What address?'
> C: 'Number nine.'
> SL: 'What name [sic] is it?'
> C: 'It was 4.30 a.m. in the morning.'
> SL: 'I know those people. They are friends of ours. Never. Mandy. Jesus, they were at a barbeque at ours on Friday night. And the two girls. Oh my God. You are joking. She's been having hassle with an ex-boyfriend.'

Lewis told the court: 'I was stunned. Initially, I just sat in the office in total disbelief and the next few minutes were just a blur.'

But it was what Lewis told the court next that was so astonishing. As he was about to leave the police station to go home to his wife, he received a telephone call from her. He said: '*She told me she was at the scene. I told her to go home.*' He then left the police station and returned home. When he arrived, his wife was already there. Lewis described her as 'hysterical, she was beside herself with grief'. It was at around 9.00 a.m. that they went to Kelvin Road together.

This was an astonishing revelation. It vindicated the four witnesses – Carol Ann Isaac, Beverley Lewis and Timothy and Manon Cherry – who all claimed to have seen Alison Lewis in Kelvin Road during the early hours of the morning at a time when she denied being there. It gave further credibility to the claims of Isaac, Lewis, Manon Cherry and Gary Beynon that Alison Lewis had appeared to be freshly showered and smelling strongly of soap when they met her.

According to the prosecution, Timothy and Manon Cherry, Carol Ann Isaac and Beverley Lewis were all 'mistaken' in the accounts they gave of seeing Alison Lewis in Kelvin Road on that early Sunday morning. But now there could be no doubt: Alison's own husband Stephen had confirmed that she was in Kelvin Road early on the morning of the murders.

Chapter 28

This confirmation from Stephen Lewis of his wife's where-abouts early on Sunday, 27 June 1999 suggested that Alison Lewis had perjured herself in the witness box, thereby reducing her credibility as a key prosecution witness. It also potentially posed a problem for the prosecution if it intended to assert that she was trustworthy in a later address to the jury. Alison Lewis clearly had some serious questions to answer, even if her husband's testimony did not amount to evidence that she was involved in the murders.

But the prosecution case moved quickly on, Mr Harrington asking Lewis if he knew about his wife's affair with Mandy Power, whether he had left his bed on the night of the murders, and so on.

Stephen Lewis' disclosure, which indicated inconsistencies in Alison Lewis' police statements and the testimony she gave in court, did not succeed in generating a response from the defence either. Instead of recalling Alison Lewis to the witness box and cross-examining her even more closely about her movements that night, they did not do so. It not only became yet another missed opportunity to blow a very large hole in the prosecution case, it meant that a chance to question Alison Lewis more closely on her movements on that fateful night were lost for good.

And how could the jury, and perhaps even the judge, miss such a vital point, which could so easily have changed the outcome of the trial? Perhaps it was the dismissive way in which the prosecution dealt with the admission, making it seem unimportant, whereas in fact it was crucial, and vital to the defence case.

Once again, Dai Morris' fate lay in the hands of a jury. This time, his legal team had no conflict of interest, nor private agreement with any former suspects, and all the evidence pointing towards his lack of guilt was available to the defence. There was every reason to believe he would receive a fair trial, but yet again he did not.

Part of the problem was that a second investigation – which had commenced when the original conviction was quashed in 2005 – produced fewer prosecution witnesses and no more hard evidence than had been available for the first trial in 2002. Altered telephone records, which the prosecution claimed had 'blown apart' Dai Morris' claim to have been in Mandy Power's home on the morning before the murders, did nothing of the sort. In fact, they went some way towards establishing that Dai Morris could have been telling the truth.

The defence team never managed to convince the jury that Dai Morris had told the same story – conceivably a truthful account – from day one. Unfortunately for Morris, he had made his admission as to how his gold neck-chain ended up in Mandy Power's house to his cousin Eric Williams, and not to the police. Moreover, the lies Dai Morris told time and again were not made to cover up the murders, but to prevent his partner Mandy Jewell from finding out about his sexual relationship with her close friend Mandy Power.

The prosecution's claim regarding the order of deaths, which contradicted the forensic evidence of expert witness Claire Galbraith, remained effectively unchallenged. This left the jury with the impression that the prosecution's version of events must have been true, when the forensic evidence showed that it was not.

In summing up the prosecution case on Monday, 7 August, Patrick Harrington told the jury that these were the worst murders ever seen in Wales. He described the killings as the 'worst type of massacre' and 'carnage'. Morris was a 'violent, lying thug' who had killed the family. He had bludgeoned the family to death with an iron pole, inflicting more than 80 blows. He said the case against Morris rested on a gold neck-chain found at the murder scene covered in Mandy Power's blood, that Morris' account of how it got there was a lie, and it was this lie that proved his guilt.

Mr Harrington said Morris had lied about the chain belonging to him until days before his original trial in 2002, and that he tailored his version of events to fit the evidence against him. Morris had earlier told the court that he had left his chain at the house the day before the murder when he had had sex with Mandy Power. But telephone records from Morris' flat showed that he was there, Patrick Harrington confidently asserted: 'His final lying account of what had happened had been blown apart.'

Harrington reminded the jury that on the evening before the murders, Morris had been drinking heavily in a pub some 15 minutes from Kelvin Road. He had also taken amphetamines, the combination of which had made him violent. Some witnesses, he said, had seen him wearing a gold chain similar to the one found at the murder scene, while another said he described Mandy Power as 'evil'. Morris, he said, had gone to the home of Mandy Power to find out more about his girlfriend Mandy Jewell's affairs after a pub customer had called Jewell a 'slapper'. When she did not give him the information he wanted, he attacked her, then turned on her mother Doris and Katie and Emily – 'total innocents who were put to death', Harrington told the jury. He said: 'The person who did that was not normal – was someone with a reactive temper which could not be kept under control.'

Concluding, Mr Harrington told the court: 'Everyone who works in the court system can become immune to man's inhumanity to man.' Then, turning to the jury, he added: 'No one involved in this case will ever forget it. Neither will you.'

On Tuesday, 8 August, Gareth Rees began his summing-up for the defence. He told the jury that they must 'forget the theatre and drama of the courtroom and concentrate on the evidence'. Rees said that David Morris had been turned into a figure of hate – a 'drug-crazed monster' capable of beating to death three generations of the same family. He reminded the jury that the only piece of evidence which linked the defendant to the murder scene was his gold chain found at the scene covered in blood. This, he told the jury, had a perfectly innocent explanation. Morris had left the chain at the house two days before the killings when he had gone to the house to have sex with Mandy Power.

Mr Rees said that the prosecution had failed to prove its case against the defendant and urged the jury members to be objective when considering their verdict. As part of his summing-up,

Rees reminded the jury that witnesses had said that Stephen Lewis knew about his wife's affair, about Stuart Lewis' peculiar behaviour in abandoning the crime scene, and that Morris had no motive for committing the crime.

Mr Rees said there were many questions surrounding Mandy Power's lover Alison Lewis, who at one stage was arrested in connection with the murders, along with her husband Stephen and brother-in-law Stuart. He told the jury they would 'have to tackle head-on Alison Lewis' fragile mental state and her obsessive jealousy.' He reminded them about the witnesses who said that Alison Lewis' husband Stephen knew about her affair with Mandy Power and urged them to remember the 'bizarre behaviour of Stuart Lewis when he was called to the murder scene and then inexplicably left very quickly. Morris,' said Mr Rees, 'had no possible motive for the murders.' He had been drinking that night but everything seemed normal. 'It was nonsense,' he said, 'for the prosecution to suggest otherwise.'

Turning to the jury, he said: 'How on earth can you be sure it was David Morris and exclude the real possibilities that the Lewises or other people are responsible?' Concluding, he said: 'If you are not sure, then the only proper verdict is one of not guilty.'

Thursday, 10 August saw Mr Justice McKinnon begin his summing-up for the jury. It would last for two days. He told them: 'These were truly terrible crimes that had been committed. Three generations of the same family had been savagely battered to death in their own home. You'd need hearts of stone not to be affected by the photographs of the injuries.' The judge described in detail the horrific injuries sustained by each of the victims: 'Ms Power, her two daughters Katie and Emily had been battered repeatedly with a fibreglass pole – their skulls had effectively been smashed.' He then added, almost apologetically: 'Words cannot convey the severity of the injuries inflicted upon them.'

Referring to the forensic evidence, which showed that the killer had tried to strangle Mandy Power, he said: 'Was that the first act of violence? Was it then that one of her children got the pole in an attempt to save the life of their mother, a pole they used to play with, but a pole that was used to kill them all?' But the forensic evidence clearly showed that the 80-year-old invalid, Doris Dawson, was the first person to be killed, *not* Mandy Power. Furthermore, Alison Lewis had clearly lied about being in Kelvin Road soon after the murders; she had smelled of soap and her hair was wet. If the villagers of Clydach had been confused by all the conflicting evidence put forward in the first trial, what were they to make of it now? And, more importantly, what was the jury to make of it? The suggestion that Mandy Power was killed first dovetailed with the prosecution's case perfectly, but the forensic evidence proved otherwise.

The judge reminded the jurors that the prosecution claimed that David Morris was responsible for the murders 'fuelled by drink and drugs ... he committed the worst kind of massacre and sought to destroy the evidence.' He reminded the jury that the defence had claimed that Dai Morris was elsewhere at the time the murders were committed, and that the defence had also pointed to the Lewises as having been responsible for the crime. Alison Lewis had been arrested on suspicion of murder, perhaps assisted by her husband Stephen, he said.

Yet again, there was no mention of Stuart Lewis, a man with no alibi, who looked more like Nicola Williams' e-fit image than his brother Stephen, and who was not where he said he was at the time of the murders.

'If the defendant was wearing the chain later found in Kelvin Road,' the judge said, 'he can't have left it there the day before…. The only inference, says the prosecution, is that he must have left it at the murder scene.' He told the jury: 'In the absence of an unknown intruder, you have seen the killer in that witness box – either David Morris, Alison Lewis or Stephen Lewis.'

By directing the jury in this way, the judge was not asking them to decide after consideration of all the evidence, if they believed beyond a reasonable doubt if Morris was guilty of the murders, but to *choose* between him and the Lewises.

In the minds of Dai Morris and his family, who had watched dismayed as the case for the defence fell apart before their eyes, there was never any doubt about the verdict the jury would bring in.

Exactly one week later, on Thursday, 17 August, the jury brought in a unanimous verdict of guilty. Dai Morris was again convicted of the Clydach murders. He was sentenced to life imprisonment, with a recommendation that he serve at least thirty years. The trial judge told him: 'You have shown no remorse. If ever there was a case for a whole life sentence, this is it. Life should be life and you should never be released.' And with the sounds of cheers from the victims' families ringing in his ears, Morris was led away to begin his sentence. It was Round 4 to the prosecution.

More than one hundred media reporters had gathered outside the Newport Crown Court, owing to the huge international interest the trial had generated. Standing on the steps of the court after the verdict was announced, members of Mandy Power's family raised their hands in the air, delighted at the outcome. Mandy's sister, Sandra Jones, happy now that she felt justice had been done, said: 'We've done them proud. They'll be looking down on us today. Nobody will ever know how much we've gone through. Hopefully, we can now go forward.'

The Power family supporters, celebrating their victory, called Morris 'a lunatic who doesn't deserve to walk the planet', while a family spokesman said: 'Once again, the verdict was the right one. David Morris will spend the rest of his life behind bars and we as a family will do everything in our power to make sure he never comes out. The last seven years has [*sic*] been a nightmare for us and have not been helped by the poster campaigns and petitions by Morris' family claiming him to be innocent. Two guilty verdicts say it all. Throughout this trial we have had to listen to lies about Mandy and hear her name being dragged through the mud.'

Speaking from the steps of the court, Alison Lewis, looking visibly delighted, declared: 'I'm very relieved obviously. This is the verdict I wanted. I feel that this second trial has at least vindicated me – but how many more juries have to find David Morris guilty before people realise that I had nothing to do with these murders and that this isn't a conspiracy by the Crown Prosecution Service, South Wales Police, or Mandy Power's family against one single man? This isn't about me, the South

Wales Police or the CPS,' she added. 'They have said they made a mistake and apologised to me. It is about the family now.'

Speaking on behalf of South Wales Police, Detective Inspector Chris Coutts said: 'Mrs Power's family has shown unbelievable strength and dignity. The community of Clydach has also felt the pain, but they have also shown spirit and support for my team.'

Debra Morris, shocked and disappointed by the verdict, said: 'We will fight this every step of the way. He has no chance in Wales, and he is up against the police.' Morris' father, Brian, agreed, saying: 'He will never get a fair trial in Wales.'

Witness Statement
CJ Act 1967, s9 MC act 1980,s MC Rules 1981, r70

Statement of:	Gail Evans
Age if under 21:	Over 21 (if over 21 insert "over 21")
Occupation:	Solicitor
Address:	10 Philips Parade, Swansea, SA1 4JL
Telephone:	01792 472180

This statement (consisting of 6 page/s each signed by me) is true to the best of my knowledge and belief and I make it known that, if it is tendered in evidence, I shall be liable to prosecution if I have wilfully stated anything I know to be false or do not believe to be true.

Dated the 29th day of July, 2004

Signature

I am the person named above and reside at the address given. I was part of the defence working on behalf of David Morris (DM) from 2nd June 2001, when I was introduced to him at HMP Swansea, until his committal to prison on 28th June 2002.

Throughout this time I was employed by Goldstones Solicitors, 9 – 10 Walter Road, Swansea. My senior supervising solicitor through out this case was David Hutchison.(DH).

DH was also the senior partner in the practice. At this time I was employed as a trainee solicitor.

I am aware that this case has now been referred to the appeals court and I offer the following information for that appeal.

Margaret Fay Scott (MFS)

Signed   Signature Witnessed By

Witness Statement
CJ Act 1967, s9 MC act 1980,s MC Rules 1981, r70
Continuation Sheet 2

During a natural break during the trial I returned early to my office, this was possibly a couple of days after Mike Renderson had given his evidence. When I got back to my office I received a telephone call from Margaret Fay Scott.

She had just read the newspapers, and particularly about the evidence that Mike Renderson had given.

She was adamant that his evidence was not correct. She recalled that after he had been interviewed by the police early on in the case, he had been asked about a chain that DM was supposed to have had on in the pub the night of the murders.

She informed me that his account was all lies because after he had been interviewed he had telephoned her to ask her whether or not DM was wearing a chain in the pub because he couldn't remember. She told him that she could not remember either.

I told her that I would have to refer it to DH. DH was in the office so I went straight to DH and told him of the telephone call I had just had with MFS.

DH told me to refer this information to the QC, Peter Rouch (PR), I was also told not to tell DM, or ring MFS back until I had spoken to PR.

I told PR the following morning whilst in the robing room of the Guild Hall Court, Swansea.

I never had any discussion with PR about whether this information should be passed to DM. From an evidential point of view PR explained to me why this evidence would not progress the case. This was because MR's evidence was helpful to the defence in the way that he had described the chain. This was consistent with DM's instructions to us. But I was made aware by DH that DM was not going to be told about this information and that it was not going to be used.

Signed _____ Signature Witnessed By _____

M48

Witness Statement
CJ Act 1967, s9 MC act 1980,s MC Rules 1981, r70
Continuation Sheet 3

David Hutchison (DH)

My employment with Goldstones commenced on the 17th July 2000. I was placed into the criminal department with DH as my supervising solicitor. However during and up until I was introduced to DM any difficulties I had I referred to Mr Gethin Humphries. My access to DH was limited during my first year, only troubling him with difficult legal issues. Once I was introduced to DM I spoke to DH on a daily basis some times three to four times a day. We used to have a conference every morning, discussing the morning mail in relation to DM, and what needed to be done that day. We would discuss at length all aspects of the case. DH would commence work each day at approximately 7.10 a.m. He would open the mail at 8.00 a.m. and we would start our discussions at 8.30 a.m or sooner.

All DH's clients are aware that the best time to speak to DH is before 9.30 a.m. and he takes many calls from clients from 8.30 a.m. up until 9.30 a.m. if he is in the office. He also takes his calls initially on speaker phone. Whoever is in DH's room at the time a call comes through, via reception is aware of who is calling. If DH does not want anyone in his room to listen to the call he picks up the handset and asks you to leave. On a number of occasions whilst working with DH on DM's case I was aware of him accepting calls from both Stuart and Steven Lewis. At the time that these calls were received I was always asked to leave the room and cannot comment on the content or length of these calls. These calls were received to my knowledge after I had been introduced to DM, this would be after the 2nd July 2001.

All incoming calls into the offices of Goldstones are logged into books kept at reception, these books in turn are kept for quite some time and should be in the office now.

Similarly all clients who attend the office are recorded into a book. There should be a record kept of when the Lewis brothers attended at the office.

I recall an incident during the preparation of DM's case when the Lewis brother's attended at the office. I do not recall the date. I was asked by DH to prepare certain papers for the brothers to collect. I recall that they wanted copies of their taped

Signed   Signature Witnessed By

AP49

Witness Statement
CJ Act 1967, s9 MC act 1980,s MC Rules 1981, r70
Continuation Sheet 4

interviews. DH was not in the office on this occasion. I met the brothers in Gethin Humphries (GH) room. The brothers are identical twins, and having never met them I was intrigued as to which brother was which. When I entered GH's room one of the brothers was sat in the window and was very pleasant saying good morning to me and thanking me for my assistance. The other brother kept his head to the floor and did not acknowledge me. They were with GH for some 30 minutes after I handed them their papers, after they left I had a conversation with GH and stated that it was probably s Stuart who was sat in the window and Steven was the miserable one, GH confirmed that this was correct, I said to GH 'maer eog yn ffoy', which translated means the guilty always run, but which meant in the context of our conversation that he was guilty because he could not face me.

I remember having a conversation with DM at the prison to this effect. This was in an attempt to cheer him up. I was not able to divulge any confidential information to DM. The conversation was an innocent one relating to DM that I had now met the brothers and that I thought that Steven Lewis looked guilty.

From memory this would have been when DM was in HMP Cardiff, between October and March (2001 – 2002), but I cannot be certain.

This is the only occasion that I met them. Generally I would be out of the office morning and afternoon visiting DM in prison.

During June, July and August of 2003, I encountered great difficulties with DH in the office these difficulties can be dealt with in greater detail if required but are relevant to an ongoing employment dispute that I have with DH. On the 8th September of 2003 I suffered a back injury, which meant that I was off work from the 8th until the 29th September. I returned to work on the 29th September and was called into DH's room in the morning at approximately 8.40 a.m. It was explained to me that I had been named in the grounds of appeal for DM. I did not see the grounds, I did not read them and was only made aware of their contents by DH.

Signed _____ Signature Witnessed By _____

Witness Statement
CJ Act 1967, s9 MC act 1980,s MC Rules 1981, r70
Continuation Sheet 5

I was asked by DH to specifically recall a conversation that I had with DM about the Lewis brothers, he was vague in the way that he phrased the question and initially I could not recall the conversation, after prompting I repeated the circumstances and subsequent conversation with DM in full as outlined above.

I should explain that I have always been apprehensive in my dealings with DH. He is a bit of a scary character and all staff are wary of him. Nobody would lie to him, and we were all fearful of his wrath. Initially I was scared that I had done something seriously wrong. When I realised to which conversation he was referring I fully outlined the events.

Mrs Catherine Stewart another partner in the firm was party to this conversation and I spoke to her subsequently about it.

I explained to DH that GH would be able to confirm what had happened. He advised me that GH had no recollection of the events.

He then said that I did not see the brothers in GH's room, I confirmed that I had, he stated again that I had not seen them in GH's room, I then said 'Dave on Richard's life they were in GH's room', he then told me that if I was asked I was to say that I had seen them in the reception area of the office. I did not reply.

I was left in no doubt that the only people who would reasonably be expected to ask me about these events would be DM's current defence team, and that as I had been named in the grounds of appeal, that this would be in the Court of Appeal itself. I was left in no doubt that the suggestion coming from DH was that I was to lie to the Court of Appeal.

I subsequently sought the counsel of Mrs Stewart, and again apologised if I had done anything wrong but again reiterated that the conversation with DM was an innocent one, she stated that she felt that I had been injudicious.

Following the events of that morning I was told that I was not fit to be in work and should return to my Doctor. He signed me off for another fortnight.

Signed _____ Signature Witnessed By _____

Witness Statement
CJ Act 1967, s9 MC act 1980,s MC Rules 1981, r70
Continuation Sheet 6

I did however make a note of this event in my diary. I was subsequently accused of losing files and other objects in the office and I have made notes as to these problems in my diary also.

I do recall that there were times that DM was dissatisfied with DH's handling of his case. He did speak to me about sacking DH, I never told DH about this. The reason for this is that I was intimidated by DH's manner in general. I was exceptionally wary of DH and of his response. What I would do is go back to DH and suggest that he go and see DM, I would outline, in general, DM's concerns. I do not recall the specific reasons behind this. I do recall a discussion about his Junior Counsel, DM had previously asked DH for the services of Huw Rees Davies as junior Counsel. This request had been denied.

I have made this statement as a result of being contacted by Ms Deborah Morris, David Morris' sister. I was asked by Deborah whether I was willing to speak to DM's new solicitor Danny Simpson. I confirmed that I was willing to assist. I was contacted by Danny Simpson, I confirmed that I would be willing to assist if my professional ethics allowed me to do so. I also requested that I be provided with copies of DM's waiver of privilege and confidentiality to the Court of Appeal and myself.

Signed _____ Signature Witnessed By _____

(1)   13/1/06

STATEMENT OF DAVID TUCKER REGARDING DAVID MORRIS

EARLY THIS YEAR, 2006, I WAS IN CWMARTIN PRISON, ON A WING WITH DAVID MORRIS, I WAS CALLED INTO A BACK ROOM OFFICE BY PRISON OFFICERS, I WAS LEFT ALONE WITH A POLICE LIASON OFFICER, HE TOLD ME IT HAD BEEN NOTICED THAT MORRIS, AND MYSELF WERE ASSOCIATES, AND SPENT A LOT OF TIME TOGETHER. I WONDERED WHERE THIS WAS LEADING TO. HE THEN SAID HE WAS AWARE THAT I WAS TRYING TO GET A STATEMENT FROM A DC JO FLETCHER, FOR THE PURPOSES OF APPEAL, HE THEN SAID SOUTH WALES MURDER SQUAD WOULD ENSURE I GOT THAT STATEMENT, IF I MADE A STATEMENT FOR THEM, TO ME THAT STATEMENT FROM DC JO FLETCHER, IS THE KEY TO LETTING ME HAVE MY FREEDOM AGAIN, WHICH HE WAS WELL AWARE OF, I HAD RESERVATIONS ABOUT IT ALL, BUT WANTING THAT STATEMENT FROM DC JO FLETCHER, MADE ME AGREE TO MAKE A STATEMENT AGAINST DAVID MORRIS, DC JO FLETCHER HAD BEEN SO EVASIVE IN GIVING ME THE STATEMENT I WAS FED UP WITH IT ALL, AT THE TIME OF WRITING THIS, THERE IS A 180 THOUSAND POUND COUNTY COURT CASE AGAINST HER FOR WITHHOLDING IT, AS I WAS NEVER GIVEN THE STATEMENT FROM HER WHICH IS WHY I'M NOW SAYING WHAT HAPPENED, IN CONNECTION TO THE STATEMENT I MADE AGAINST DAVID MORRIS THE POLICE LIASON OFFICER GAVE ME A ROUGH OUTLINE OF THE STATEMENT I WAS TO LATER MAKE AT WORCESTER CITY POLICE STATION, I NOTICED I WOULD BE IMPLICATING MYSELF IN A CONTRACT BEATING THAT I NEVER COMMITTED, AND RAISED THIS, THE POLICE LIASON OFFICER SAID IT WAS TO ENSURE I GAVE EVIDENCE IN COURT AND DIDN'T MESS THEM ABOUT, IF I DID, THEN SOUTH CID WOULD CHARGE ME WITH ATTEMPTED MURDER SECTION 18, AND IN COURT IT WOULD BE ON RECORD ANYTHING I SAID WOULD NOT BE USED AGAINST ME IN ANY COURT OF LAW. I ASKED HIM WHY HIM AND SOUTH WALES MURDER SQUAD WERE GOING TO ALL THIS TROUBLE, TO GET A JAIL CELL CONFESSION I ALSO ASKED IF THE CASE WAS WEAK AGAINST MORRIS, HE LOOKED GRIM WHEN HE REPLIED TO ME, HE SAID IN A LOW VOICE "IT WAS EASIER TO CONVICT MORRIS, THEN TWO POLICE OFFICERS". I SAID WHAT ARE YOU ON ABOUT, HE SAID "SOUTH WALES MURDER SQUAD SPENT OVER 18 MONTHS GATHERING EVIDENCE AGAINST A WOMEN POLICE OFFICER AND HER PARTNER, BUT MORRIS'S NAME COME UP, DUE TO A CHAIN HE HAD LEFT BEHIND AT A EARLIER TIME, THEN WHEN THE MURDERS HAPPENED, SO THEY USED HIM AS THE FALL GUY TO AVOID A SCANDAL IN THE

② 13/10/06

STATEMENT OF DAVID TUCKLEY REGARDING DAVID MORRIS

POLICE FORCE. HE THEN WINKED AND SAID ' FORGET ABOUT MORRIS
AND WHATS WHAT IN THE CASE, JUST DO YOUR PART AND YOU'LL GET
YOUR STATEMENT WHICH WILL HELP YOU PROVE YOUR INNOCENCE, AND
GET YOU BACK HOME." HE ALSO TOLD ME TO COVER THEMSELVES THE
SOUTH WALES POLICE WOULD PICK ME UP AND TAKE ME TO WORCESTER
POLICE STATION IN A CAR THAT WOULD BE TAPE RECORDED, ALSO
THE INTERVIEW AT WORCESTER POLICE STATION WOULD BE FILMED
IF YOU WATCH THE FILM, I SMILE AT THE PART WHERE I SAID
MORRIS HAD A EVIL LOOK, I SMILED AT HOW LUDICROUS THE
WHOLE THING SOUNDED, ALSO AT THE END I SAID WHEN I WAS
BROUGHT BACK INTO INTERVIEW ROOM TO SIGN + READ STATEMENT
THAT IT WAS A GOOD STATEMENT AND I COULDN'T HAVE DONE
BETTER MYSELF, OR WORDS TO THAT EFFECT, IN CASE THIS DAY CAME
WHEN I CAME BACK TO LONG LARTIN PRISON I WAS TOLD I WOULD BE
SENT TO BIRMINGHAM PRISON UNTILL THE END OF MORRISS TRAIL,
HAVING GIVEN EVIDENCE I WOULD THEN BE SENT TO HMP DOVEGATE
ALSO TO BE GIVEN STATEMENT BY DC J. FLETCHER WHEN I
WAS IN BIRMINGHAM PRISON I HAD SECOND THOUGHTS ABOUT ALL
OF WHAT I'VE WROTE, AND I TOLD PRINCIPAL OFFICER JONES
OF K-WING, CONTACT SOUTH WALES MURDER SQUAD AS I DON'T
WANT ANY PART OF HELPING THEM LOCK UP A INNOCENT
MAN. HENCE WHY I WAS NEVER BROUGHT TO GIVE EVIDENCE
AGAINST DAVID MORRIS AT NEWPORT CROWN COURT. BECAUSE
OF HOW I'VE BEEN TREATED BECAUSE OF THIS, AND HOW LONG
LARTIN ARE SENDING ME UP NORTH TO A PRISON TO CAUSE
ME PROBLEMS, + DIFFICULTIES FOR VISITS, BECAUSE OF COUNTY
COURT CASES AGAINST THEM, AND DC J. FLETCHER, MY LIFE
MAY BE AT SERIOUS RISK, SO I WANT THIS ON RECORD SO
DAVID MORRIS IS AWARE OF HOW FAR THE PRISON, AND
POLICE, ARE PREPARED TO GO IN KEEPING HIM IN CUSTODY
TO AVOID THE SCANDAL OF TWO POLICE OFFICERS BEING
CONVICTED FOR THE MURDERS, ALSO THE IMPLICATIONS OF
THE COVER UP, + SUBSTANTIAL AMMOUNT OF COMPENSATION
POLICE WOULD HAVE TO PAY MORRIS.

Tucker

4

As for the pole, Alison said in her statement it was under the shed.

She said she put it there because one of the girls hit the other one with it

Or it may have been Louis Pugh who said it I'm n really sure like I've already said there is so much to remember and i haven't got any statements here to help me remember. I've got no paper work at all. And the days i spent in court were like a daze. When my trial was going on i was being kept in the block. I felt like a robot. Up at 5am unlock at 6am search then shower, serched then taken to reception strip serched and given an A cat suit to put on handcuffed then put in the van and taken to court i think i was in the van for about 1½ hours then put in a cell strip serched again then given my clothes. At the end of the day it was all the same but backwards - and no shower. Then i would have to try and sleep, but its the same in most prisons, The block comes alive at night, And people are shouting and screaming out the windows untill early hours of the morning So i didn't get a lot of sleep. I was put back on normal location towards the end of my trial after complaining that i was falling asleep during the trial, But by then i had missed a lot of what went on, Its hard to concentrate when your tired. When the trial was over, it just didnt sink in that i had been found guilty again, Not for a few weeks, I was just happy that i never had to go through all that every day i just needed to be left alone and not pushed from pillar to

5

bst any more. Sorry i started to go into one there. Its just people dont realize the half of what you have to go through even before you get to court. Its all mental torture. If you maintain your innocence in prison. Then your placed on basic (permanent Punishment. Every 28 days they ask if your guilty or not. If you say not guilty then your kept on punishment. So you can put that in your book for all ne people who think that I'm guilty. If i cant get justice and get out of this liveing hell. Then I'm going to be on punishment for the rest of my life, hat'll make them happy. I'm sorry that wasn't aimed at you but its best you know how I feel.

Chapter 29

This time there could be no question of conflicting interests or wrongdoings within Morris' legal team, even if there had been a huge amount of documents and materials in this extremely complex case which made it difficult, perhaps even impossible, for them to comprehend the matter in its entirety. But this incontestable fact notwithstanding, Dai Morris has continued to protest his innocence. If he truly did not commit the murders, how could he have been found guilty by a unanimous jury decision in the new trial *which he had demanded*?

There is no single answer to this question. Instead, the failure by the defence to achieve a not guilty verdict was, once again, the result of a complex combination of reasons, some of them common to both trials.

One such reason, which became clear only *after* the second trial ended, concerned the widespread belief that because Dai Morris was twice convicted of the crimes, it was doubly certain that he had carried out the killings. The first conviction confirmed the second.

Both trials were momentous national media events, especially in Wales, and there could not have been a single jury member in the Newport trial who did not know that Morris had already been found guilty of the murders once before, but had 'got off' on a legal technicality. Standing on the steps of the Newport Crown Court after the guilty verdict was announced, Mandy Power's sister Sandra Jones concluded her address to reporters when she said: 'Two guilty verdicts say it all.' The next day, another sister, Julie Evans, declared: 'Once again, the verdict was the right one.'

Newspapers and online news forums repeated the notion that Morris was twice convicted. On 18 August 2006 a passage from *The Observer* read: 'A builder was jailed for life yesterday after being convicted for a second time of bludgeoning to death four members of a family with a 4ft-long fibreglass pole.' Almost a year later, BBC News, in its online edition dated 11 July 2007 covering Morris' failed appeal against his convictions, stated: 'He was convicted for a second time by a jury in August last year following a retrial at Newport Crown Court.' The impression conveyed by all these statements is the same in every instance: that Morris was twice convicted of the murders. It was the truth, but it was not the *whole* truth.

Morris' first conviction was quashed by the Court of Appeal in Cardiff in 2005 because the judges agreed that Morris had not got a fair trial owing to a conflict of interest involving one of his legal representatives – his solicitor, David Hutchinson. Under British law, every person accused of a crime is entitled to a fair trial. This is a cornerstone of Britain's great legal system. Dai Morris' trial in Swansea was shown to be unfair and, for this reason, his conviction was *quashed*. In other words, it was set aside as though it had never existed. The only trial that mattered in law, if not in public opinion, was the 2006 trial in Newport. The outcome of the earlier 2002 Swansea Crown Court trial no longer had any relevance and should have been disregarded.

But to many people this ruling was perhaps a concept not easily understood. In their eyes, Dai Morris was properly convicted of the crime in Swansea, but had got off the hook on a legal technicality, a loophole in the system. This was quite wrong and it also constituted a misunderstanding of how the law works. When Morris was convicted in Newport Crown Court, it should have been regarded as a *first* conviction. It was quite wrong to regard the quashed Swansea conviction as the first of two proper convictions.

There can be few people in the civilised world who would seek to hold up a quashed conviction following an unfair trial as evidence of guilt, yet that is exactly what happened in the case of Dai Morris. He started his second trial at Newport under the dark shadow of his first conviction and therefore was a victim of extreme prejudice. Perhaps Brian Morris had been right after all when he said that his son would 'never get a fair trial in Wales'.

Another reason can be attributed to the flawed manner in which South Wales Police ran the murder investigation. The case against the Lewises was dropped for just one reason, according to Morris' former solicitor Simon Jowett. The reason was *insufficiency of evidence.* This course of action was allegedly taken on the advice of senior counsel, even though there was significant evidence against the Lewises to arrest them, including testimony from an eyewitness who placed Stephen Lewis near the scene of the crime at the time of the murders – although it could just as easily have been Stuart Lewis – and the discovery of Alison Lewis' DNA on Mandy Power's thigh and on her vibrator.

'The police did a complete U-turn when Dai Morris appeared on the scene,' Simon Jowett said. 'They decided he was guilty and built a case around him.' They did this, even though Morris' DNA and fingerprints were nowhere to be found in the house and, after a year-long investigation, they still were unable to find any evidence against him. It was an intellectually dishonest prosecution, based on purely circumstantial evidence.

Part of the reason for the conviction also lies with the defendant. Morris was his own worst enemy, who brought much of his trouble on himself. His history of convictions, some for robbery and violence, spanning more than two decades, made him an unpopular figure in the village of Craig Cefn Parc when his criminal record became public knowledge. Even his own defence counsel, Peter Rouch, described him as 'no angel' at the original trial.

Well known to the police as a petty criminal, but more recently for minor domestic squabbles involving Mandy Jewell, Morris was despised by some of his neighbours and several residents of Craig Cefn Parc.   They were among the people who would give what was undoubtedly the most damning evidence against him in both trials, testifying under oath that he was wearing his gold neck-chain in the New Inn on the night of the murders – the only piece of solid evidence linking Morris with the crime.

One of these people, Michael Randerson, suspected Morris of being involved in the theft of his cars; furthermore, he actively disliked Morris, who had shamelessly chatted up his girlfriend in the New Inn on the night of the murders. Randerson, his girlfriend Fay Scott alleged, lied about remembering that Morris was wearing his gold chain that night in a statement given to detectives twenty-one months after the event. Other witnesses also questioned more than eighteen months later included Philip Turner, Morris' neighbour, who hated him; David Howell Thomas, a friend and employee of Turner, who was unable to see properly even with the aid of his glasses; Sharon Jameson, whose husband hated Morris; Janice Williams, a drug-addicted alcoholic, sexually rebuffed by Morris, who gave several contradictory statements to the police, but only those incriminating him were ever produced in court.

All these witnesses had an axe to grind, and testifying against the man who had become Public Enemy Number One in Craig Cefn Parc was a sure-fire way of getting him out of the village and locked away for good. It suited everyone – villagers, police and prosecution alike.

What casts doubt over all these witnesses' statements – quite apart from any personal grievances they may have held against Morris, coupled with the inordinate delay in testing memories and taking statements – is the almost complete absence of any witness with whom Morris did not have some history of conflict.

These witnesses included Fay Scott, with whom Dai Morris spent some time talking in the New Inn on the night of the murders and who might be expected to know whether or not he was wearing the gold neck-chain later found at the crime scene, and publican Glyn Hopkin, who was stone-cold sober and might also be expected to have known if he was wearing such a chain. There were other people in the bar that night who may have known who Dai Morris was, but no one else, other than these few who loathed him, came forward to claim that he was actually wearing a gold neck-chain that was similar to, if not the same as, the one that prosecuting counsel held up in court.

There is no reason to believe that the inexperience of Gareth Rees QC, his trial tactics or his handling of this very difficult case, placed Dai Morris at a disadvantage when compared to the more experienced Patrick Harrington QC, nor is there any suggestion that Mr Rees did not at all times do his best for the accused.

And it was the duty of the jury to decide, upon consideration of all the evidence, whether or not the prosecution had proved its case against the *defendant* beyond reasonable doubt. That was all they were required to do. It was most certainly not their job to decide if the Lewises had committed the crime. Stephen Lewis, the jury had been told, had an alibi for the time of the murders which the jury could accept, and this left just Alison Lewis and Dai Morris in the frame.

The jury was put in the position of having to make a stark choice between a former policewoman with an unblemished record who was a lover of Mandy Power, and a drunken, drug-taking criminal with a history of violent crime. The outcome was inevitable.

A year later, on 11 July 2007, Morris lost a bid to challenge his conviction at the Court of Appeal. But his 'whole-life' sentence was quashed and replaced instead by an order that he serve a minimum period of 32 years before he can apply for release on parole. His application for leave to appeal his conviction was rejected by the judges' ruling, which stated that there was 'no arguable grounds' for a challenge. And because Morris continually protests his innocence, he will not be considered for release and may never be freed.

Chapter 30

When, in 2009, Brian Thornton, senior lecturer in journalism at Winchester University, took an interest in the case, Dai Morris' luck appeared to have taken a turn for the better. Thornton, who is closely involved with the Winchester Innocence Project,[*] obtained Morris' case files from his former solicitors and started working through them with his students. What he has discovered so far is little short of astounding.

In forensic tests carried out at the crime scene, Thornton's team discovered documents that showed DNA *had* been discovered at 9 Kelvin Road. Male DNA was found in a number of locations throughout the property; also on the murder weapon, the two spent matches used to start the fires, the silver watch placed on Mandy Power's wrist, and even on the clothes she was wearing at the time she was attacked and killed. Furthermore, basic-level DNA testing indicated that all the items revealed traces of cells with the male, Y chromosome, though *none* of the DNA found matched that of Dai Morris.

The scene of crimes officer consulted by the author was right when she said, 'in a crime of this brutality "Tracking down and eliminating every bit of biological debris left behind would have been impossible, even for the cleverest criminal".' This dispels completely any notion put forward by South Wales Police that Morris had wiped away all traces of his DNA and fingerprints, or that he was forensically aware.

A more advanced test, known as Y-STR analysis, was, astonishingly, never carried out, even though this would have confirmed conclusively whether or not DNA found on the items came from Dai Morris. Instead, items that did *not* reveal male

---

[*] A BA Journalism student organisation at Winchester University which investigates alleged cases of wrongful imprisonment and, where appropriate, seeks to overturn convictions. See: www.innocencenetwork.org.uk

DNA were subjected to Y-STR analysis which, inevitably, revealed nothing at all.

The Y-STR analysis, which would have conclusively eliminated or incriminated Morris, could and should have been carried out immediately after his arrest. Yet not only was the test not carried out, but the very existence of the discovery of male DNA discovered in 9 Kelvin Road *not* belonging to Morris was never even mentioned at either of his trials.

What might the effect have been upon either of the Swansea or Newport Crown Court juries in 2002 and then again in 2006, had they been made aware of this crucial piece of evidence? Male DNA was found all over the crime scene, and even on the murder weapon itself, but none of it belonged to Dai Morris. Would they have twice brought in a guilty verdict, or might this evidence have introduced an element of doubt leading to Morris' acquittal? South Wales Police had this evidence in its possession within three weeks of the murders and they knew its likely effect upon a jury. But they were determined to convict, and it was no doubt for this reason that they chose not to reveal its existence.

Morris' case for innocence is reinforced by his insistence to his legal team that he be given the conclusive Y-STR test because he insists he has nothing to fear.

Three weeks after the murders, when addressing reporters, Martin Lloyd-Evans told them: 'the killer may have been male or female, and that more than one person could have been involved.' Forensic scientist Claire Galbraith also expressed her opinion that the killings 'might have involved more than one attacker. Since the killer took the precaution of wearing a sock over at least one hand whilst wielding the murder weapon, it is clear that he or she was aware of the type of incriminating evidence which might be found, leading to their identity becoming known. Why, then, was male DNA found on so many items including matches, the silver watch and the murder weapon? Was it because the murderer had decided to set fire to the house and assumed that all trace evidence – DNA and fingerprints – would be destroyed? Or could it be that the DNA belonged to an accomplice? This second person, a man, may have helped out with the clean-up operation, and might have been confident that fire would cover all evidence remaining, or he was not forensically aware, or he was simply careless? Only further investigation on this point will tell.

Another significant discovery made by Brian Thornton and his team was that the police had tampered with evidence from the police HOLMES database (Home Office Large Major Enquiry System). This is an information technology system used mainly in the investigation of major crimes, such as rape, grievous bodily harm (GBH) and murder. He discovered that the text from several thousand pages of records emanating from HOLMES, some containing crucial information, had been cut and pasted into Notepad (a Microsoft application) where they could be – and were subsequently – altered.

One such document – Message 23 – was entered into the HOLMES system the day after the murders. It came into the murder inquiry incident room from a detective and read as follows: 'I've just been contacted by an informant [David 'Pancho' Powell] who stated that he knew Mandy Power and she was gay and she has been drinking in Farmers PH [public house] Clydach. Informant stated three weeks ago he overheard conversation Mandy was having with 2 females who stated that her and her kids had been threatened by her current lover's husband who was a police officer.'

The informant Powell, a neighbour of Mandy Power, later gave another statement in which he said: 'I questioned her as to the threats and she said… "This person has threatened to do us in". She definitely said "Do us in". I took that to mean to beat her and her daughters up. I advised her about going to the police, but she stated "I can't". Mandy then went on to explain that she was involved in a relationship with another woman and that it was this woman's partner who made the threats.'

But the cut and pasted version of Message 23 – known as Action 92 – stated: 'source of information stating that Mandy Power [was] being threatened'. It did not identify the person making the threats, nor give the reason why they were made.

The recent discovery of this evidence suggested that not only was the man on trial innocent, but that South Wales Police knew from the outset that he was.

The results of Brian Thornton's five-year investigation and incredible findings were publicised by journalist David Rose in *The Mail on Sunday* on 23 November 2014.* The article provoked a storm of protest at the police handling of the case and, as a result, the Criminal Cases Review Commission (CCRC) agreed to launch an investigation into the claims. Their investigation – which was said to be fast-tracked – took over two years to complete. It concluded on 30 June 2017 when Morris' lawyers were given *provisional* notice that his case was unlikely to be sent for appeal on the *existing* evidence, and that it was 'not suitable for hearing'. A CCRC spokesman made it clear that this was not a *final* decision.

But this surprising turn of events is not necessarily the end of the line. Morris' lawyers were given two months to submit further information if they think it may influence the decision of the CCRC, although this period of time may be extended.

Whichever course his lawyers choose to take, whether it be acquiescence to the decision of the CCRC, which seems unlikely, or to continue with the fight, one thing remains certain: Dai Morris will continue to protest his innocence.

As this account of the murder investigation shows, the evidence in favour of the defence is convincing, and the case for a miscarriage of justice is overwhelming. Meanwhile, Dai Morris, now 55, waits patiently in prison, hoping that one day his freedom will be granted. But prisoners who refuse to admit their guilt are punished for it. They serve longer prison terms and receive fewer privileges, less time out of their cells, fewer visits from family, reduced or no daily access to the gym. The prison service states 'minimisation of offending and denial of offending are good indicators of continuing risk,' so prisoners lose their parole opportunities also, with no expectation or hope of early release.

The pressure on an innocent prisoner to admit guilt is enormous, yet this is the stony path that Dai Morris has chosen. He says: I'll stay here for the rest of my life, if that's what it takes, because I will not admit to something I didn't do.'

---

* www.dailymail.co.uk/news/article-2845510/Who-REALLY-murdered-married-WPC-s-lesbian-lover.html

In his closing address to the jury at the Swansea Crown Court trial in 2002, Peter Rouch QC memorably told them: 'Some cases cry out for a motive, they scream out for a motive, and this is one of them.' But the case of David George Morris is far more than that. His is a case that screams out for justice.

Epilogue

This account of the Clydach murders and the injustices it exposes has been an incredible and a complex story to tell. It is not just another run-of-the-mill miscarriage of justice where all that might be demonstrated is that some cog in the machinery of justice was out of place. In this case, the entire machine broke down, and multiple injustices combined to commit one of the worst miscarriages of justice Britain has ever seen.

This case is one that falls into that unusual category where not only does the convicted person maintain his innocence, but, exceptionally, he points to another person as the likely perpetrator of the crime. It was never my intention to produce evidence to show that somebody other than Dai Morris might have been responsible for the Clydach murders: that is the job of the police and the Crown Prosecution Service. It was my objective solely to consider the investigation of the South Wales Police in its entirety and to consider the evidence presented at the trials in order to ascertain, as far as was possible, that Dai Morris was treated fairly and was not deprived of his human rights.

This objective turned out to be impossible, however, because Dai Morris and the Lewises, former suspects for the crime, are inextricably linked in this terrible, tragic saga. I could not, in all good conscience, examine carefully the case leading to the imprisonment for life of a man who may well be innocent, while at the same time overlooking evidence which showed that someone else might have been responsible for the crimes.

When I began my research into the Clydach murders, I had no preconceived notions about the identity of the killer. There was a great divergence of opinion on this point by an unusually large number of intelligent people. But, perhaps, like many in Britain's mostly law-abiding community, I had faith in the country's legal system and I secretly felt that because Dai Morris was convicted on two occasions of the crimes, he must be guilty of the murders, and justice had been served. So it was primarily to satisfy my own curiosity, as well as that of my friends, that I set out to examine the case more closely in order to discover the truth for myself.

I thoroughly expected to quickly find incontrovertible evidence supporting the jury's guilty verdicts, proving beyond reasonable doubt that Dai Morris was the killer. But what I discovered was nothing of the sort. Instead, my research revealed a police force willing not only to arrest an innocent man, but to charge him with murder on the basis of his criminal record, and very little else. For me it was unthinkable that three police officers, sworn to uphold the law, could possibly have been in any way involved in the murders.

But taking the history of wrongful convictions in the United Kingdom as my starting point, any illusions I held about the integrity of the police were very quickly shattered. I discovered that a number of police forces were literally a law unto themselves, although institutionalised corruption involving South Wales Police gave that police force the unenviable record of being the worst of them all. It seemed to me that the police were more concerned with achieving convictions, and lowering the crime rate, than they were with ensuring that they had the right person for the offence. I was shocked and unsettled by this unnerving discovery.

Whether this systematic corruption applied to Dai Morris' case remained to be seen. He had, after all, been convicted of the crime not once, but twice. I asked myself: how could the justice system, which I had devoted my entire career as a solicitor to supporting, drop the ball on two separate occasions? In my view, the odds were infinitesimally small.

The first Crown Court trial of Dai Morris, held in Swansea in 2002, was indeed unfair. Surprisingly, given the catalogue of corrupt behaviour on the part of South Wales Police, it was not, on this occasion, all due to wrongdoing on their part. At that point it was still possible for a good defence team to show that the evidence the police had gathered was thin, and not enough to convict him. It was an unfair trial because a member of Dai Morris' own defence team, solicitor David Hutchinson, represented Morris in circumstances where he should not have done so. Hutchinson acted for the Lewis twins at the same time as Morris, and he had developed a relationship with them that went far beyond the usual solicitor-client relationship. As a consequence, Hutchinson failed to act in Morris' best interests and did not represent him either properly or professionally.

The retrial held four years later at Newport Crown Court offered a chance to remedy the injustice. This time, entirely different but perhaps related factors led to his conviction. But the shadow of the quashed conviction hung over the Newport Crown Court trial, in which the jury members knew that Morris had already been convicted of the murders. In addition to their inevitable prejudice, South Wales Police produced witnesses who gave vital if dubious evidence to the court which the defence chose not to challenge. Given the nature of the evidence with which the jury was presented, it was not hard to convict him again.

While a righteous justice system can mitigate the effects of a corrupt police force, it cannot defeat the combined force of the police and an establishment that is determined to convict. The British justice system is vulnerable to the integrity of its people. It took two trials to derail justice and irrevocably change the path of Dai Morris' life.

Who the Clydach murderer *really* was, what the motive might have been, and if anyone else might also have been involved may, some day, once again become a matter for the police. How South Wales Police conducted its protracted and flawed investigation into the Clydach murders should be a matter for further inquiry by its regulators. What is certain, and what my research for this book has astonished me by revealing, is that Dai Morris' retrial was also unfair, and yet another miscarriage of justice has taken place.

Chronology of key events

| 5.00 p.m. | Mandy Power and her two daughters are collected by taxi from 9 Kelvin Road and are driven to the home of her nephew, Stephen Jones, to babysit for him and his wife who are attending a wedding anniversary party. |
| 10.00 p.m. | Barbeque at 8 West Crossways, hosted by Alison and Stephen Lewis for their neighbours, ends unexpectedly when Alison, who had fallen asleep, wakes up and announces that she is going to bed. |

Saturday night 26 June/Sunday morning 27 June 1999

The night of the murders.

Sometime after midnight on Saturday 26 June	Detective Inspector Stuart Lewis absents himself from his office in Cockett Police Station for three hours. His police car also goes missing. Alison Lewis' car is seen outside 9 Kelvin Road by a Cefn Coed Hospital staff member.
12.30 p.m.	Taxi driver Kevin Duffy drops Mandy Power and her daughters at 9 Kelvin Road and sees her open the front door using a key.
12.45 p.m.	Rosemary Jones and her son Wayne Jones hear a car pull up outside 9 Kelvin Road. Someone gets out and lets themself into the house while the car drives off. They see the shape of a figure behind frosted glass and the lights going on and off.
2.20 p.m.	Returning from a night out in Cardiff, Nicola Williams sees a man carrying a bag and wearing what appears to be a police jacket walking in the direction of Kelvin Road. Her description fits Stephen Lewis, but the e-fit image composed with her help by police technicians looks more like Stuart Lewis.
	Bedroom fires are started at 9 Kelvin Road.

3.00 a.m.   Stuart Lewis returns to Cockett Police Station. Later, he denies that he ever left.

3.50 a.m.   Kitchen fire started at 9 Kelvin Road.

4.20 a.m.   Neighbour Robert Wachowski hears banging noises and sees smoke. Another neighbour calls the fire services.

4.27 a.m.   Fire Service HQ in Carmarthen receives the first 999 call reporting a fire in 9 Kelvin Road.

5.00 a.m.   Stephen Lewis is woken by his alarm and gets up for work.

5.18 a.m.   Stephen Lewis is picked up by Police Constable Gareth Thomas and is driven to work in Neath.

6.00 a.m.   Timothy Manon watches from his house in Kelvin Road as Alison Lewis approaches his wife and buries her head in her shoulder.

                 Manon Cherry meets Alison Lewis in Kelvin Road and notes that she is freshly showered and smelling of soap.

                 The owners of Clydach Cabs hear the news about the fire at 9 Kelvin Road. Because they are unable to contact Carol Ann Isaac and Beverley Lewis by telephone, they drive to Morriston to tell them personally.

                 Carol Ann Isaac and Beverley Lewis are woken at their home in Morriston and told about the fire. They drive immediately to Kelvin Road.

                 First news of the murders is received at Cockett Police Station. Fifty officers are assigned to the case and detectives leave for Kelvin Road. Alison Lewis claims that this is the first time she learned about the deaths, by telephone.

6.30 a.m.	Carol Ann Isaac and Beverley Lewis arrive at Kelvin Road. There is just one police constable on duty. They meet Alison Lewis in the home of a neighbour, Christine Williams, and console Lewis. Both women note Lewis as being freshly showered and smelling strongly of soap.
7.00 a.m.	Police surgeon Carl Harry arrives at 9 Kelvin Road and pronounces all four victims dead. Dai Morris and Mandy Jewell hear about the murders in a telephone call from Alison Lewis.
7.15 a.m.	Gary Beynon, a gay friend of both Mandy Power and Alison Lewis, receives a telephone call from Alison Lewis telling him that Mandy and her family have died in a fire.
7.30 a.m.	Gary Beynon drives to Alison Lewis' home in Pontardawe via Kelvin Road. He describes Alison's appearance as fresh, as if she had recently showered or washed.
Noon	Nicola Williams reports to the police her sighting of a mystery man with a bag walking near the scene of the murders.
28 June 1999	Detective Superintendent Martyn Lloyd-Evans holds a press conference at Cockett Police Station.
30 June 1999	Detective Superintendent Martyn Lloyd-Evans makes a media appeal for information. No mention is made of the man Nicola Williams saw walking near the murder scene at the time of the murders.
1 July 1999	Twenty members of the victims' family are escorted by police around the murder scene at 9 Kelvin Road.
2 July 1999	Earlier media appeal results in around 500 telephone calls being received. Several callers mention Dai Morris.

3 July 1999   Detectives working round the clock have taken 130 witness statements and spoken to 200 people.

7 July 1999   Alison Lewis is admitted to Cefn Coed psychiatric hospital. She is observed receiving sexually explicit texts from an old girlfriend. She is also aggressive, necessitating the use of restraining measures by eight members of staff.

                Nicola Williams helps police technicians to compose an e-fit image which closely resembles identical twins Stephen Lewis and Stuart Lewis.

13 July 1999   Detective Superintendent Martyn Lloyd-Evans appears on BBC *Crimewatch* and appeals for information. While on the television programme, he does not show the e-fit image produced by Nicola Williams.

17 July 1999   The longest forensic investigation at a murder scene in Wales ends. In addition, 1,000 people are interviewed, 280 witness statements taken, 300 messages received. Detective Superintendent Martyn Lloyd-Evans receives 'negative' forensic report, giving rise to the theory that the murderer was 'forensically aware'.

21 July 1999   Alison Lewis leaves Cefn Coed Hospital.

30 July 1999   Funeral for the four victims takes place in Clydach, with the Reverend Nigel Griffen officiating. Burial takes place at Coedgwilym Cemetery, Clydach.

7 September 1999 BBC *Crimewatch* records a full reconstruction of the crime, including fire engines and police cars rushing to the scene.

14 September 1999 The BBC *Crimewatch* reconstruction is broadcast on television. Detective Superintendent Martyn Lloyd-Evans appeals for help but still does not reveal Nicola Williams' e-fit image of the man she saw.

1 October 1999	Gary Beynon sees Alison Lewis and a former girlfriend in a close embrace dancing in a Swansea nightclub. When she sees him, Lewis' demeanour changes in an instant to one of grief.
20 February 2000	Anne Powell, mother of Alison Lewis, pleads for her daughter to be left alone, as rumours about her continue to circulate.
11 March 2000	Dylan Thomas Theatre in Swansea is booked as a venue to give transparency to the police investigation. The event is presented by journalist Vincent Kane, Nick Ross presenter of *Crimewatch*, and criminal psychologist Adrian 'Cracker' West.
25 March 2000	DNA testing commences and samples are taken from people with access to 9 Kelvin Road.
11 May 2000	Headstone is placed on the victims' grave in Coedgwilym Cemetery.
25 May 2000	Detective Superintendent Martyn Lloyd-Evans addresses Clydach villagers, assuring them the hunt for the killer is almost complete. A total of fifty-eight police officers are now working full-time on the case.
Mid-June 2000	Police release an e-fit image of a woman they want to interview. She does not come forward, nor is she ever traced. No mention is made of the e-fit image composed by police technicians with the help of Nicola Williams.
21 June 2000	A news conference is held at Cockett Police Station. Robert Dawson speaks of his disappointment at the lack of arrests.
23 June 2000	9 Kevin Road is sold for £7,000.
27 June 2000	One year after the murders a mobile incident room is set up in Kelvin Road. Detective Superintendent Martyn Lloyd-Evans assures villagers that they can expect results.

4 July 2000	Alison Lewis, Stephen Lewis and Stuart Lewis are arrested on suspicion of involvement in the murders. An angry mob of 150 people surrounds Morriston Police Station, where it is believed that Alison Lewis is being held.
8 July 2000	The Lewises are released on bail after four days in police custody.
31 July 2000	Police Chief Sir Anthony Burden publicly expresses his confidence in and support for the investigation.
9 September 2000	Detective Superintendent Martyn Lloyd-Evans flies to Quantico in Virginia where he meets with offender profiling experts and learns 'valuable lessons'.
7 October 2000	The Lewises' police bail is extended until December.
12 December 2000	The Lewises' police bail is extended until January 2001.
10 January 2001	Police announce that they are close to discovering the origins of the gold neck-chain.
23 January 2001	The Lewises will not be charged with involvement in the murders, but the Lewis twins remain suspended from duty.
8 February 2001	Alison Lewis admits on HTV Wales that she knew personally several police officers involved in the investigation and had worked with Detective Superintendent Martin Lloyd-Evans at Llanishen, Cardiff.
9 February 2001	Telephone calls flood into HTV Wales offices demanding a public inquiry.
19 February 2001	Off-duty policewoman Deborah Powell receives key information from Kim Crowley concerning Dai Morris.

Mid-March 2001	David Hutchinson launches civil claims for the Lewis twins.
20 March 2001	Police arrest Dai Morris on suspicion of the Clydach murders and take him to Morriston Police Station for questioning. David Hutchinson is instructed to represent Dai Morris. Mandy Jewell is arrested on suspicion of conspiracy to pervert the course of justice and is taken to Neath Police Station. Shirley Morris, Dai Morris' elderly mother, is taken into police custody in Swansea where she is held for 11 hours helping the police with their enquiries.
21 March 2001	Police are given a further 12 hours to continue questioning Morris.
22 March 2001	Police descend on a property used by Dai Morris at Arennig Road in Swansea, which is searched for evidence. Nothing is found.
23 March 2001	Dai Morris is formally charged with the Clydach murders.
24 March 2001	Dai Morris is committed for trial at the Crown Court in Swansea by Mr Howard Morgan JP.
5 November 2001	Dai Morris enters a formal plea of not guilty to the charges at Swansea Crown Court.
8 April 2002	The trial is delayed by two days because of the Queen Mother's funeral.
10 April 2002	Morris' trial commences at Swansea Crown Court, with Patrick Harrington QC for the prosecution and Peter Rouch QC for the defence.
28 June 2002	Morris is found guilty on four counts of murder and is awarded four life sentences.
1 July 2002	Wendy Morris launches a petition to clear her former husband's name.

Chronology of key events

December 2002   Michael Mansfield QC is hired by the Morris family to represent Dai Morris in an appeal.

November 2003   BBC *Panorama* investigation discovers similarities between the case of Dai Morris and other miscarriages of justice. The programme is highly critical of South Wales Police.

October 2004   Three Appeal Court judges sitting at Cardiff give Morris leave to appeal.

14 February 2005   Appeal hearing takes place at the Court of Appeal in Cardiff, with Michael Mansfield QC representing Dai Morris.

4 May 2005   Morris' convictions are quashed and a new trial is ordered.

18 May 2006   Retrial commences in Newport Crown Court, with Patrick Harrington QC for the prosecution and Gareth Rees QC for the defence.

17 August 2006   The jury returns a guilty verdict in the second trial and Dai Morris is convicted of the murders for a second time and sentenced to life imprisonment, with a recommendation that he serve at least 30 years.

11 July 2007   Morris loses a bid to challenge his convictions, but his whole-life sentence is quashed, replaced by an order that he serve a minimum period of 32 years before he can apply for release on parole.

14 November 2014   Morris' case is referred to the Criminal Cases Review Commission (CCRC) where it is given Priority 1 (urgent) status.

30 June 2017   Provisional decision taken not to refer case to Court Appeal. The deadline for the submission of a response is the end of August 2017.

04 August 2017   Case to continue...

Appendix

This is a list of miscarriage of justice cases from 1985 involving South Wales Police. It includes cases where a convicted individual was later cleared of the crime and has received either an official exoneration, or there is a consensus that he or she was unjustly punished, or where a conviction has been quashed and no retrial has taken place, so that the accused is assumed to be innocent.

Paul and Wayne Darvell, 1985

On Friday, 14 June 1985, the battered body of Sandra Phillips was discovered on the floor of the sex shop she managed in Swansea. She was the mother of four children, one of whom, Grace, had celebrated her fourteenth birthday on that day.

A year later, on 19 June 1986, two homeless brothers, Wayne Darvell, 30, and Paul Darvell, 31, both of low intelligence, were convicted of the crime and sentenced to life imprisonment, with a recommendation that Paul serve at least 20 years and Wayne 15 years.

Five years later, in March 1991, the BBC programme *Rough Justice* cast doubt on the evidence-gathering methods employed by the police in the case. This led to an inquiry involving the Devon and Cornwall police force which uncovered an appalling catalogue of unethical and illegal practices carried out by the South Wales Police detectives involved in the murder investigation.

They discovered that Wayne Darvell had been bullied into making a statement implicating both himself and his brother in the crime, a statement that the detectives knew was untrue. Electro Static Detection Apparatus testing of detectives' notebooks showed that their notes had been compiled at much later dates than the detectives had claimed and, in one case, a detective who claimed that he had written his notes immediately after an interview produced as evidence a notebook that was not actually issued until two months later.

Exculpatory evidence, including a bloody palm print which did not match either of the brothers' palms and would therefore have cleared them, was suppressed by the prosecution and kept hidden from defence lawyers. Photographs and negatives of the palm print, which would have proved the Darvell brothers' innocence, were destroyed.

Secretly taped conversations of the brothers' discussions in their cell, strongly suggesting their innocence, were not given to defence lawyers and they later disappeared. Two detectives who claimed to have seen the Darvell brothers near the murder scene were proved to have been lying when the detectives' diaries were examined and showed that they were working elsewhere at the time. An earring, said to belong to the murder victim, was planted in the back of a police car used to transport one of the brothers to the police station.

In 1992, the Court of Appeal in London quashed their convictions and the two brothers walked free. That evening Robert Lawrence, Chief Constable of South Wales Police, said he 'deeply regretted' the miscarriage of justice and vowed that he would reopen the murder investigation.

Three South Wales Police detectives involved in the murder investigation were charged with conspiracy to pervert the course of justice and were committed for trial at Chester Crown Court. It was alleged that they had forged notes and had given false evidence which led directly to the Darvell brothers' conviction and subsequent imprisonment.

Following an eleven-day trial, during which their defence counsel claimed that their actions had been 'sloppy' rather than criminal, all three officers were found not guilty.

At the time of writing, more than twenty years after Chief Constable Robert Lawrence's momentous but ultimately empty statement that he would reopen the case, no one has been charged with Sandra Phillips' murder and the trail has gone cold. Grace, just a child of fourteen on the day of her mother's death, is now 46 years old. The identity of her mother's brutal killer still remains unknown.*

* After the Devon and Cornwall Police inquiry commenced, I found myself in Exeter police station representing a male suspect for the murder. By this time the photographic negatives of the bloody palm print, which might have provided a match, had disappeared and no other evidence linked my client to the crime. No admissions were made during the interview, though the answers he gave were very odd. Later the same day he was released without charge. But as we were being led out of the police station, the sergeant accompanying us said to my client: 'Don't you feel bad that two men were sent to prison because of what you did?' After deliberating for a moment, and perhaps realising that he was no longer under caution, he casually nodded and replied 'Yeah'. He then exited the building and returned to Swansea. He was never reinterviewed in connection with the murder.

Darren Hall, Michael O'Brien and Ellis Sherwood, 1987

Following the killing of Cardiff newsagent Philip Saunders in his shop in 1987, three petty criminals, Darren Hall, aged 18, Michael O'Brien, aged 33, and Ellis Sherwood, aged 30, were arrested and charged with his murder. The prosecution case rested entirely on Darren Hall's 'confession' that he was 'the lookout for a robbery that went wrong'. Despite the lack of solid evidence linking any of the three men to the crime, they were all found guilty and sentenced to life imprisonment.

When the case was reviewed by the Thames Valley Police, their report was scathing of South Wales Police detectives' investigative methods, and it subsequently formed the basis of an appeal. Thames Valley Police uncovered numerous irregularities, flagrant breaches of police protocol and unacceptable investigative practices. In one case, a detective had handcuffed eighteen-year-old Darren Hall to a hot radiator in order to force a confession from him, and he had been denied access to a solicitor for several days. Hall and his associates also disappeared from the station's custody records for hours at a time when they were being subjected to abusive off-the-record interrogations. Incredibly, detectives offered Michael O'Brien £10,000 to perjure himself by testifying falsely against South Wales Police's prime suspect, Darren Hall. The Criminal Cases Review Body said that South Wales Police had shown a 'systematic disregard of proper procedure'. By the time their cases were quashed by the Court of Appeal in 1999, and they were released from custody, these three innocent young men had spent eleven years in prison.

Stephen Miller, Anthony Paris and Yusef Abdullahi, 1988

Having been wrongfully convicted of the murder of Cardiff prostitute Lynette White in 1988, and sentenced to life imprisonment, Stephen Miller, Anthony Paris and Yusef Abdullahi were released from prison by the Court of Appeal in 1992.

An investigation by the BBC *Panorama* programme, which led to the appeal, discovered numerous irregularities in the handling of the case by South Wales Police. There was no direct evidence against any of the suspects: no DNA, fingerprints, a weapon or even a motive. Stephen Miller endured nineteen interviews, during which he was shouted at, threatened and bullied. It was only under the most intense pressure that he broke down and confessed to the crime, also implicating his co-defendants. Before this point, he had denied involvement 307 times.

After the release of the three men, the case was reopened. In 2002, after the development of Second Generation Multiplex Plus, forensic scientists obtained a reliable crime scene DNA profile. In 2003 the profile enabled the police to identify the real killer, a security guard and client of the deceased, who confessed to White's murder. He was sentenced to life imprisonment.

Eight police officers involved in the original investigation were charged with perverting the course of justice. In addition, some of them were charged with perjury. Two civilian witnesses who had lied under oath were also charged. But before the trial began, a box of vital evidence in police custody of Detective Chief Superintendent Chris Coutts went missing. This left the court with no choice but to acquit the defendants. Less than two months later the missing documents turned up in the office of DCS Coutts.

Jonathan Jones, 1993

In 1993, Jonathan Jones was convicted of the murder of Harry and Megan Tooze, his girlfriend Cheryl's elderly parents, by blasting them to death with a shotgun. Despite being elsewhere at the time, and despite having no motive, Jones was found guilty of the crimes on the basis that his thumbprint was found on a saucer, part of a set owned by the couple, and the staggering, unfounded theory put forward by the police that he wanted to get his hands on the money his girlfriend stood to inherit.

In 1996, Jones was freed by the Court of Appeal when it was established that money could not have been a motive because he and Cheryl Jones earned a sizeable income, she had £6,000 in savings, Jones' alibi had never been disproved, and the glasses that he always wore revealed no trace of the victims' blood or brain tissue. It was a case 'based on suspicion, speculation and conjecture', yet it cost Jonathan Jones almost three years of his life.

Annette Hewins and Donna Clarke, 1995

Annette Hewins and Donna Clarke were convicted of causing the death of three people in Merthyr Tydfil by arson, even though there was no forensic evidence against them, no fingerprints and no independent witnesses to the crime. The two women were sentenced to 13 years and 21 years imprisonment respectively.

In the investigation that followed, it was shown that during 30 hours of questioning, South Wales Police detectives had bullied Clarke, an immature and vulnerable teenager, into making a false statement, thereby implicating her friends in the crime. She admitted lying under oath, but said she did so only because detectives had frightened her into signing the statement.

CCTV footage recorded at the garage where the petrol was bought showed that the petrol Hewins purchased was leaded. However, the fire was started with *unleaded* petrol. The police knew this was a serious flaw in their case but they chose to ignore it. Crucially, they failed to pass on this evidence to the defence lawyers.

After their release from prison, Annette Hewins said: 'They [South Wales Police detectives] targeted one person and built a case around them. They convinced themselves that someone is guilty and ignored any evidence that pointed to other perpetrators. Yet, innocent people, and the victims' families, have had their lives ruined.'

Acknowledgements

It wasn't even my idea. Four, or perhaps five, years ago, a small group of us, all good friends, would meet up regularly to pass the time in convivial surroundings. Sooner or later, one of them would bring up the subject of the Clydach murders in order to discuss the minutiae of the case, the individuals involved, and their many doubts surrounding the verdict. Inevitably, one of them would say to me, 'You ought to write a book about it.'

But what was there to write about? There was no doubt that it was an interesting story; one of the most brutal, horrific multiple murders ever committed in Britain, and the imprisonment for life of a man who swore he was innocent. And since he was *twice* convicted of the crimes, my faith in British justice – the finest system in the world – convinced me that he must, therefore, be guilty, no question. So, in my mind, there was nothing to write about.

However, it was as a result of my friends' persistent encouragement, and the seeds of doubt which they planted in my mind, that I became curious and decided that I would, after all, take a closer look at the case. What I discovered during three years of research truly shocked me and shattered my beliefs in the integrity of Britain's legal system. It also led directly to the publication of *The Clydach Murders: A Miscarriage of Justice* which, without the inspiration of my friends, would never have been written. And to them, I give my sincere thanks. You know who you are.

I would like to thank past and present members of Morriston fire service for providing me with their first-hand recollections of that terrible night, painfully recalling events I'm sure they would rather forget, and one very kind – and patient – female scene of crimes officer who helped me with current forensic detection techniques.

I also thank the several lawyers, police officers, witnesses and other individuals who came forward providing useful help and advice, in particular Debra Thomas who, on several occasions, provided me with invaluable information and vital documents, some of which appear within the pages of this book.

My special thanks go to my friend and lifetime literary agent, Jonathan Williams, who enthusiastically endorsed the project from the outset. His support was, as always, invaluable. He is professional, optimistic, highly supportive and very helpful, and I am extremely grateful to him for his guidance throughout.

And my special thanks go also to my publisher, Mick Felton of Seren, for very kindly agreeing to publish this book in the first place. With over thirty years of publishing experience, Mick's advice and suggestions in all matters surrounding the production and publication of this book are both impeccable and gratefully received; especially for his hard and dedicated work during the editing and publishing processes, to ensure that the quality of this book in all respects was as good as it could possibly be.

I give my thanks also to marketing and communications officer Rosie Johns at Seren for her hard work also, and being always available to offer help and advice.

And, as always, my special gratitude and love goes to my long-suffering family for putting up with me, in particular my wife Yvonne, who has always been there for me.

If you have moved or affected by the content of this book please feel free to share your thoughts with others. If you have specific information which you believe may assist in the search for justice, please email me at: theclydachmurders@gmail.com